# STRENGTH TO YOUR SWORD ARM:

## SELECTED WRITINGS

## ALSO BY BRENDA UELAND

*If You Want to Write*

ME

*Mitropoulos and the North High Band*

# STRENGTH TO YOUR SWORD ARM:
## SELECTED WRITINGS

BRENDA UELAND

INTRODUCTION BY SUSAN ALLEN TOTH

HOLY COW! PRESS • DULUTH, MINNESOTA • 1993

Portrait painting of Brenda Ueland by Eleanor Falk Quirt
Back Cover—the colorful Crest of Arms is a northern European design
which was cross-stitched onto a dark blue background. This embroidered
tapestry was a family heirloom that Brenda Ueland displayed in her home.
The double-lion figures that wield raised axes symbolize qualities of
courage, strength, and royal authority.

Special thanks and acknowledgment to the Editorial Board for Strength To
Your Sword Arm: Selected Writings—Bruce Carlson, Paul Johnson,
Gabrielle McIver, and Jim Perlman.

First Printing, 1993
10 9 8 7 6 5 4 3 2 1

Library of Congress Cataloging-in-Publication Data

Ueland, Brenda
    Strength to your sword arm : selected writings / by Brenda Ueland.
        p.    cm.
    ISBN 0-930100-50-6
    I. Title
PS3541.E4S77    1992
814' .54—dc20                        92-54181
                                      CIP

Publisher's Address:                 Distributor's Address:

Holy Cow! Press                      The Talman Company, Inc.
Post Office Box 3170                 131 Spring Street
Mount Royal Station                  Suite 201E-N
Duluth, Minnesota 55803              New York, New York 10012

This project was supported, in part, by a grant from the National Endowment for the Arts in Washington, D.C., a Federal agency.

# TABLE OF CONTENTS

Preface / *Jim Perlman*    ix
Introduction / *Susan Allen Toth*    xiii


## I. MINNEAPOLIS SCENE
What Makes a House Beautiful    3
My House on 44th Street    4
Remodeling My House and the Workmen    7
On Roses    9
Opening Day    11
A Baseball Game at Nicollet Park    13
The Best Boys    16
Minnesota vs Nebraska at Memorial Stadium    18
The Ice Follies    21
The Circus Unloading in the Meadow . . .    23
Elaine Norden and Women as Tycoons    25
Girls Working on the Railroad    27
Olden Times    30


## II. PORTRAITS
Robert Penn Warren    32
Paul Robeson    34
John S. Pillsbury    37
Colonel Ole Reistad    39
Countess Mary (Part I & Part II)    43, 45
Carl Sandburg    47
Officer Joe Ryan    50
Dr. Francis Bull    52
Dr. Piet Kolthoff    56
Dr. William O'Brien    59
Kate Tucker    62
Kieth Emery    65
My Brother Torvald (Part I & Part II)    68, 71
Mr. Bruce Carlson of The Schubert Club    75

## III. CHILDREN

Children: How to Be Good to Them    80
Discipline and Children    82
On Scolding Children    85
Until All Teachers Are Angels    88
There is No Resting Place Down Here    89
Parents Must Be More Fun    91
My Advice to a Boy of 18    94
Gaby, Sandra and Graduation    96


## PHOTOGRAPHS


## IV. FEMINISM

The Regrettable Herd Instinct    105
A History of Women    108
20 Million Hunters: An Aspect of Feminism    118
Fat and Thin Women    124
Abortion    132
On Prostitution    135
Fallen Women    138


## V. ANIMALS

My Dear, Dear Cat Friends    141
Florence Murphy and Sam    147
Pogo    148
Lion Farm    149
Report on the Poor Animals    151
Bullfighting and Rodeo Riders    155
The Least of These    157
"Humane" Societies    160
The Victims    163
The Medical Scientist's Worst Enemy    168
Fireflies    173
How to Cut the Throat Properly    175

## VI. SPECULATIONS: SPIRITUAL AND PHILOSOPHICAL

What Do I Believe?   178
Walter Russell, the Sculptor   180
Dr. Henry M. Simmons   182
Monsignor Fulton Sheen   187
Scandinavian-American Banquet and Kierkegaard   190
The Art Institute Show   193
One of the Very Few Masculine Feminists   196
Different Ways of Praying   198

## VIII. WELL-BEING

On Making Choices   200
Tell Me More   205
On Using New Words   211
On Fighting and Bravery   213
Being an Optimist   216
On Drinking, Nags, and Scolds   218
Why Men are Cross When They Come Home   220
Confessions of a Badly Dressed Woman   223
Confessions of a Secret Teetotaller   227
On Two Kinds of Moderation   234
New Year's Resolution   235
A Spree on Gasoline   237
On Running Up Pike's Peak   240
My Failure at Pike's Peak   243
On Walking   246
Bill Roessler and How to Walk, Dance   248
Every Fine Garden Had Such Things   251

# PREFACE

*"I am 93. Have written two books.
Have about ~~five~~ six million words published . . ."*
—Brenda Ueland,
Letter to Robert Giroux, January 14, 1985

A mong the dozens of notebooks containing hundreds of newspaper clippings, among the thousands of unbound handwritten and typed sheets that only begin to suggest the sum total of one writer's work, there is Brenda Ueland's penned letter (in large, scrawled form) to publisher Robert Giroux. Written two months before her death in March, 1985, this note describes the vast repository of one of the most prolific and wildly original Midwestern (and American) authors of the twentieth century. Although Farrar, Straus & Giroux would turn a blind eye to Brenda's repeated requests for publication consideration, the "project" was already well underway by Bruce Carlson whose attractive Schubert Club editions of ME and If You Want to Write, helped to carry forward our awareness of Brenda's book-length offerings into the 1980s. In 1987, Scott Walker's Graywolf Press initiated a paperback reprinting of If You Want to Write and the book has since sold over 140,000 copies with no end in sight. It was with this spirited rekindling of a broad-based audience hungry for more of Brenda's writings that I received a telephone call one Spring day in 1989. "This is Bruce Carlson calling from The Schubert Club. We've seen your books and we think you're our man." Soon I was drafted for work by the inner circle of Ueland supporters: Bruce Carlson, Paul Johnson (whose chance meeting with Brenda began a writer's friendship), and Brenda's daughter Gabrielle McIver (known to friends as "Gaby"). We became a working group, a support group, and met frequently at Gaby and Jim McIver's home for meals and serious discussions about a wide range of topics (including the latest progress of the Minnesota Twins). Over the ensuing three years, we gathered together, selected and edited the materials you see herein.

Of course, one of the most difficult questions an editor faces when confronted with thousands of pages of material is how to make choices and then order that material in a manner that is pleasing and accessible for the reader. This gathering brings together some 80 articles, short essays, and newspaper columns that Brenda Ueland wrote and published during a period from the late 1930s (a scene describing a circus unloading in Kenwood Parkway) to the 1984 portrait of Bruce Carlson. Within this timeframe, we have tried to represent Brenda's vast array of interests between two covers. Let me assure you: there are hundreds (and hundreds!) more pages that *could* be included: we simply chose what we liked best and organized the writings around six or seven large topics. The book begins with familiar scenes described in Ueland's native Minneapolis, to intimate portraits of interesting personalities, to advice-giving about raising children, and on to more deep thinking as inspired by feminist issues, spirituality, and emotional and physical well-being. A section on "Animals" is perhaps the most strident and forceful in its denunciations of animal experimentation for scientific research. We believe that this book can be read straight through with pleasure from the beginning or opened at random to focus upon a particular subject or theme.

The general reader may also want to know where and when each of these individual writings may have first appeared. This is a slippery proposition at best, as we discovered that Brenda often wrote one newspaper column in one year and then returned to it some other time revising and updating it, only to republish it as a "new" piece. For example, Ueland might compose a newspaper column in a 1950s edition of the *Minnesota Posten* (a Norwegian-American newspaper) and then later revise and republish it in her 1970s *Minneapolis Tribune* column. While this may prove frustrating to literary historians and others, we decided to "free" each piece from its moorings in time and place, and leave each one undated so as to let them stand (or fall) on their own merits. In general, though, the writings in the "Minneapolis Scene" section were written and published during the late 1930s and early 1940s, the "Portraits" section spans the 1940s to 1980s, articles about children and feminist thought are from the 1950s to 1970s. Brenda composed most of her anti-vivisection writings during the late 1950s and early 1960s and published them as a series in a long-running column entitled "Report on the Poor Animals" in *The Minnesota Posten*. Many of the articles on "Well-Being" were composed and published during the last twenty years of Brenda's life with her pieces on climbing Pike's Peak written when the author was in her mid-eighties. Almost all of Brenda's newspaper columns are preserved on microfilm at the Minnesota Historical Society in Saint Paul, Minnesota if anyone cares to pursue these matters further.

About style and content: as any reader of this book will soon find out, Brenda's "original mind" extended to creating new words, new expressions of speech ("like a bug in a monkey nut") as well as nontraditional grammar and punctuation. Where textual editing was necessary, we did so only to give clarity and authority to the writing and never to intentionally change meaning. Brenda was something of a master of the parenthetical statement and oftentimes would overrun and restructure a sentence to drive home a point or make a profound insight. The reader will also notice Brenda's frequent allusions to historical figures: heros, classical writers, musicians, philosophers, poets, dramatists, and visual artists are all mentioned as she makes her way through each article and argument. This is no mere name-dropping—Ueland was a careful reader and interpreter of many historical works and used this material to add depth and authority to her viewpoints. In some respects, it may be interesting to compare the substance and vitality of Brenda's work with that of another Midwestern "force"—her contemporary, Meridel Le Sueur. Or to contrast Brenda's large vision of humanity and constantly evolving presentations with that of Walt Whitman whose final version of *Leaves of Grass* was published during the first year of Ueland's life.

Finally, a project as huge and all-encompassing as this couldn't have been accomplished without the able-bodied assistance and talents of several people. Beyond the obvious merits (and wisdom!) of our editorial board, we also note the contributions of Tracey Johnson and Anthony Signorelli who each transcribed portions of the book from newspaper columns into a computerized system. Marian Lansky of Clarity in Duluth, Minnesota, developed the design and format for this volume. We were assisted in our research by the support staffs of the Minneapolis Public Library's Minneapolis Author's Archives and the Minnesota Historical Society. The National Endowment for the Arts awarded us funding to support this project in a time of severe financial restrictions. To all who helped, our sincerest thanks!

And now, on with the show!

—*Jim Perlman*, Publisher

# ADMIRING BRENDA UELAND'S HANDSPRINGS

When I first read these selections from Brenda Ueland's writings, I felt before long that I was being pulled irresistibly, forcefully—though sometimes under protest— into the orbit of her personality. To read Brenda Ueland is to feel you are in her immediate presence, talking to her, arguing with her, and listening, half-mesmerized, with a mixture of admiration and irritation, curiosity and amusement, and laughing-out-loud pleasure.

She is no stylist. Direct, almost abrupt, she sometimes writes in a passionate flow of words that tumble over each other. Her adjectives frequently rush on as if they were a stream that could batter down an opponent. In her enthusiasm, she is apt to find everything recurringly "wonderful." She repeats favorite anecdotes, phrases, and aphorisms, occasionally cribbing from her own earlier writings. Because so many of these collected pieces were written for newspaper columns, they can seem hasty, unfinished or truncated.

Yet Brenda Ueland herself, high-spirited, tempestuous, funny, contradictory, overwhelms such criticisms of her prose. Unabashed and persistent, she talks to her readers as if to old, deeply interested friends. She assumes without hesitation their intimate understanding. Such friends, she somehow makes us feel, don't need or expect any superficial polish— just straight, honest, compelling talk. So her repetitiousness, for example, eventually comes to seem part of her ardor in promoting her favorite causes, her heaped-up ecstatic adjectives the inevitable result of her fiery optimism, her meandering organization inextricable from the quirkiness of her lively mind.

What one reads Brenda Ueland for, in the end, is not just what she says or even how she says it, but for the stimulation of her company. She makes one want to get to know her, to observe her, and to learn from her something about how to live a full, rich, and exciting life.

And she is eager to tell us. In fact, as any reader of this collection will soon see, she can hardly be stopped! In her autobiography, ME, first published in 1939 to little notice and then successfully reissued by The Schubert Club in 1983, Brenda Ueland describes her first forty-seven years. She admits in her opening pages that despite having known a few famous people, she does not plan to focus either on them or on external events. "There is nothing especially interesting in my life," she writes, somewhat disingenuously, "but my inner life, like everybody's in the world, is interesting. I have much to say about that. I have many thoughts about how I and others might become better and happier." And off she goes, careening happily from family anecdotes to vignettes of New York City just before and after World War I to her unconsummated love affair with famed Arctic explorer Fridtjof Nansen to her lifelong pursuit of creativity and originality.

Born in Minneapolis in 1891, to a family that proudly looked back to her distinguished Norwegian grandfather, Ole Gabriel Ueland, a leader of Parliament, and parents who continued his civic example, young Brenda grew up in a large and enlightened family. In her portrait, "Dr. Henry Simmons," she writes lovingly: "My parents were political idealists, feminists, democrats. They wanted their children to be light-hearted and athletic, to live outdoors and eat oranges and apples. My mother thought the girls should not be the menials of the boys and so the boys made their own beds and the girls were on the football team in the pasture."

Encouraged by her remarkable mother, who, besides raising seven children, was a tireless and influential worker for child-labor laws, women's suffrage, and other liberal causes, Brenda Ueland followed her own wandering lights. She went East to college, first to Wells, and then, when she yearned for broader horizons, to Barnard in New York City. After graduating and working as the first woman reporter on the *Minneapolis Tribune*, she used her savings to go to Europe. Returning to New York, Brenda Ueland cut her hair off, studied art and lived in

Greenwich Village.

Of her years in New York, Brenda Ueland remembers somewhat wistfully in ME, "There began for me one of the gayest, most jokey, intoxicating, free and jolly existences perhaps that has ever been experienced." Writing for the magazine EVERY WEEK, and then eventually free-lancing, she met Willa Cather, John Reed, and other noted Villagers. She had her first love affairs (with her usual hyperbole, she once told an interviewer that she'd had "more than a hundred lovers" during her long life), and she married for the first time.

From this marriage Brenda Ueland had her only child, a girl named Gabrielle, "Gaby" for short, after her famous Norwegian grandfather. In the section of this collection called "CHILDREN," Brenda Ueland explains at length her unusual ideas about encouraging and nurturing children. "Parents Must Be More Fun" ends with a typical explosion of enthusiasm: "I say to those youngish parents who are exhausted by their children and, with pale, neurasthenic frowns on their foreheads, are always pleading, 'Plee-ase go to bed dear...Plee-ase now Jack, Sally, Jane, go in the other room dear, and look at television."

"'No,' I say, 'you are doing it wrong. You are failing as parents. You should be so vigorous, healthy, in the pink of condition (cut out all the smoking and drinking and coffee breaks), so inexhaustible, rambunctious, jolly, full of deviltry and frolic, of stories, of dramatizations, of actions, of backward somersaults, or athletics and tomfoolery, of hilarity, that your children at last, after hours of violent exercise, worn down by laughter and intellectual excitement, with a pale, neurasthenic frown on *their* foreheads, cry: 'Plee...eeease, Mama, go to bed!'"
This impassioned burst of advice shows Brenda Ueland at the top of her form—and a fit, dauntingly energetic form it was.

After her marriage failed, and the Depression made free-lancing precarious, Brenda Ueland returned with Gaby to Minneapolis. There she remained, writing and teaching, for over fifty years, until her death in 1985 at the age of 93. She married and divorced twice more, and at the end of her life she shared her small, cozy house near Lake Harriet in south Minneapolis with her daughter and Gaby's husband, Jim

McIver. Gaby McIver admits her mother was not always easy, "but," Gaby comments wryly, "she was endlessly interesting."

In "My House on 44th Street," Brenda Ueland happily boasts about how hard she worked to make this old house habitable. It suited her personality, she felt: "I have a square room that is glass on three sides and one can see a piece of Lake Harriet. 'The Captain's Room' I call it because I can look through my binoculars at the whales on Lake Harriet. (I was a sea captain in one incarnation and am going to be one in the next.)" Although this popular city lake is edged with trees and home to ducks and geese, it is also ringed by substantial houses and a paved path whizzing with bicyclists and skaters. Only Brenda Ueland would be able to imagine whales on Lake Harriet.

During her later years, Brenda Ueland became a familiar figure around Lake Harriet, where she walked for several miles each day, dressed in her idiosyncratic style, usually a combination of sturdy men's wear, sensible shoes, and eccentric accessories. Writer Karin Winegar, who became one of Brenda Ueland's beloved younger friends, recalled in the *Minneapolis Tribune* after her death: "By the time I met Brenda, she resembled a Zorn, a Norwegian troll. She refused to wear new clothes, preferring comfortably ragged jackets, pants held together with safety pins and old running shoes . . . And yet her good humor, intelligence and enthusiasm gave her an allure that was unmistakably sexy. She had clearly been a terror in her prime, and I was a little relieved that she and I were not competing for anyone's attention."

In her eighties, Brenda Ueland began to receive fresh recognition, partly as a feminist icon, partly as as prescient commentator on health and fitness, and very much as the author of a small book, *If You Want to Write*. This inspirational handbook, aimed at encouraging would-be writers by showing them how to trust their creative instincts, had been first published in 1938.

With enviable self-confidence, Brenda Ueland announces her qualifications for writing this book in her introduction: "For many years I had a large class of people at the Minneapolis

YWCA. I think I was a splendid teacher and so did they." In a postscript, she even produces her own bravura blurb: "At that time when I was writing the book, Carl Sandburg, an old friend, was at our house. He liked the book. He said: 'That is the best book ever written about how to write.'" It is tempting to speculate how Sandburg, who also knew how to promote himself, felt about this inserted testimonial.

When *If You Want to Write* was reprinted in 1983 by The Schubert Club and in a 1987 paperback by Graywolf Press, a new generation of readers evidently agreed with Carl Sandburg. Won over by Brenda Ueland's democratic zeal, constant reassurance, and cheerful exhortations to "Let her go! Be careless, reckless! Be a lion, be a pirate! Write any old way," these Ueland fans and apprentices propelled the book's sales to what now exceeds 140,000 copies. This is recognition indeed.

Feature stories about Brenda Ueland in the Twin Cities press during the early 1980s transparently show that their subject relished attention. At the beginning of ME she admits, with an irresistible candor, "All my life I seem to have had two forces working in me—pushing me, making me search, search and never rest. They give me an energy that sets my mind wrangling and struggling and arguing and discussing things, whenever I am alone. One energy seems to be the wish to be important and admired . . . The other energy is that I want to *be* what is admirable inside, whether anyone admires me or not."

This tension between egotism and idealism enlivens many of her essays. A reader is never quite sure at any particular moment whether Brenda Ueland is saying something genuinely admirable or is waiting, with disarming eagerness, to be admired. When is she ferociously (or gaily) arguing mainly for the sake of attention? How many—all, some, any—of her passionate assertions does she really believe? Is she exaggerating outrageously for effect? What is she probably leaving out? Only one thing is sure: Brenda Ueland is having a ball. In *If You Want to Write* she says, "Writing is not a performance but a generosity." With Brenda Ueland, writing was often both.

Brenda Ueland loved to perform. In a diary entry of 1932, she notes: "I walk, stop at the sandy beach and try hand-springs and do them better than before, even getting to my feet. This is good." When I think of Brenda Ueland, I often picture her twirling hand-over-foot on the beach of a Minneapolis lake, showing off for herself—and, in a sense, for her eventual readers.

On that day in 1932, she was forty-one. Before it was fashionable to be fit, Brenda Ueland promoted exercise, healthy diet, and meditation. In her mid-eighties, she attempted a run up Pike's Peak, an exploit she describes in two essays included here, "On Running Up Pike's Peak," and "My Failure at Pike's Peak." Of course, she knew she hadn't really failed. She won admiring publicity for simply trying at age 84. Her grandson-in-law, a doctor, told her, she reports: "There is not a doctor in the U.S.A. who would *allow* you to go up on the top *even in a car*, because of your age." But she showed *them*: one day in training she hiked ten hours up the mountain, without, she claims with justifiable pride, "the faintest qualm about the hazards of old age." After all, she reminds us, "in Minneapolis I walk at the rate of a mile in twenty minutes steadily for 9 miles, without a rest, and do not get tired. The lower legs are splendid."

Brenda Ueland was an almost fanatic walker, and she believed that walking could cure many ills. In "A Spree On Gasoline," she wishes she could establish a kind of monastic order for young people, like the French Cistercians who had vowed never to ride. "Now if our high school students walked and/or ran everywhere," she went on hopefully, "think how wonderful they would be! Red cheeks, long legs, wide flashing smiles. Dauntless and helpful."

Exercise was essential, Brenda Ueland felt, to keep her "creative fountain" clear. She often writes about this fountain, which others, she says, might call spirit, or intelligence, or imagination. "If you're very tired, strained, have no solitude, run too many errands, talk to too many people, drink too many cocktails, this little fountain is muddied over and covered with a lot of debris," she admonishes in "Tell Me More."

Smoking is one sure way to muddy the fountain. In "New

Year's Resolution," she advises smokers, in her most exuberant battering-ram prose: "Say that you resolve not to smoke. Think, 'Oh the bliss, the freshness, the athletic bounceyness, the clear slippery eyes, the iridescent sparkling intelligence when I don't smoke! Think of it! To get out of that horrible old straight-jacket, sucking in that stuff until your mouth tastes like a motorman's mitt and you feel that you have a combined case of slow poisoning, gangrene, steeple-head and impacted teeth."

Alcohol is also anathema, she explains in an essay both amusing and hectoring, "Confessions of a Secret Teetotaller." After drinking "the glass of poison," she warns, "your voice rises and clatters out of you." She relentlessly holds her own party behavior up for unpleasant scrutiny: "This is when you giggle, whack men on the arm with your fan and say, 'Naughty boy!', when you talk in a loud, unhearing voice about 'conditions all over the world.'"

Yet even in her teetotalling fervor, Brenda Ueland is not easily pigeonholed. In this same short essay, she suddenly avers that, in fact, she loves to give cocktail parties herself, "and when I do, I always want everybody to drink to beat the band . . . Say people took to serving lukewarm Ovaltine or iced Postum at cocktail parties—No, I just love cocktail parties. The thought of stepping into a room full of amiable uproar with pretty women with new hats on—that is one of the pleasantest things in life."

Brenda Ueland is always reluctant to appear a goody-goody. One of her most endearing stories, tinted by her exaggerative flair, is how she satisfies her occasional cravings for fudge sundaes. "I go downtown to the most opulent, sinful ice cream emporium in town," she confesses, "and have a double fudge sundae. Then ashamed to ask for more I go home, change my clothes, put my hat on backwards as a disguise and come back and have another one."

When Brenda Ueland exclaims how she likes to see pretty women in new hats at cocktail parties, she might have added that she would probably not have counted herself among them. Pretty she was—or, rather, strikingly handsome, judging by early photographs—but she paid little attention to fashion. In "Confessions of a Badly Dressed Woman," she claims that she was the first woman in the country not only to cut her hair short but also to wear sailor pants and slacks, men's double-breasted chesterfield coats, shorts, and bare-backed handkerchief halters. (Here, too, her delight in spectacular exaggeration is evident. In "The Regrettable Herd Instinct," she ups her own ante: "I dress about 25 years ahead of the fashion. I can prove it. I was the first woman in the Western World to have my hair all cut off.")

Reading about Brenda Ueland's defiant wearing of men's pants, observers of American popular culture may be reminded of another performer, an actress who also became known for her outspokenness, independence, and trend-setting trousers. Brenda Ueland would have enjoyed twitting Katharine Hepburn about the copycat title of her own blithely egotistic autobiography, ME, published forty-seven years after the original.

But Brenda Ueland certainly did not want to be only, or even mostly, remembered for what she wore—or didn't wear. (Though indignantly denied by her daughter Gaby, stories still circulate in Minneapolis about people who claim they saw her sunbathing nude outside the old family home on Lake Calhoun.) She saw herself as a spiritual writer, a woman who could teach others how to live their lives. In her essay "On Making Choices," Brenda Ueland urges her readers to find an unshakeable moral core for all their actions and decisions. "But we must try to find our True Conscience, our True Self, the very Center, for this is the only first-rate choice-making center. Here lies all originality, talent, honour, truthfulness, courage, and cheerfulness. Here only lies the ability to choose the good and the grand, the true and the beautiful."

Of course Brenda Ueland did not think this True Self was stodgy, puritanical, or self-denying. "Now in making choices," she counseled, "never be grim. Think of life as a river, a smooth-flowing, golden Heraclitean river. Know that you will make dreadful mistakes with almost every choice. Hurrah! Congratulate yourself for making daring, honourable, ridiculous mistakes." To Brenda Ueland, life offered constant and exciting challenges. "The choices turn up every few minutes, every hour," she writes. "To choose bravery or flight? To choose your natural carefree, rollicking self, or to choose your cautious, pussy-footing self?"

Courage, daring, honour, truthfulness, "the good and the grand": Brenda Ueland fiercely espoused chivalric ideals. Her highest praise is to compare someone to a knight. "Now from the earliest childhood I have loved heroes, brave men, fighters, Vikings," she writes in "Bullfighting and Rodeo Riders," and in "On Fighting and Bravery," she pronounces firmly, "Courage is the greatest quality of all." Her creed is perhaps best summarized in two lines of "On Drinking, Nags, and Scolds." She proposes: "To change oneself or the world for the *better* requires two things: 1. A continuing vigorous restlessness of the intellect and the imagination and 2. A continuing jovial courage." She sometimes ended her letters to dear friends, "Strength to your sword arm!"

She often sees herself as a knight riding into battle on noble causes—albeit a jovial knight, one with a rollicking nature, one who was "jokey," another of her special words of praise. In ME, she relates how William Blake appeared to her in a dream one storm-ridden night: "Blake was thundering to me to be a wild lonely galloping horse, compact in myself, in my life and my work; not to be just a tenderly loving woman, being bled of anxious love by others."

When a cause struck at her heart, Brenda Ueland rode out with all flags flying. The essays in "ANIMALS" are only a few of the enraged indictments she levelled against vivisectors. She wrote some of her gentlest and most loving essays about her pets (see "My Dear, Dear Cat Friends"), and some of her most scathing about people who abused animals. Although she lived in a state where hunting is a revered fall pastime, she threw down her gauntlet before those unknightly men and women. "Since I was six years old I have felt nothing but indignation and contempt for hunters and sportsmen," she writes in "Bullfighting and Rodeo Riders" and concludes stingingly: "Perhaps the most angering thing in these exhibitions—

man cruelly conquering beast—is the entire absence of fairness, of chivalry, of knightliness, of grandeur, of grace, of *noblesse oblige.*"

It was not that Brenda Ueland longed to be a man so that she could emulate one of her heroes. "No," she wrote in "Twenty Million Hunters," "it is women who are chivalrous. We are Knights. We love, adore beauty and defenselessness and try, with passionate ferocity, to protect it."

Brenda Ueland's feminism, like everything else about her, was distinctly her own. In "A History of Women," she excoriates the traditional Biblical view of women: "There is a persistent ungentlemanliness, a lack of feeling of justice and kindliness towards women, in the Old Testament." Moses and Abraham, she points out rather sadly, were not knightly. With relief she turns to Jesus. "The divinely balanced nature, man *and* woman, together and equal, was manifested in Jesus. He was on our side."

Although some men were her heroes—Sir Tristram du Lyonesse, Roland, Olav Trygveson, Lord Nelson, Garibaldi, and others—she was sure that paternalistic society had damaged many men. "They must worry about their hardness, their dry know-it-allism, their destructiveness," she cautions. She saw men as somehow allied with Science, which she hated, feeling it was opposed to "the good and the grand." "Men should be happy because women will rescue us from Science, that horrible idolotry" she says, dismissing scientists as "gross literalists," "computers of everything," and mere "measurers collecting rocks on the moon."

Decades before the so-called "men's movement," Brenda Ueland worried about the stunting of men's emotions. "Perhaps that is one reason that men as they grow older are so much less interesting and so much less fun than women," she says in "There Is No Resting Place Down Here," for men tend to become "emotionally arthritic, rheumatic in all their emotional joints." In "Tell Me More," an essay on the importance of listening, she evokes a haunting picture of men who have lost this ability: "Now this non-listening of able men is the cause of one of the saddest things in the world—the loneliness of fathers, of those quietly sad men who move among their grown children like remote ghosts."

But gloom and ghosts don't linger long in Brenda Ueland's work. She is an unabashed optimist, which she defines in "Being an Optimist" as someone with a "cheerful, flexible, liquid, open, bouncy mind." Even her nostalgic essays are seldom melancholy. When she writes about bygone days in Minneapolis, her memories sparkle. One of her funniest short anecdotes, related both in ME and in "Confessions of a Badly Dressed Woman," describes how she and her sister-in-law Julie once dared to go downtown bare-legged. But they were so shaken by public reaction that they turned around and took the streetcar home again!

In "Olden Times," Brenda Ueland magically evokes the Sunday afternoon parade of horses and carriages that went by her childhood home. "Remember it was a soft dirt road then and the stately elegant procession came noiselessly along. We would watch for Mrs. Thomas Lowry in her victoria with her black horses and silver harness, her red-faced coachman on the box . . . Mrs. Lowry, with a black lace parasol lifted gaily against the sun, would bow and wave a tiny lace handkerchief."

This kind of condensed but lively description shows Brenda Ueland as a writer at her best. Just when an essay begins to sag, she will suddenly draw an unforgettable brief picture—Robert Penn Warren casually swimming back and forth with her for hours in Lake Harriet, Nansen dashing to her back porch in sub-zero weather for gulps of fresh frigid air, World War II women workers at the railroad yard lunching in an old box car, a professor in his formal academic robe looking like "a kind of Minnesota beefeater."

Along with sharp vignettes, Brenda Ueland offers the pleasure of her company. In her essays and articles she often seems to be thinking aloud, and a reader overhears remarks and observations that are startling, honest, absurd, and unexpected by turns—and sometimes all at once. Who else would justify sloppy clothes with this tongue-in-cheek grandiosity? "The reason I dress as I do is that I have to tone myself down. Otherwise people would go wild . . . Whenever I appeared downtown they would run amuck—men leaving their wives, etc." Who could better this description of the breast stroke? "You sink under water each time and with a convulsive paroxysm of backbone and muscles, you come up glaring and snorting, mouth open like Neptune's, or a shark's."

What other reporter would describe the Ice Follies: "It is as though everybody were continually shouting 'Whee!'" Or attend a baseball game and admit: "Kansas City got one run and we got none. But it seemed to me a fine game. Anyway, I don't think about scores and prefer to gaze in every face." Or instruct children not to steal because it is "unaesthetic, i.e. it requires sneaking and padding about and pussyfooting in the most slimey unattractive way."

Who could fail to like a woman who, in "Remodeling My House and the Workmen," reports the following pungent exchange? "Mr. Craig is six-feet-two: a gaunt fiercely short scraggly mustache. One day he was carrying out the icebox and I was steering it and he said over his shoulder:

'My wife has never done five minutes work like this in all her life.'

I shouted: 'Throw her in the river! To thunder with her! Get someone like me!'

'Naw,' he said, the cigar at an acute angle and this chin against the ice box as it tipped down the stairs; 'I like that kind of woman.'"

It may or may not be significant that when Brenda Ueland was helping her furniture mover carry out an icebox, she was in her vibrant sixties. What matters more is her zest, her shouting, her elation in reporting what she did and what she said and what he said back. In almost all of her work, Brenda Ueland calls out to the reader and asks for response.

"Don't be grim!" she cries. "Be careless, reckless! Be a lion, be a pirate! Be a knight! Strive for a cheerful, flexible, liquid, open, bouncy, spirit! Keep the fountain clear! Now watch me doing hand-springs by the lake! Pay attention! Listen to me! *Listen* to me! " She would be delighted, but not surprised, that readers still do.

—*Susan Allen Toth*

Susan Allen Toth was born in Ames, Iowa and is a graduate of Smith College, the University of California at Berkeley, and the University of Minnesota, where she received her Ph.D. She is currently a Professor of English at Macalester College in Saint Paul, Minnesota. Among her books are: *Blooming: A Small-Town Girlhood*, *Ivy Days: Making My Way Out East*, *How to Prepare for Your High School Reunion and Other Mid-Life Musings*. Her most recent publications include: *Reading Rooms: America's Foremost Writers Celebrate Our Public Libraries* (edited with John Coughlan), *A House of One's Own* (written with her husband, James Stageberg), and *My Love Affair With England*. She lives in south Minneapolis (near Lake Harriet), with her husband and her daughter, Jennifer.

## WHAT MAKES A HOUSE BEAUTIFUL

A house is pretty and charming because of the spirit of the people in it. It does not matter if the interior is Louis Quinze or Early Pullman. This sets me trying to define what makes an ugly and disagreeable house.

Well, what makes a house ugly to me is closed windows in beautiful weather; darkness; stuffy veils of curtains shutting out the jocund day, and bad air and a stagnant bad smell. All this can be due to a fussy fear of the lady of the house that opening windows will let dust in, or fade the rugs (which proves she is more practical than loving) or it can be due to a general unhealthiness of the people themselves: not only overstuffed chairs but overstuffed people full of steaks and chops, with stale cigar smoke in all the plush drapes.

And a disagreeable house is one with frigid indirect lighting, or rooms lighted by horrid unbecoming lights in the ceiling, and with muddy colors everywhere, and putty and liver-colored walls. People who live in such a house look like their house, you will see, if you take notice. They have muddy complexions and they are cross and commercial. No sunlight in their souls.

◆

# My House on 44th Street

❖❖

I have bought a house near Lake Harriet, a kind of bum old house but I could afford it. And anyway, I like it because it's old. High ceilings. They don't press down upon one's skull. They give you a feeling of dignity, the lifted head, elegance, courtliness.

And it has a yard two hundred feet deep and full of weeds, golden rod, apple trees, a monstrous oak, thickets. Many people say, "Oh, I don't like so much yard—all that hard work!" But that is the very thing I like about it: plenty of hard work. One gets so strong and lively then. As gangsters name themselves Floyd ("Pretty Boy") Nelson, I like to give myself soubriquets: Brenda ("Harvard Five-Foot Shelf") Ueland; and Brenda ("Do it the Hard Way") Ueland. And Brenda ("the woman who never gets tired") Ueland. My theory is that the less work you do, leaning feebly on labor-saving devices, the weaker, dimmer and feebler you get. Something in it.

Now ownership is a wonderful thing. I've never owned a house before. I feel an astounding, unquenchable energy. Why, I am an incandescent fountain of fiery gumption. On the second floor of my house I have a square room that is glass on three sides and one can see a piece of Lake Harriet. "The Captain's Room" I call it because I can look through my binoculars at the whales on Lake Harriet. (I was a sea captain in one incarnation and am going to be one in the next.)

I put up my storm windows myself. They are old warped windows covered with the most slobbery cheap paint jobs by those dreadful people (renters, I suppose) who will paint over a couple of pork chops and think it looks all right. So I took a razor and scraped off every bit of paint, even the microscopic dots, and washed them all and polished them all until they shone like diamonds.

"The man" could not come to put them on and was

angered at the absurd helplessness of my sex—how when we find a nail sticking where it shouldn't we have a black-out and mentally cry: "Help! A man! A Carpenter! Ten dollars!" So I borrowed one of those long ladders, carrying it six blocks, ("The kind the fire department has without the hooken," I said to myself) and put on my own storm windows, washing the regular windows high up in the air, very much like those funny men in vaudeville of long ago, swaying and teetering and humming. But it was easy.

And when I could not get a monstrous kitchen cabinet into my house, instead of running in a panic to a carpenter (twenty dollars), I bought a Swedish saw for seven dollars and sawed it in two myself. And pretty soon I got on to how you saw: you relax and don't push. And then by using encyclopedia volumes I actually eased the heavy top half of the cabinet on to the bottom half. "How engineery!" I'd say to myself. "Stresses and strains. Leverage. I get the idea. Easy does it. Queer how I know this without a course. This is what Archimedes meant when he said, 'Give me a lever long enough and I'll lift the world.' "

And when my aged windows stuck and could not be opened, what do you think I did? With a kind of excitement, a dread, I would put on my glasses and try to figure out why the window stuck. I discovered that a strip ran along the side. I took it off, with my new hammer and screw driver, trembling with anxious trepidation. (Oh, the terror that I'd never get it back again!) And I refitted them all so that now they slide like noiseless, greased pistons. It did not even take much brain power—just three to five seconds of attention.

"A rat in a maze, that's what you are," I kept thinking to myself. "Yes, a scientist's rat looking for the way out, and I am the especially bright one that finds the hole."

I put my stormdoor on the front door, fitted it in very nicely, after quite a struggle. It is warped and would not shut entirely. No carpenter for me! I just bought a plane and fixed that bulging place, a cinch! saying to myself, "Brenda, you are a very clever chimpanzee. Or will be, if you keep it up." And I thought of the wonderful chimpanzee the scientist had. He hung a bunch of bananas from the ceiling and gave the chimpanzee a stick to knock them down. The chimpanzee looked up at the bananas, refused the stick, and seized and lifted the professor to get the bananas.

By next spring I bet I can build my own garage.

◊

# REMODELING MY HOUSE
## AND THE WORKMEN

❖

I have been remodeling my house and now it is all done. There is a new fireplace and five huge windows on the East and South. All day until sundown there is a great yellow triangle of sunlight on the floor. That's what I like.

But the best thing about it is getting to know the workmen so very well. Alfred Olson, the carpenter, and Trygve Larsen who built the whole brick chimney in two days, on Saturday and Sunday. Now and then he would shout "Mud!" and Leslie Larsen (tall, slim, laughing, handsome, and blue-eyed) would bring up a fresh pie of cement mixed to perfection. The chimney is a work of art and where it becomes smaller at the top there is a kind of Egyptian design, as though it had been built for a Pharaoh.

Then there is Russell. He is Irish and Czech. He comes from a farm near Mora, Minnesota. He loves nature and wishes that he had a farm right now; drinks buttermilk and is incapable of getting either mad or tired. One Saturday he came and dug my cellar a foot deeper, tossing the sand out the window and I shovelled it away from the window to keep the opening clear. I say to the men: "I will do the heavy work, so don't worry about that. YOU are the artists."

Then there is Johnny Olson, very thin and light, really only jockey-size, and he worked fast for those eight hours every day, carrying those fat wheel barrows full of cement, sometimes through deep sand. He has a way of looking at you steadily with a gentle, questioning smile through lovely sapphire-blue eyes. I watched him making a grand stairway of cement that comes curving in a parabola over a sloping lawn and, for the most part, he measured with his eye alone. What perfection! What geometry in that stairway! Einstein could spend columns of mathematics on it, if he cared to.

Johnny Olson said: "When you were in Norway, did you see King Haakon's palace?"

"Yes."

"You remember the wrought-iron fence around it?"

"Yes, Beautiful!"

"My father made it. His name was Ole Peter Olson."

Johnny Olson, I learned later from Trygve Larsen, once fell and broke his back and was supposed to be dead. But here he is again, working with prowess and skill. He says remarkable things. I am always asking him the next day, "Just how did you put that?"

"God hates a coward," he says. What a wonderful phrase. I have inscribed it on my coat-of-arms.

And I must tell you about Mr. Craig—Archie D. Craig. I have known him for several years because he has a five-ton truck and has moved my furniture a couple of times. And when I broke up my cement-and-cobblestone driveway in June, he and his son, Tom, carried it away. He comes and carries anything enormous that you want carried, and takes it away.

Mr. Craig is six-feet-two: A gaunt fiercely short scraggly mustache. Always smoking a cigar held in his short teeth. With that denim cap and its dashing upturned visor, he looks rather like a Civil War general. He is a very droll man and we argue about the comparative prowess of Scotchmen (himself) and Norwegians (me). One day he was carrying out the icebox and I was steering it and he said over his shoulder:

"My wife has never done five minutes of work like this in all her life."

I shouted: "Throw her in the river! To thunder with her! Get someone like me!"

"Naw," he said, the cigar at an acute angle and his chin against the icebox as it tipped down the stairs; "I like that kind of woman."

◆

# ON ROSES

❖❖

T alked to Carl Holst, chief of the Rose Garden, a tanned young man in GI working trousers. Topaz-brown eyes and the outstanding thing about his looks (I hope he will forgive me) is his remarkable double-fringed, tan-colored, tangled eyelashes. He shows me white roses, whiter than Death, than magnesium fire, whiter than phosphorus, named "Frau Karl Druschski." Shakespeare said something about a rose smelling as sweet by any other name, but "Frau Karl Druschski" or "Kaiserin Gustav Wilhelm" is better than some name like Mrs. P. K. Peebles.

Carl Holst showed me the "Peace Rose" which is yellow in the bud and early blossom and gradually blushes into pink. And he showed me the "Crimson Glory," so red, so perfect it "makes the rash gazer wipe his eye," as the poet George Herbert said.

And Carl Holst says, his hand gently lifting the red rose as if by its pretty chin, as if it were a beautiful countenance, "and early in the morning when there is dew on it, it couldn't be prettier if it were covered with real diamonds."

As he walks about in the sun he seems to know every single rose's face—how it feels this morning, if it feels exuberant and happy. There is a place along the fence where the roses are still unnamed. They have just recently been bred and they are being tried out. Are they beautiful and sturdy enough? If so they will be given a fine name like "President Truman" or "the Empress of Cathay."

He says that a man from New Jersey came way out here to Minneapolis for his vacation, and came every day to the Rose Garden. And a bachelor from St. Paul comes over and spends whole Saturdays and Sundays taking notes, lifting the pretty blushing roses to gaze at them.

The President of the National Rose Society came. But the

names of these people I must investigate further. I bet that every rose fan alive is benign, tall, romantic, and handsome, a very perfect gentle knight.

From Marie Vind: "The pretty yellow roses in the side of the Lake Harriet Rose Garden are Rosa Hugonis, sometimes called 'the Golden Rose of China.' So you were right about their 'more poetical name' and almost right in calling it 'The Huguenot Rose.' By the way why don't you make more sketches? I liked your drawing of 'the hat lady' in Saturday's column. P.S. There is a Harrison yellow rose but it is single and pale yellow."

Well, I have gone to the Rose Garden and studied their names now. Some names are not poetic, like that of the rose named "Dr. Van Fleet." Shakespeare said it didn't matter at all what a rose's name is. But is this so? Say you put it in Sonnet XCIX:

> The Dr. Van Fleets fearfully on thorns did stand
> One blushing shame, another white despair;
> A third, nor red nor white, had stol'n of both
> And to his robbery annex'd thy breath. . . .

The roses in the Rose Garden are the most beautiful things you ever shuddered before. There is Le Rêve—the Dream; the Talisman, rose-colored but turning to bright gold in its inner circle; the Clio (she was the Muse of history), a single rose on a tiny decorative tree, a most beautiful death-pale white-pink. And there is the Captain Hayward rose, dashing and bright red.

> "Sweet rose, whose hue angry and brave
> Bids the rash gazer wipe his eye. . ."

That is the only way to describe the red-brightness of the Captain Hayward. There is the Goldfinch Rose and the Sunset—O yellow, yellow!

◆

# Opening Day

❖❖

The first baseball game was yesterday afternoon. A grey wet London day with wet rain suspended in the freshened air. All morning I was telepathically aware of the boyish prayers of grown men for good weather. Mr. Mike Kelley's and Mr. Rosy Ryan's.

But the rain was held in the sky. Cars were parked for six blocks in every direction and men poured through the gates—everybody so well dressed and stock-brokerish and stylish and sportish, this first day. People pushing through the turnstiles were grinning and joking; everybody hurrying through the dank cold corridors and shouting wisecracks to friends ahead.

A huge crowd. The band from Fort Snelling. The diamond as pleasant as a Spring lawn.

What do I know about baseball? A man named Mr. Kelley owns the Millers. (Is that why they are called Kels? I guess so). He is the financial backer and hopes his team beats all the others and that all the games are nerve-wrackingly exciting so spectators will fill the grandstand and have a pleasant summer.

Mr. Kelley's manager is a big famous man named Rosy Ryan, so called because he had rosy Irish cheeks when he went to Holy Cross College at Worcester. He was a famous pitcher for the New York Giants. I can't imagine a better manager and disciplinarian for young athletes, stern and intelligent like a warm-hearted Commando colonel.

Then there is Mr. Parke Carroll, aide-de-camp of Mr. Ryan. He says there is only one thing I can do for him—become a fan. Well, I will. And am. Though I haven't been to many games since I played myself.

Now when I see a baseball game I see the slugging, the unbelievable catching; the lazy tired way they reach for bullets in the air; the pitcher's long meditation and his extraordinary sprawling-grasshopper windup and explosion. The catcher like a gladiator. The umpire so near he'll get his teeth knocked out if he isn't careful.

I love sitting in the sun or soft fog, gazing at each man and his antics and feeling his anguish when he strikes out.

Well, that is what I see in baseball. Though Alice Duer Miller, the pre-eminent novelist, told me that mathematics (she has a Ph.D.)—calculus, Einstein, the fourth dimension, etc.—are a cinch. But baseball is very difficult, deep, involved, involuted, abstract, and metaphysical.

But for Mr. Carroll's sake I will learn it all.

The soldier's band played. Mayor Kline threw the first ball. Chief of Police Hilner sat in his box.

I saw Mrs. Mike Kelley on the roof near the press box. And Red Lowden with a blissful perpetual smile, as though he were eating a pink ice cream cone in Heaven.

The Millers had sparkling new uniforms, white and piped with red. (Kansas City wore a singularly unbecoming, dull, underwear-grey). Rosy Ryan stood often with his hands in the air. (Was it some cryptic signal or heart-breaking anxiety?).

Kansas City got one run and we got none. But it seemed to me a fine game. I expected much worse from the pained dithyrambs of the sportswriters predictions. Anyway, I don't think about scores and prefer to gaze in every face.

Loren Bain went to Edison High School. Otis Clark has terribly long legs. Jack Aragon is the catcher: what a romantic name! And Mike Blazo—must put that name in a novel.

They seemed to count on Bill Ebranyl in emergencies. Fred Vaughan has a competent, piratical nose. Bill Schaedler is six feet three and seems vague and innocent.

Of the others I will tell you when I know them better.

◆

# A BASEBALL GAME AT NICOLLET PARK

**⁂**

A baseball game is a pleasant way to spend a summer evening. You park your car on a shady street and then walk to Nicollet Park—past a big man in a pink shirt and arm-garters, watering the grass; people fanning themselves on wooden front porches; past the blank yellow brick building with rust-colored boards on all the windows. . . the streetcar barns.

The sky is full of fawn-colored clouds against azure and lemon yellow and the palest star beginning to twinkle over the western bleachers. At the gates people stream in. Just beyond the turnstile nice Rosy Ryan (the big manager of the Millers) says "Good evening!" over the bare heads and T-shirts.

Men in their working clothes. A naval officer with his cap on sloppily. Many women. Pretty girls with manes of curls and in slacks, some so swarthy along their noses and under their earrings you know they have been in Lake Calhoun. In the box seats a few dizzily smart knock-outs, as though this were the Polo Grounds in New York.

Everybody said Louisville would win. The sky darkened with dramatic leaden clouds against the fair lemon color, and then the white artificial lights turned everything to daylight, and the twin umpires, in black with tiny caps like Tweedledum and Tweedledee, began to function.

Our pitcher was a young man named Jungels. Could it come from the French word, "jongleur?" He seemed to be very good. About five innings passed and the Louisville men (the Colonels) couldn't get anywhere. Whenever they hit Jungel's ball it was not a dead-center swipe but on a corner (as if it were to rip the corner off) and the ball made a high parabola to the darkening sky until a dim, leaping outfielder always caught it. "Out!"

Then Jungels seemed to blow up. He walked a couple of

them (Ladies: this means he pitched four balls that were so bum and inadequate that the batter was allowed to go to first base). Three men on bases, then, a perfect mess for Mr. Jungels. But he pulled out of this because one of our men, Andres, very easy, athletic and competent-looking, caught a foul, and gave them only one measly run, the one Jungels himself forced by a "walk."

Then the Louisville Colonel Gleeson knocked his home run: that meant 2 to 1 against us. At this point I figured Mr. Jungels and the Millers would have a psychological break-down and begin to slump a little. But not at all. Jungels got even better. Though our side had a trying experience: Somebody (Barna?) knocked a home run and it sailed over the high fence. Yet what happened? At one place an Ewald Dairy painted cow sticks up high in the air. The homer hit the cow and was not a homer.

But we had a player named Buster Maynard (you can see his ferocious pep—his jaw, his sharp nose, his vigorous steel neck show this). He bunted, then stole a base. There he was, on second.

Then our man, Ray, walked (I explained that). Then our man, Danneker got to first and Buster tore to third, but he stopped there in dancing fright because Tom Sheehan, the manager (coaching and yelling along the sidelines) told him to go no further. He could have easily got home. This was an awful blunder.

But we had luck. In this dither of leaping men and screeching fans, Colonel Albright threw the ball to first so wildly that Colonel Al Flair couldn't catch it. Pandemonium busted. And Buster Maynard came running home and Ray right after him. Then our slouching easy-does-it man, Andres, hit a level bullet about six feet from the ground, and going a mile or so, our McCarthy came in home. The score: 4 to 2. We beat.

Walking homeward along Thirty-first Street, everybody happy and peaceful. A Mister and Mrs. hastened ahead of us, both in enormous khaki pants and much the same plump build, only she wore ruby earrings, a gauze-flowered blouse and had a permanent. But I could feel what happy people they were. They both like slacks, like summer, like ball games, and they'd go home and have a cool drink.

And I thought (imagining that I was visiting Siberia) "What an American crowd!" Unaccompanied men in work clothes, or a certified public accountant wearing one of those composition hats that look like masticated sawdust! A happy janitor beside us, blissfully gnawing and breathing forth a black cigar. And to everybody, everybody else was an old friend.

❖

# THE BEST BOYS

❖

**Y**esterday morning 80 young ball players, (17 years old or less) came to Nicollet Park and tried out for a dazzling reward: On August 28 there is a game at the New York Polo Grounds between the East and West—between the best boy players in the country. The managers will be Babe Ruth himself and Ty Cobb himself. The game is sponsored by the *Daily Times* and *Esquire* magazine.

Yesterday they were finding the best boy from Minnesota, the Dakotas, and northern Wisconsin, and they had gathered at Nicollet Park, each with "chaperons" (some very hearty bluff red-faced American Legionnaires).

Last year young Roger Brown was sent to New York. It is a kind of masculine Cinderella story. They live in the Waldorf; they are taken to every theater, sight, fiesta; they shake hands with La Guardia, chiefs of police, world champs, actresses, generals. Then the game at the Polo Grounds before a million cheering, razzing fans. And Ty Cobb to talk in your left ear and tell you what to do!

At Nicollet Park in the cold, blazing yellow sun, every face was dead serious with Parke Carroll of the Millers (a piercing gaze and good-natured smile) and Managers Rosy Ryan and Ray Blades of St. Paul to pick them out.

First the boys sprinted for them and then there was a confusion of pitching, batting, fielding.

A boy of 11 had come to the tryout and it was a bitter blow when he found he was too young. So Eddie Jones of the *Daily Times* made him a bat boy, which meant he sat in the dug-out with them all. "Elwood Satterval," he told me his name was, from Thirty-eighth Avenue South. "Are you on a team, Elwood?" "Yes. A team we got up. I'm catcher."

At noon Bobbie Summers and Barbara Flanagan and I of the *Daily Times* carried milk and sandwiches to them, and a sturdy man told me he was the "chaperon" of a wonderful boy— "Clare Picha. You pronounce it Pee-ha. He's wonderful—good catcher, pitcher." And the husky chaperon said his own name was Ben Maier "of the Twin City Ford Plant Legion Post."

In the afternoon game we saw that No. 12 was excellent, a solid boy with yellow-gold hair. Whenever he was to bat they waved to the outfields and began yelling, "Out to the fences! Get back, guys. Send 'em out to the fences!" This was Ronnie Knutson of St. Paul.

And before our box seats, a handsome boy was pitching to another one labeled "Bearcat," and two little boys beside me said, "That's Critch of Washburn. He's a good boy. I bet he gets it." I got them to spell his name, or try to. It is Crichton, the Admirable Crichton—Dick.

Just then a foul came banging straight at us and hit a very little boy on the head with a horrible "clunk!"—a pale little boy with a 10-cent jockey cap on. "Let him have the ball. Give it to him, the poor kid!" everybody said. He didn't utter a sound, just looked about at our concerned faces with forget-me-not blue eyes and it was hard to keep the tears out of them. He pocketed the brand new ball, smiling. I gazed at him horrified, but he seemed to be all right.

"I wisht I got hit," said the small boy beside me. "What's your name?" I asked. "Michael McInerny." And Michael's friend was Bruce Baxter. "We're eleven and ball players and the same nationalities, part Irish, part Norwegian. We know Elwood, sure... Well, there goes Critch to pitch," they said. But Crichton made some subtle kind of failure that they could explain, but I can't. And the judges chose Clare Picha. But the Admirable Crichton was an alternate and so was Ronnie Knutson.

❖

# MINNESOTA VS. NEBRASKA AT MEMORIAL STADIUM

❖❖

Т
he first football game was on Saturday. (O! the golden weather.) What fun to sit there in that sea of good-nature and enthusiasm, of 50,000 Minnesotans; and in the sparkling air with the sun's golden needles flooding one's face. And to watch the cheerleaders, is so fascinating and delightful. A whole bevy in white flannel trousers would come handspringing and bounding across an angle of the green field like whirling leaves. There was a Nebraska girl cheerleader who was very rhythmic and entertaining, in a red jacket (with an N on it), kicking her spindly legs in saddle shoes, her sharp elbows waggling in the most delightful jazzy way.

I don't know much about football, albeit more than a lady friend of mine who says: "All I know about it is that all the boys fall down." It is so interesting in this first game of the year to see the good players emerge, the unknown personalities, the freshman neophytes, whose ruddy jowls will some day be seen in the sports pages from coast to coast. And in the first game the uniforms (the golden Minnesota ones and the white Nebraska ones) are as unflawed, as immaculate as if it were a musical comedy. Now it is hard for "personality" to show itself in football games because of their suits—the identical helmets and bulbous shoulders make them all look like robots. To women it would be a much more interesting game if we could see if they had red hair or yellow, crew-cuts or curls, snub noses or what.

But the first boy who caught my eye was Number 5 and I could not unpin my gaze thereafter. This is Faunce. He is light—only 170 pounds—not hulking like a buffalo. He has a spring and elegance, a steely daintiness. He always stands very straight and has an unflagging, undownable lightness, as if built on platinum springs. It is so pretty and smooth when he runs. And he threw the most satisfactory forward passes I have ever seen.

Now, to my eye, most forward passes are an uneasy, chancy kind of thing, and I always feel as queasy about their success as if I had thrown them myself. But this Faunce boy—he would stand back there (he is a halfback and presently you heard in the murmuring around about, "He's the Flash of Fergus Falls")—he'd stand there with the ball in his steely hand, and then with the most prolonged deliberation, as if his head were a cake of ice with ears on it, while they were thundering all around him, he'd throw it.

It seemed to go as straight as steel to the exact point—to big Bob Sandberg (world-famous athlete, Olympic champion shot-putter). Sandberg would catch it, as if the others helplessly leaping up and down, were kindergarten children. And sometimes Faunce, waiting to throw the ball, decided after deep thought that Sandberg hadn't arrived at the right point in time. So Faunce would carry it himself. And he *always* got somewhere—slipped and sprung through whole ranks of the enemy.

The Nebraska boys (in lily-white) seemed fine at first. But as our score piled higher than 15 and dirt got on their suits, discouragement and fatigue bowed them down. And besides, our team has 98 men on it. Substitutes are numbered as the stars of the firmament. And more and more of these champing masses of substitutes (full of nine hours sleep, meat and potatoes, nothing to do) would be whirled into the game as the danger of Nebraska's scoring subsided.

And it was quite obvious that all of them—like Mark Heffelfinger, Jack McNeil, Malosky, etc.—had all read Ralph Henry Barbour's books wherein the freshman-sub always makes a touchdown in the last 30 seconds. But three Nebraska players were wonderful—Richard Hutton, Sam Vacanti and one named Bill Moomey. (And I am indignant that no Minnesota sportswriters would bow to them the next day. No, not one!)

Beside us in the grandstand were sitting two boys, rather quiet, who could not help but let out a cry when Moomey ran through our team. So I asked if they were from Nebraska. "Yes, ma'am." It seems Nebraska is a good school but has only 10,000 in it. (The loud speaker was shouting "26,000 students have registered in Minnesota.") I spoke of how cute their girl cheerleader was, that skipping, spindle-shanked fascinating creature across the field. "A tactless compliment," I thought later.

◆

# THE ICE FOLLIES

❖❖

To the Ice Follies! It is the most astonishing exciting, skyrocketing, flowery spectacle you ever stared at with an open mouth, a girandole glittering with ornament: Golden nymphs in buskins, demi-gods and rajahs on skates, hussars and bull-fighters, Bowery toughs in green-and-rose cheeks. There are two monstrous pussy-cats on skates followed by a doleful skunk with button shoes and weak ankles.

And think of it!—all this in our plain old Arena with CrackerJack packages crumpled on the floor and yells about pop! It must be because I have not seen the Ice Follies for a few years that I am so staggered. They have made such advances. Take the rhythm. Before it was vague and blurred but now they tap-dance on skates with Bill Robinson's precision. There is a huge orchestra, the music a flood of dulcet strings and French horns playing Chopin, Tchaikovsky.

The Ice Follies started here ten years ago. There were three local boys—Oscar Johnson (chemist at a cake plant), Eddie Shipstead (typewriter salesman) and Roy Shipstead (garage attendant) who liked to skate in Como Park and try to do tricks. In 1933 they gave their first show here, the Greater Arena Ice Show they called it. Now there are 165 in the cast and 17,000,000 people have seen it in ten years—an unsurpassed theatrical record.

But is it worth it? Oh Heavens! It is better than Broadway, than movies. Here the girls are flying right past your nose, in their glitter and sequins and cellophane halos and diamonds and golden fringes—just a few feet away. They are solid flesh and blood—extraordinary athletes at that—and healthy and sound with comely muscles, because skating is natural and free exercise. Ballet is artificial and the calves knot into bunches in time. But not skaters' muscles.

Just their faces show it. In opera or ballet the smiles are

always a little dry-gash and agonized. But these girls, skating and flying, going backwards at 60 miles an hour on one silver point, cannot keep from smiling with wild frolicksomeness. It is as though everybody were continually shouting "Whee!"

Take Bobby and Ruby Maxon. I never saw such grinning delight. Take Bobby Blake who skates "an impression of George M. Cohan," all Cohan's rhythm and waggishness, but instead of dancing on a stage that is 50 feet by 30, Bobby Blake is Cohan at 60 miles an hour over a hockey rink big enough for 22 roughnecks.

There is Pluto (Disney's dog) on skates. You laugh till you wheeze and wipe your streaming eyes with your wrists. There is a girl named Ginger—Heavens, what a creature!—"with ruddy limbs and flourishing hair," a soft huge mop of reddish hair, tresses and plumes, floating in the wind like Venus' curls. Now chorus girls behind footlights must be encrusted with grease paint but these well-knit, handsome, fresh-faced children you can see as they are.

You may think that I write this because I am expected to say something nice. Not so. The house is sold out. You can't get a ticket if you try. I mean what I say.

There were four of us in a box. Ditty Shearer (beautiful mother of two) kept groaning out: "Oh why, why didn't I learn to figure skate! . . . Why have I wasted my whole life, those years spent on Home Economics B, on studying Plato . . . Why, why was I always trying to be a novel character instead of skating!" And at last she said sadly, "I suppose even if I'd spent my life skating I'd only be the one in the skunk suit."

When we clambered awkwardly out after seeing those 165 comely creatures flying like angels, like falcons, like seraphim, with beatific smiles of ease on their faces, I heard a woman mutter: "Why they do things on skates I couldn't do in my shoes with four wires!"

◆

# THE CIRCUS UNLOADING IN
# THE MEADOW NEAR KENWOOD

❖❖

I walked through the woods by Cedar Lake and through the M. & St. L. tracks. A few wild roses left and killdeer flying over the marsh. I met a handsome old lady with blue eyes and slim as a jockey, cutting hay with a sickle. "For my rabbits," she explained.

"I am going to see them set up the circus tents," I said.

"I'll be over later," she called after me.

The tents for the zebras were already up. A few Minneapolis fathers were standing about, a child hanging on to each hand. "Oh!" cried a little boy. "Look at the great big *mouse!*" He had caught sight of the kangaroo.

The elephants were getting water and an old keeper was sitting on his heels right under them. Elephants! the strangest and most endearing animal, swaying absurdly on rubber legs, feeling tenderly around with their trunks, lifting dirt to spatter on their heads. Now and then you are aware of a small eye with its monstrous lashes. It's looking at you.

I ventured to speak to a young man sitting on a bale of hay: Melvin Plunkett from Texas. He is the seals' trainer. "I'm tired," Mr. Plunkett said, "because I've got so much on my mind." And I followed him when he went to tend the hippopotamus, who seemed to be miserable, resting his snout against the iron bars and sighing with boredom.

It is lovely in the morning sun and you walk around tactfully with eyes down because behind every red-and-gilt wagon circus people are dressing and washing. Indian women laughing. A sad blond boy with a cowboy hat. Somebody scrubbing a milk-white horse with a pink nose.

Then I saw a dignified elderly lady with fragile gold earrings washing clothes in a pail. "Do you wash their clothes?" I asked. She was indignant at the idea. "I wash only my own clothes," she said reprovingly. "I am in charge of the wardrobe.

Sixteen costumes alone cost $47,000." She told me that her name was Mrs. MacFarlan.

Now this circus is especially proud of its horses. "Talk to Alabama," Mrs. MacFarlan said. I found him sitting on a wagon-flap in the sun, a thin man in riding boots. Alabama is a Kentucky gentleman named Campbell who loved horses and 30 years ago ran away from college to join a circus.

A henchman came over to say that blankety-blank, dash-it-to-blank, etc. just when they wanted to wash the horses there was no water. But Alabama, undashed, said: "They's a stream over there"—pointing toward Kenwood Parkway—"water from here to hell-and-gone. So what do you want? That stream will do fine, yonder under them trees." And he went on placidly telling me how he was a bachelor and wished that he could get married. Was I married?

Then a truck got stuck in deep mire and the boy came moseying over with an elephant. The elephant was told to give it a push. So he did, kneeling and putting his lovely, puzzled, noble forehead against it. The truck rolled out like a toy. Nothing to it.

The main tent was rising. First, it was all spread on the ground—weathered rumpled canvas. A crowd of small boys went around, with a few roustabouts, and lifted the short poles. Presently the tent was so high that the work-elephants could get under it, each dragging harness on the slack of his pants, and chains in the dirt.

At last the drab tent is high in the air. And behold, it takes on that beauty—flags and pennons! And one thinks of Saracens, the Crusades, and knights' pavilions and tournaments and jousts. Of Sir Lancelot du Lake and Charlemagne.

But most of all one thinks of the Fourth of July when we were ten.

◆

# ELAINE NORDEN AND
# WOMEN AS TYCOONS

❖

D owntown is fascinating on a summer night. It is still light even at half past nine. You can see everything that your daytime nervousness obliterates: the Beaufort Hotel on Third Street and its delicate wrought-iron porch over the sidewalk. And through the plate glass front you see the night clerk and the shiny desk and the brass spittoons and the fireman's chairs in the lobby. Now it is old, seedy and derelict. But it is like a fashionable hotel in New Orleans in 1860, with Mark Twain in there or Sam Houston, loosening their brace of pistols. And next door there is a harness store.

At Schiek's for dinner, myself mournful that the huge room with the mahogany bar, the stained glass jewels, the large square tables with white cloths, the mediaeval weapons on the walls—that it is all being changed. "Being improved," says Mr. George Polities, the new manager. He says they will build new kitchens out in the left in that vacant lot. Mr. Polities (a Greek name and how perfect for him and his job!) tells Elaine Norden from Chicago how he had a famous restaurant down there. It was fixed up like a submarine, he said.

Elaine Norden of the Campbell-Mithun advertising agency in Chicago, tells how she was interviewed by a Texas columnist lady "whose syndicated columns go to six million people." And it struck me how although I know Elaine Norden much more than that other columnist, and call her "a tycoon of tycoons," it never struck me that she was "material" for a piece "about the successful business woman of today."

"So she interviewed you," I said, "and came way from Texas to do it. I know just what you said to her, I bet"?

"What?"

"You said: 'I think the business woman of this day and age has a splendid opportunity to advance if she will really try,

25

cooperate and coordinate with the conditions of today, and handle everything a hunert percent, in spite of the fact that the average business man resists the forward drive of the business woman.'"

E. Norden, indignantly: "I said no such thing!"

"Well, what did you say?"

"I said that women in business should quit blaming men for non-success. If they get less far than men, they are to blame. It is timidity. Men dare to risk huge sums on new enterprises. Women tend just to want a safe job and a salary. No piratical nerve! No gumption! No risks!"

I argued: "You often hear of some remarkable woman, say in Jones, Jones & Jones Investment Bankers—how this invisible woman behind the scenes knows all that business, round and about and through and through, and without her omniscient brain, and hours and hours of work, the whole structure of Jones & Jones would collapse. Jones and Jones, swaggering about in their $150 suits at the Minneapolis Club and on all the executive boards in town, would just be lost."

"Okay and very true," said Elaine Norden, "but Miss Simpkins, the patient, unegotistical female wonder behind the House of Jones & Jones is to blame for her own anonymity. If she had true gumption she would go out and start a Simpkins, Simpkins & Simpkins. But she is scared to. Won't take the chance. A typical female."

❖

# Girls Working On The Railroad

❖❖

**A** cold day with snow blowing from the north, and Miss Blanche Hosp took me to the Soo Line yards. She works in the employment office of the U.S. Retirement Board, and sends women workers to the railroads. They shovel coal, unload cars. At the Northern Pacific they are even yards clerks. That is, they work at night spotting freight cars, and they walk miles in rain or blizzard, stumbling out of the way of express trains.

Miss Hosp loves railroads. "They say I am a regular gandy"—one of those migratory railroad workers of old.

The Soo yards are on Central Avenue North. Huge dim repair shops, the roundhouse, skeins of tracks. We walked over the snow to the "rip tracks" where boxcars are repaired.

The women were having lunch in an old boxcar, heating their coffee on an iron stove. Thirteen of them: in pants, bright kerchiefs, plaid shirts. The oldest was Sandra Varnay in a man's cap, her hair concealed, a red face and glasses and a joking gruff manner. And everybody laughs at every word.

"Spell your name," I said.

"Varnay—it's French. But I'm Finnish and brought up in Norway." Lots of joking then about how no wonder she was so tough and enduring. She sorts scraps all day, lifting hunks of iron weighing from 10 to 100 pounds. And as I asked my insolent, prying newspaper-questions, she said her daughter is married to a lieutenant. And so she lives alone.

"Where's your husband?"

"I drowned him." (Hilarious laughter).

But then she said seriously that she had worked before in a dry cleaning place, but this work was much better because it was out of doors. Did it really make a difference? Yes, yes! They all said it did. You feel healthier, stronger, than in all your life. And there was a kind of piratical ring in their voices. And they all grin jovially and often. Now on indoor faces it would be a smile but in these weather-red faces it is a grin and their teeth seem smaller than other people's and white and perfect.

I said to Elizabeth Canfield who has a handsome intellectual face like that of a young actress, "What are you wearing?" She showed me, opening the layers at the neck: a striped sweater next to the skin, a wool shirt, a reefer, etc. Mary Kalina (blond with wide cheekbones) and Anna Holubka (a rosy face, tiny childish white teeth in the widest smile you ever saw) spelled their names for me.

"You two have an accent."

"We're Russian."

"Oh, Russian! Isn't that just right?" The whole thing was Russian, the day, the snow, the women roly-poly in jackets-upon-jackets.

Then their boss, Mr. Sobraske, came in. "She is a Riveter's helper." (She is a fine looking, serious, smiling girl). "And Marion Barbelen here—she's driving a tractor crane." Marion—more beautiful than any girl on the stage because of that red face, that health flashing off frame and face! And Hilda Kyostia—blond, studious looking, Finnish—drives a tractor crane, too.

They are all so nice. And they look so round-faced, young. "I bet you are all 16." "Oh ya? Sure!" "Sixteen! I'm 32!" said Dorothy Hanson. Her husband is fighting in Italy. And there was Beniata Said, so pretty but still pale and a little subdued because she is a new girl.

"Do you go to high school?" I said to Lois Thompson and Eileen Peters.

"No, we quit."

"School is bad for the health," I said. Hearty laughter. "Ya it is! You said it!" And the country girls scowled and really meant it and no fooling.

There was Dorothy Shaw and Eleanor Bristow. "They're engaged to two brothers.

"I suppose," I said, "that after the war it is back to the 10-cent store." Yells of NO! They are farm girls, Eleanor said; that is why they like outdoor work. That was startling to me, a city person, that staunch farm-patriotism.

When we went out doors, Mr. Sobraske said: "Now Marion, come on and show her." She made an embarrassed face and climbed lightly into the yellow crane tractor, showed us how she worked it—up and down and opening its jaws. And after that the slim roseate Marion, a bunch of curls sticking out over her perfect nose, chugged away on her fat-wheeled mechanical elephant to lift two-ton boilers all afternoon.

Oh yes, and they get 65 cents an hour. Six days a week and every other Sunday—that's about $35 a week.

❖

❖❖

**M.** bought an old Bible in the bookstore at 9th Street and Marquette. It had belonged to "Dr. Charles Steizle" and there was a yellowed clipping from the *Minneapolis Journal* of 1898 saying that Gladstone had died that day. And these nostalgic ads! *Wanted*—horse-shoer and good wagon-repairer. *Situation wanted*—male. Young man of 22 wants work of some kind; educated and honest; will work hard and cheap for three dollars a week. *For sale*—A Lady's first-class outfit at half price. Bang-tail horse, harness and phaeton for $100. At 1025 Harmon Place: *House to rent*—six-room house with city water; stationary washbowl and closet inside; fine neighborhood; part modern; lawn and garden; only $16 a month.

I was orating to Barbara Flanagan of the *Daily Times* about the olden times when there were no automobiles, only horses and carriages. There was no din of combustion engines all around us day and night, that ugly, constant unpoetic roar. "Think of this, Barbara," I said, "at this minute I could hitch up a horse on a pitch dark night in mid-winter, affix the tugs, all the straps around the shafts, each in its especial way."

When I was about five I remember being in love with a mounted policeman whom I called Smith-ride-Horsey. His beat on his noble bay horse was from Captain Ewing's dock at 34th Street and Lake Calhoun Boulevard, to our house on the south shore. (Captain Ewing, an old sea-dog with a full beard and yachting cap, rented rowboats for fishing.)

Then on Sunday afternoon we all went down to our lower terrace where Lake Calhoun Boulevard turns off to go to Lake Harriet, to watch the stream of horses and carriages going by. Remember it was a soft dirt road then and the stately elegant procession came noiselessly along. We would watch for Mrs. Thomas Lowry in her victoria with her black horses and silver harness, her red-faced coachman on the box. (Oh the bright complexions in those days of policemen, teamsters, icemen, ladies in carriages. All faces are greenish now from riding in airtight automobiles.) Mrs. Lowry with a black lace parasol lifted gaily against the sun, would bow and wave a tiny lace handkerchief. There was Mrs. Gilfillan's carriage, the Rand's carriage, the C. J. Martin carriage.

Some had a black horse and a white horse prancing before their carriage, or spanking bays champing foam. Some had two men on the box. I even remember a tandem or two; a little groom who sat behind with his arms folded and was called for some reason "a tiger." The dashing young men in spidery phaetons drove swaying pacers with a high check-rein. ("How cruel!" we'd cry) and no blinders. There were calico horses, chubby horses, tall thin horses named Nellie, horses with straw hats on.

I was telling Barbara these wonders ("I was born too late!" she groaned) and began to think how the saddest thing of all is to have lost all the poetry of sound.

"With automobiles (not to mention the heavy blanket of carbon monoxide over the land) we cannot hear," I said, and began to enumerate: The soft distant clopping of horses' hooves at four o'clock in the morning when the milk wagons began to come into town. Frogs. Wagons creaking musically up Richfield Road. Cocks crowing far far away, and nearer and nearer as the sun rises. Oarlocks on the lake. Thunder pumpers in the swamp. Hoot owls in the moonlight. The faraway wild melancholy train whistle (I always thought it was an Indian war cry). The roar of freight trains coming over the water when there was a slight north wind. Fish jumping. Mosquitoes' tiny bugles. The rustling of leaves before a thunderstorm. The lapping of waves, breathless and unrhythmical. Somebody playing the piano in the evening. Porch swings going "Eee-eee-eeekk." The North wind, the West wind and all the zephyrs.

"Well cheer up, Barbara," I said. "There's always the radio. And sound effects."

❖

# ◄ PORTRAITS ►

## ROBERT PENN WARREN

M r. Robert Penn Warren is Southern, a Kentuckian. His friends call him Red. He teaches English at the University. Girls in his class say he looks like Leslie Howard. And one Sunday he came over to swim at our beach on Lake Calhoun.

There is one thing about my swimming: I cannot get tired. I claim that I will beat anyone from the age of 1 to 99, if they will only go far enough. It is not that I go very fast—they just won't be alive.

So that golden afternoon I swam far out beyond the red-capped buoy and looking back, why there was Mr. Robert Penn Warren.

"Shall we swim over to Thomas Avenue?" he asked.

"Okay."

I kept thinking anxiously about him as I ploughed along. "Is he sinking? Oh, these tall men—they have no specific gravity. Can't float. They get blue lips . . ." and turning around to tow him in, there he is *ahead* of me!

"Let's not go in to Thomas Avenue," he said. "How about swimming over there?" pointing across to Thirty-Fourth Street, about a mile.

"Fine."

"Well now," I thought (and buckled down to it and breathed hard that endless distance), "now he is a goner. Poor Mr. Warren. I am afraid he will be too proud to yell for help. Men don't like this sort of thing—to be beaten." I looked around over the wide water, in panic, for him. Where? Far away he had reached the shore and was waiting.

"Instead of walking home," he said, Southern-gentlemanly and reticent, his curious eyes on the far horizon (you can't tell the color of them and there is a black rim around his iris), "shall we swim?"

"Very fine."

Thus we tacked back and forth all afternoon.

And so I knew he could write a wonderful book. And he has. *At Heaven's Gate*. It is just out, published by Harcourt, Brace and Howe.

"I bought Marie them things," says one of his characters, a young Kentuckian in the most beautiful dialect ever spoken: "I bought her a necklace and it was all gold. It had a sparklet in it and it had a shine like a diamint, you let the sun git it clear. . . Marie was one of them little women, and quick when she aimed to. She was lak water laying in the sun and it deep and nary a riffle. But a little wind, and a sparkle runs all over the water. I bought a necklace to wear on her bosom for that sparkle that was in her."

A serious, true and remarkable book.

"How do you feel with a new book out?"

"I never think of them again."

And that's right. As Plotinus said: "Keep your eyes always toward the One (perfection) and love that, and let your works, flawed or fine, stream out behind. Never look back."

❖

# PAUL ROBESON

**H**oney-comb ice on Lake Harriet, all blown to the south shore, soaked and dark like sherbet, whispering and tinkling. Three gulls sailing one above the other like Cupid's bows. Two robins, their chests horribly engorged, glide swiftly over the grass on tiny wheels. The little waves break nervously. Breathlessly against the shore; it is almost in rhythm but not quite—broken time. They slap the stones and gurgle back as under a boat, worrying the rim of foam on the sand.

Oh, this gemlike translucence, this lively, lovely air! The willow trees are each in a golden cloud like a goddess in a nimbus. Swedenborg said that when we die we don't know it. I feel that perhaps I have died and gone to Heaven.

Paul Robeson singing at the Symphony. I talked to him. The odd thing is that he was willing to see me because he heard that I was Norwegian. (I will explain it in a minute.) He is such a Titan, a Colossus, that for him the rules of exclusion were waived and he was allowed to stay at the Nicollet Hotel.

He is huge, his shoulders so broad and mighty that you cannot guess his height. His face is black, his eyes wide apart and they have an energy and a glare. Once in a while he will smile and it is like the sun coming out. And the perfect arch of his teeth, that wide architecture. I think: "No wonder he sings like that: It can resound under that arch," for in the Symphony concert his immense voice mingled with the trumpets at their loudest and yet it was tender and human.

Now before I die I want to do something for colored people. I have always loved and admired them. To me they have always been "the most generous race," the largest in spirit and the most patient. As a child it always consoled me (for the unfeelingness of white men) to watch Negro teamsters with their horses—that deeply warm, including, jokey feeling that they had as though their horses were their dear friends, Mr. Smith and Mr. Jones.

Then, I have that most necessary knowledge of guilt: We went far away and took them out of their green kingdom in Africa and made slaves of them. And now see how we treat them in our knavish white way! And finally as a matter of common sense I think it is no answer to any problem to keep people down. The only thing to do is to lift them up quickly, as fast as we can. Give them education, opportunity, admiration, friendship. And how do you lift up anyone, children or human being or creature? By respect, by honoring them, by bowing low to them. By taking away humiliation. Humiliation is a terrible force that rots anyone, children, servants, employees, races. It is one of the most destructive forces in the world. It is interesting that the Russians have seemed to know it best of all. Read Dostoevsky.

Here are some of the things Paul Robeson told me:

"As for myself I have always been proud of being a Negro, even before I learned that we, too, have an ancient culture, a history. It goes very far back. But most poor colored people think they are just the children of howling savages."

He is forty-five. His father was a slave who ran away and became a minister; his mother was a school teacher. He has degrees from Rutgers and Columbia University. Walter Camp called him "the greatest defensive football end that ever trod the gridiron." Eugene O'Neill offered him the leading part in "Emperor Jones." In London he played Othello opposite Mrs. Patrick Campbell. He likes to study phonetics and his Russian is flawless. And he is learning Norwegian. "Such a liquid, clear, beautiful language," he says, "the most beautiful I have ever heard."

At the Symphony concert he sang the death scene from "Boris Godounow" by Moussorgsky and I think it is because Pushkin wrote the great drama. Pushkin, who is Byron and Shakespeare combined to the Russians, was a fiery officer who died in a duel at 37, a great poet, a great genius. His heroine Tatiana in "Eugene Onegin" was the forerunner of the great heroines of Tolstoy and Dostoevsky, and she represents a far greater conception of Woman than was to be found in English literature. Pushkin had curly hair, a dark face and a fierce generous heart. His great-grandfather was Hannibal, a Negro prince at the court of Peter the Great.

But now I come to an interesting thing. Paul Robeson loves Norway. He said that in three countries, Spain, Russia and Norway, they accepted him entirely, with the most candid, free affection and liking. "I could feel that I was not even exotic to them. Black? It was nothing to them. It was as if I were just somebody with brown eyes. They all knew my songs, called out from the audience for 'Old Man River,' for all of them. They had all my records. They took me skiing on Sunday in the mountains above Oslo."

What made him especially happy was this: "They are the most pure Nordic stock of all and I am the very opposite—from the Equator and black. Their immediate, generous, easy friendliness makes me believe that race hatred is taught, is inculcated. It is not essential or natural or necessary."

❖

# JOHN S. PILLSBURY

J ohn Pillsbury—he has a handsome nose with a straight line from the forehead like Apollo's, glass astride it, a flushed face and grizzled curls. But how to describe his nature? Well, I think he is this kind of man: Say that Chiang Kai-Shek was coming to Minneapolis with Chinese Communists, and President Truman and Philip Murray and General MacArthur, and the whole world depended on the result of it, and some Minneapolis man must be in charge to make them all feel kind-hearted and genial and honorably fair to each other, who would it be? John Pillsbury of course.

He was born on Second Avenue and Tenth Street (the handsome old house is gone) and "went to the Washington school where the courthouse now stands," he says. "Didn't you go East to school, Mr. Pillsbury?" "Oh, no—straight through the Minneapolis public schools. Sure. They were tough, too—I mean you had to use your fists; but that's good, too. Then to the University."

Now for three and a half years he has been the smiling, Herculean co-chairman of our War Bond drives and has helped raise unbelievable millions among us, as though it were as easy as pie. To be chairman, he says, "is just a matter of choosing smarter people than yourself to do it, then *you* take the credit—" (with his transparent, beaming grin). And he "liked that chairman job because of the hundred fellas I didn't know before. I'd say that is what I like best—knowing people."

Just then Mrs. Pillsbury came into his office and there was a brief colloquy about how he must call for skates at the Arena ("For our youngest boy," he explained) and when she left he handed me a picture of his six children, writing their names in the margin, with their numbers: "John—he's No. 1, Edmund 2, Ella 3. . ."

"I suppose you were a very severe parent," I said, because

he is the most absurdly kind-hearted man.

"We had two rules for the children: Be nice to servants and polite to my friends. If people came and a child wouldn't smile or be nice—'Upstairs you go!'"—genially swinging an imaginary child out of the room.

He says that he has "always loved life—music, athletics." He played football and baseball. He thinks Brahms No. 1 and 2 are about the best there is. "Oh, I like modern music (hastening to be kind, to be fair to all good things). I really do. Or try to. But I'm glad to go back to Brahms."

He does not smoke now, but says, "I used to be a pretty good judge of fine cigars," and he tells how when he was alone in London as a young man he would go to the theater and it seemed less lonely because of the cigar. And I can imagine him jovial and rejoicing in the elegant ballet in a magnificent box but full of that vague suffocation that is loneliness for Minneapolis, Minnesota.

But his most earnest belief he describes in this way: "If there are 12 well-chosen people on a committee and all of them agree, but I disagree with all of them, I conclude that I may be wrong." That is, he believes that the cooperative, generously appreciative-of-others spirit is the only way to get good work done, to make progress, and to go on to the next, in this anxious world.

"Have you any special heroes?" I asked—(that gagging interviewer's question!) "Oh, I guess not—but I always admired Stassen." And then suddenly he sprang to his feet and began to stride around on lively, athletic legs. "Come upstairs and see our penthouse—"where the Pillsbury Company has enormous glass iceboxes and they make fancy things out of Pillsbury flour.

◆

# COLONEL OLE REISTAD

Colonel Ole Reistad, the Commander of the Royal Norwegian Air Force, stayed in my house. He is a blond man blazingly sunburned with a tremendous span of shoulders and his short military hair is pale gilt and he has one of those piratical noses with a slight bump on the bridge. Oh, but I admire that Colonel Reistad. I have no space to tell his war exploits but here are a few things:

When he arrived in Minneapolis at the airport he wore no hat. It was late October. He likes the sun, and you could not keep him indoors. The rest of us seem to feel comfortable only indoors. He seems to feel so only out under a rather cold sky. Nansen was the same. It depressed him because people "were like bugs running from box to box." And Nansen was in this house, too, one winter full of blizzards. There was a great party for him and he kept leaving the company, the reception to go out to the sub-zero back porch drifted with snow, to breathe that air with gasps of relief and longing.

As for Colonel Reistad—the first time he was here it was in November and Lake Calhoun was what Inga calls "wolfy"— sharp grey waves like snavelling slashing fangs of cold teeth biting at the sky. When I came down to breakfast I found Selma looking out the dining-room windows at the lake, with puzzled eyebrows. "Well now, that Colonel Reistad, he went out." He had run around the lake and then gone in swimming. Then when he came in April: It was time to take him downtown to make his radio speech. I looked out and there he was on the lawn, the sunlight on a million yellow stars of dandelions, running light figure-eights in shorts and tennis shoes.

And he ate apples and drank milk and nothing could express his continuous astonished scorn that people should be such tomfools and self-enfeebling idiots as to sit indoors and to smoke or drink. Which was no fun anyway. And a dull, homely, sedentary thing to do. Drinking, he said, was always done in the darkest and ugliest places.

When the reporters came to interview him he always had them sit out in the cold sunlight with him.

He told me that in Norway the Norwegian boys, retreating and fighting the Nazis who had suddenly swamped and taken Norway had hoped to join the English at Narvik and take a stand. Their hearts sank and hope fled when their eyes fell on the British troops. They were pale little fellows, cockneys most of them and they were dejected and unaccustomed to the whole business. In contrast, the Norwegians had a kind of farmer-sturdiness.

Colonel Ole was even a little dubious about the prowess of Canadians and Americans, especially because of "this golf," he said. When they were showing him around St. Olaf College and bare-legged girls were swinging golf clubs on the greensward—

"This damn golf!" he whispered to me. "Here," he said, "they have all this big expense, these big fields and clubhouses. But the little boys carrying the heavy bags are the only ones who get strong. Then they must have all these highballs afterwards. There should be a law that no man under sixty-five be allowed to play golf. It makes them *think* they are getting strong, when it is not so. It is a very bad thing."

Then he described a fine game they play in Norway. "You should play it," he said to me. They would all of them men, women, boys, girls, athletes, farmers, grandmothers, expectant mothers, go out in the mountains each one carrying a map and a compass. They would choose a point ten miles across country and then race for it.

"This is a very fine thing," he said. "You learn to know your country and how beautiful it is. And you get very strong. You are outdoors, and you have to be very clever or you will get lost and have to sleep outdoors in the mountains all night." A splendid, salutary experience, he thinks for all. And he also said that church was a fine thing, or would be, if only people built their churches eight miles away in the forest and then walked to church and home again every Sunday. They would most certainly have a great religious experience every Sunday.

With Colonel Ole, an Olympic champion ski racer and one of the great athletes of Norway, it is not just physical prowess that is important but it is a philosophy, it is what happens to the soul. He is a Renaissance man. A strong body means a strong, courageous soul. All uneasiness, foxiness, craft and falseness one throws out the window. "The fox looks out for himself but God looks out for the lion." In training his young athletes in Norway for the Olympics he insisted that they train always after hours, after their day's work or before. The whole point to making them athletes is to make them better farmers, fishermen, or wives and mothers.

And here is a letter he wrote me just now:

"You told me to take off a few days and go skiing. But I have had no time for that.

"The only day I really was on skis again was when we had big military 20-miles cross-country competition up at Vesle Skaugum in Northern Canada. We had to run with heavy pack, gun, and shooting on target ten times.

"That was a terrible rain-weather and a very, very heavy run. Over 100 boys took part in the competition and they wished that I should start. So I did and had a hell of a time, untrained as I was and had not taken part in any competition since the Olympic games in 1928. I took it very hard and did all I could to speed up. I was the oldest that went through this competition, 46 years old, and most of the others were mostly 20 years younger. But after a race of over 3 hours I managed not only to win my class, but the race and get the best time of the day. I think I myself was most surprised. I had never thought it was possible to best this well-trained youth over 20 years younger.

"I really think I have never been more pleased with a race in my whole sporting life because I was a little afraid that I was too rotten for such heavy things after all this office work and no competition in 14 years.

"But I can assure you I could feel it for some days afterward.

"I have got a dog, 'elg hund,' real Norwegian or Norwegian-American you may call him for he is born in the U.S.A. He is very fine, 2 years old and will go back to Norway with me and become a Norwegian citizen of the future.

"We are building up a new camp now in Muskoka. I go on inspection trip to the west of Canada to our boys at Moose Jaw. I got a wire just now saying four of my pilots have landed safely in England a few days after they took off from Newfoundland. That is going very fine."

Ole Reistad.

❖

# COUNTESS MARY
## PART I

I have found such a romantic and moving friend, the Countess Marja Smorczewska. But now her name is just Mary and she gives one tea and sits by the afternoon fire sewing (her hands are sturdy, somewhat reddened, boyish, work-used hands) and telling stories of Poland. The stories happened only a few years ago, but they might have come out of Napoleon's time, they are so wild and lovely, such terrible stories of forests, bitter snow, wolves, of horses and carriages, of country palaces like Versailles in the mediaeval wilderness, of the shining Nieman river with Lithuania on the other side. Her voice is warm and generous and as she goes along the stories grow so amazing, or horrifying or beautiful that I think: "Why, this is Anna Karenina telling me stories!" for Tolstoy described Anna as having just such dark blue eyes, merry and pensive, and dark bronze hair. "And she is like a Gibson girl," I think to myself—the short nose and round, endearing chin.

But there is such a pallor and sadness in her face. Her son in the Polish army she has not seen since 1939, nor seen her daughter for many, many years. Members of her family are lost in Siberia, in displaced persons' camps, or dead or murdered. In 1939, the Russians rolled over her estate and then the Germans. The frightful Gestapo lived in her house.

"But darling . . . More tea, darling . . . a little Madeira . . . Yes, darling . . ." (The Slavic word for "darling" is sprinkled all through Tolstoy and Chekhov.) She tells of stag hunts, breakfasts in the forest prepared by herself and her footmen and maids. "Oh, with a most beautiful Polish boy blowing the huntsman's horn! . . . Yes, darling, I am partly Russian"—descended from the old Russian nobility that settled in Poland centuries ago, and in her bedroom she shows me a portrait of a French court beauty with witty black eyes and a towering pompadour—"my French great-great-grandmother."

She said, with a lovely smile, "Oh the country! Flowers and animals and the summer air and the evening breeze and this beautiful sound of insects in golden summer! Because I am a farmer . . ." She bred famous white Arabian horses with long silken tails and manes and showed me a photograph of a milky pair drawing a carriage, and pointing at their harness chains—"These were pure gold and given to me by my father, Count Grudsinki II." And he once gave her an estate because she was not happy having only society life in Warsaw—"to put on some splendid toilette and go to a party until 4 o'clock every morning."

The estate had a walled garden and she "had even in it wild animals, yes, wolves." A "horse-wolf" cub had been given to her by her foresters. "They have heavy, tearing jaws—very bloody—and they tear out horses' throats as they gallop—" (Troikas, of course.) But she brought it up among her adored dogs.

She was married in England to her Polish count who was a student at Oxford—a huge, fashionable wedding—and told of the orange satin gown all sewn with pearls that extended from her shoulders into an immense, distant, dragging train.

She told of peasants on her estate who were geniuses, artists—wonderful wood-carvers. "They have carved choir screens in St. Peter's in Rome . . ." And a magnificent sarcophagus for herself.

She spoke of her great health, and there is not the faintest hint of a nervous effete aristocrat about her, or that snobbish whine of the exiled white fallen into hard work.

No, she is an aristocrat in her soul and that means she is exactly like a true democrat, absolutely identical in spirit. She says the great landowners in Poland have married into each others' families too much "and were spoiled, out of balance. Sometimes there is a brilliance that could go just one little step over into insanity."

But she and her husband loved the country and worked hard and that saved them.

◆

# COUNTESS MARY
## PART II

In writing about the Countess Marja Smorczewska I got something awry? But that's good. Because here she writes this enchanting letter:

Dear: I am sure you will not mind if I make some corrections. Only my grandmother's family came from Russia, "Kniaz" (prince) family that left Russia with similar families and all settled in Poland in the beginning of the fifteenth century. This is all that is partly Russian in me!

I bred with success Anglo-Arab horses for land work and the Polish cavalry. All my work for many years was destroyed, as well as my neighbor's, by Russians in 1939. The harness which you admired in the picture was once a work of our famous Polish workman-crafts in Wilno (given now to Russia). They worked out the skin "round," like a cord, but wonderfully soft, then decorated it with hand cut bronze and burned in gold. Such work could stand for generations, but is not gold.

My father came from an old knight's family. They worked their land, but their lives, hearts, blood and swords have been for service of their Polish kings and country from 1450. We have an unfortunate geographic position and our borders have always been in danger. His family was presented a count's title in 1786 by Prussia and for this reason we never used it.

My father, who was charm and goodness itself, gave me his own summer place on the Nieman away from everything, surrounded by forest and walled, so I kept all sorts of wild animals. I was out of place in the city and longing for the country. At times I would run away from my hard work of running the estate, or business connected with it in Warsaw offices, and just relax. Looking only on a big river, surrounded by beautiful nature, even for a few days, just made one strong again.

Our taxes have been tremendous. The more you put into

your land, the more you increase in stock and factories of sugar, or mills, the more you have been taxed until it ruined many, because the prices of wheat were low. All this was real work for a woman alone.

Dear splendid toilettes and parties until four in the morning—that was a silly old St. Petersburg custom. They would after an all-night party, drive for a breath of fresh air and speed in troikas down the side of the River Neva. But troikas we never used in Poland; it would be an abuse for a whole nation using Russian-way harnessed troikas! We have our own beautiful way of harnessing horses, and one of them is called Batagty—four horses together, head by head, and their harness covered with silver work or brass.

You know, Brenda, I can write pages about geniuses of the Polish peasants and their most amazing sense of proportion and beauty. My friends have been wood carvers for three generations, so I arranged a studio for them, bought rare wood, and books on antique furniture. They made not only furniture, doors, ceilings, but screens and confessionals in churches, and pulpits. But, dear Brenda, I am sorry but it is a long way from St. Peter's in Rome.

Yes, we made coffins for ourselves from our own forest oak, strong big coffins, carved lovely, but not for vanity, but just to save the family trouble so as to be ready in case someone dies unexpectedly. And a good oak coffin is a good home to drive to Nirvana and durable for every soil. In my coffin someone now probably enjoys keeping grains for chickens, or potatoes. Such are the jolly jokes of life!

Be a good sport, darling, and admit that every artist—as you are—rides also a beautiful horse "with long silken tails and manes," white, inoffensive—and his name is "Licentia Poetic." I thank you, dear, for giving so much attention to my humble person. I appreciate your kindness very much.

Mary.

◆

# CARL SANDBURG

**C**arl Sandburg is here. The last time it was to help get airplanes for Norway and from the train we disappeared into a movie to "Fantasia," and he loved that. He is so extraordinarily joyfully generous about other peoples' work and always carries a fistful of clippings to show you. After the movie he likes to go into a drugstore and buy candy, or a hardware store, and he bought me a knife with a more-than-three-inch blade "because you're a Corsican," he said.

The first time I saw him—I look it up in my diary:

Saturday, March 15, 1935. Joe and Dagmar Beach let me come over. Carl Sandburg is there. Before he came downstairs, Joe spoke of his eyes: "They are light, queer twinkling eyes." He is big and toes-in, like a fighter or a ballplayer. His hair is thick, unmanageable like a boy's. The slippery bangs keep falling in his eyes. Mongolian Swedish eyes full of pale light. Wonderful looking, like an idealized sculpture of Labor.

He has written some definitions of art, fifty-two of them, and has me read them. One of them said that art is a burst of a golden rocket against a gunmetal sky. But it is better than that. Later we drive to our house, and going around Lake Calhoun—"Can't we stop a minute? The gunmetal sky," he says. There it is. It is true—the pools of water on the ice reflect the sky, gunmetal and watery pink. And the lights at twilight are big rectangles. He looks across the lake for a long time. In dead silence.

And once in a while, he has written me a letter: "Sept. 13, 1938: You should have compassion that this summer I have written the story of the assassination of Lincoln. Anyhow and ennyhoo, unless I hear from you I shall wire you as to what train whistle to listen for in October."

He worked ten years on the Lincoln book. I know that at the end there was a kind of desperation that something might come between himself and getting it done. You can understand if you knew the labor of it. For example, Lincoln was assassinated on a Friday night and he read 300 American sermons delivered the following Sunday—just to search into how the country felt. So you can see behind each sentence in the Lincoln book there was search, search, testing for accuracy and truth into the past and then distilling all that chaotic ocean into clear, musical, noble sentences.

*Another letter says: "I have reached 2 o'clock in the afternoon of Lincoln's last day. . ."*

When the six volumes were published, someone said to him "It is so very American." "Yes. It's a book about a man whose mother could not sign her name, written by man whose father could not sign his. Perhaps that could happen only in America."

Then I was in his house on Lake Michigan. I was driving home from New York and all Europe had fallen. England was holding off the Germans alone.

August, 1940. I drive along the desolate highway from Chicago to his house and find it at last, in the soaking rain. A warm, lovely, familiar house high in the wooded dunes above the booming shore of Lake Michigan. There is his wife, two daughters, a girl to help, a little dog like a fox, two great cats on the upstairs bed in the sun. They went up to a high attic, an aerie, to find him. At dinner, the soft roar of Lake Michigan. Rain on the windows.

*He is for fighting, for helping them in Europe. O! I am so glad about that. . . He told about the man who wrote a book about him. He'd write how when Carl was a boy and confirmed at the Lutheran church, he wore a rose and the other kids did not. "Well you got that from my brother and sister," said Carl. "They saw I was different and that is how they put it."*

The truth was, he said to me, he wore a brown suit because his father couldn't afford a black one. Because two boys had died that year of diphtheria and the expense— coffins and a lot at the cemetery and the doctors—"And so I wore a brown suit." A long silence. "So he said I wore a brown suit and a rose." A gentle voice and then a shout of laughter. He has a curious laugh—not mirth exactly. It means sweetness, tolerance, rising above something, and irony. . . He gave me two hand-hewn nails for Gaby.

He has a wonderful voice and I always think of Isaiah. And once I heard him swear and it is like thunder and music and wild as a pirate's. It was at the Beach's and someone had mentioned a skunk of a man who works for labor's cause and injures it by his bad character. The voice rang and lifted the roof of the house an inch or two. Then he looked at Dagmar sadly, reproaching himself: "Dagmar, I got no call to holler in your house!"

But these few things tell nothing, nothing about him. He is a great man.

◆

# OFFICER JOE RYAN

**J**oe Ryan is a police officer and for two years he has been president of the Central PTA. He is a big man, an athlete, a deadshot; and an angel, that's all. I hope he will forgive me for being rhapsodic. But to know him cheers you up. You begin to think there may be thousands of Joe Ryans, invisibly working and thinking as he does, with such insight and wisdom.

He is sergeant of the park police and goes cruising around with his partner, and often when he sees me walking around the lake, he stops to talk. The other morning I came upon him at the canoe dock at Lake Harriet and he said: "I wonder why they do this—" rubbing some dents in the canvas of a canoe. Some boys had pounded nails into it. He wasn't mad. He was just trying to understand this dishonor and absurd cowardice of injuring something fine for no reason at all.

Then he said that there are things in kids' lives that we don't know about. And told this story:

"We were cruising around one morning and saw a boy, about eleven, looking down into the water. We could tell something was wrong. We found he was a deserted child. His mother had run away to Chicago, his father long before that. He lived in a boarding home. He had been kicked out of school because he kept behaving badly. And the boy cried as if his heart would break when we were talking to him.

"We told him to go home, eat his lunch. We'd go over to the school and see if we could fix things up for him.

"He started for home and we headed for the school. But on the way we heard a radio call which told of a shooting nearby. We went to the address. It was the boy's home. We found him on the dining room floor dying. He had shot himself with a rifle. Well—" Joe Ryan's bluff red face showed his feeling over this—"No child should be allowed to get in that state of mind. If we had only taken him home—" He cannot get over it, that feeling of regret.

Joe Ryan (Irish, 6 feet 2, blue-eyed, very blond) lives on Zenith Avenue near Fiftieth Street. And this is how he happened to get into the PTA. When his boy Tom was in third grade at the Riley school he came home one day, saying there would be a PTA meeting and wanted his father to go.

"Well," I said, "Tom, I'm not much for a tea party, you know. But Tom wanted me to go, so of course I did. At the meeting they were talking about buying a movie for visual education and Mrs. Spear, the president, asked for opinions on it. As nobody spoke up, I got up and said all the teachers seemed to think it was a fine thing. 'So I suggest that we buy it.' Do you know what? They put me on the budget-and-finance committee—you get it, don't you?—to see if I could hang on to money as well as spend it." (Laughs.)

His feelings about all children are revealed in what he says about his own (Tom and Mary). Whenever they want to do something that he thinks is a mistake, he listens with sympathy and says: "Well, Tom, you can if you want to. But this is what mother and I feel about it . . . And they have always known what money we have, exactly where we stand. When Tom was six, I was painting the house and he said, 'Can I paint?' 'Sure you can, Tom,' I said and got him a little brush. Pretty soon he could paint as well as I could, though not so fast. Tom and I are painting this house now. He's 17, plays football at Southwest." And he says: "Both Tom and Mary Ellen will go to the University. I am kind of proud of Mary Ellen." (Laughs.)

As for Joe Ryan, he went only through eighth grade. I said: "Your father must have been nice." "Yes. He was just a working man. I played the drum when I was a kid and would practice in the same room, and he read his newspaper and never said a word. He was a wonderful man. And my mother was just like that."

Joe Ryan knows our neighborhood and our children, and the trouble they get into; since he has been PTA president of the Riley School, of Southwest High School, and now the PTA for the City of Minneapolis.

# DR. FRANCIS BULL

r. Francis Bull of the University of Oslo spoke at the American-Scandinavian Foundation dinner and I will tell you a few impressions. You see in his soul he is not only a learned professor of literature and a great modern Scandinavian critic, as Georges Brandes was aforetime, but he is even more a poet. The glory of flying through the azure sky and over the sea and the towering Rockies! He spoke of how man's ancient vision of soaring through the sky has become a hard reality, with four motors. Apollo in his chariot, and the golden-haired Phaethon. And Elijah and Daedalus, the mythological inventor of flying, whose young son, Icarus, donned the wings and soared so near the sun that the wax melted and he fell into the sea.

"I shall fly out to Seattle and then to New York and then to Norway. Is not that a wonderful thing!" said Dr. Bull, his eyes giving off a fine flash.

At the dinner he talked to us all about Grini prison in Germany and how that hellish and terrifying experience "was also rich, because we found there was such greatness, goodness, unbendable truth and courage in ordinary men."

He taught literature there to the Norwegian prisoners of the Nazis, hundreds of them, whipped, tortured, taken out to be executed. He said it had taught him how to teach. In order to make these prisoners feel what he himself felt about literature, he had to break through mere "lecturing," that sedate, wordy distance between himself and his pupils. He had to speak like a poet, a skald, a prophet, with wildly impulsive sincerity and with grand truth and daring. Then his listeners— huddling in the dark, and listening for Nazi guards—perceived the glory that is in Shakespeare, in Ibsen's *Per Gynt* and *Brand*, in Dante.

The most illiterate men began to see the whole point and

meaning of literature. One day he was reciting from memory (all his lectures had to be given from memory, and I am told he knows all of Ibsen by heart) some parts of the Bible and a tough, cynical ruffian of a man said in astonishment: "Does it say that in the Bible? Now that's really good!"

In 1945 when I saw Dr. Bull in Norway right after Liberation he was pale and had that sickly mottled color that all Norwegians had due to semi-starvation and four years of suffering. When I interviewed him I started by saying: "Ole Gabriel Ueland er min bestefar. Ole Gabriel Ueland was my grandfather." He was delighted and astonished for this Ole Gabriel Ueland was a great farmer-statesman but he had lived so long ago. I imagine it was like saying, "George Washington was my grandfather." So I added gravely, "And Olaf Trygvasson (a Viking hero who lived about 1000 A.D.) was my great-grandfather." He liked this. Then he gave me a volume of Wergeland's wonderful poems to read on the voyage home on the Stavangerfjord.

He is a very tall and big man but his substance is somehow sensitive, lucent, and poetic rather than hard, solid, muscular. He has clear comely features, a straight and delicate and childlike nose and dark hair and then light blue eyes. One thinks of wild Gaelic poets who had that coloring. His manner is remarkable because he is so generous, eager and there is a constantly outpouring torrent of excited interest in every single person that presses to meet him. There is no skin of reserve between him and anyone. There is not the faintest touch of guardedness, aloofness, caution, criticalness. It is very extraordinary. I have never known any person who had this quality to such a degree—so unstanchably outgoing and unpretentious and radiant. I imagine the saints had it. I can see why Odd Nansen called him "St. Francis" in Grini Prison.

And yet he is so clear in his fine mind, and never sensational or unctuous, and he sees people clearly as they are. But he never seems to be judging them. He has a kind of grandeur and love for them just because they are alive and human.

When I drove him to the airport we passed the Ole Bull

statue: "I liked that so much when I was in Minneapolis before." I asked if he was related to Ole Bull. Oh yes, he said. It was the very same family. He told me a story of Ole Bull and Bjornson, the great Norwegian poet. They were both in Italy, the Seventeenth of May, Norwegian Independence Day, and there was to be a fine celebration. Now Bjornson wished to include other Scandinavians in Rome but the two great men disagreed. Ole Bull said finally with mighty anger: "I like you Bjornson, but you like the Swedes too much!" To Ole Bull it should have been an immaculately Norwegian celebration and he would have no part of it.

And as the day approached, Bjornson sent his little boy, Bjorn, to Ole Bull's house with a note, asking if he would not please change his mind. Ole Bull read the note, invited the little boy inside and got out his violin and said:

"Let me show you why I do not agree with your father. This," he said, "is Norway!" And he began to play "The Chalet Girl's Sunday" and other things with such fire of passion and magic that you could see and feel the Necken, the elves, the trolls, the Hulder, the mountains and Tor the Thunderer himself.

As we drove along toward the airport he exclaimed, "Glittering Lake Harriet, with a large diamond trembling on every wavelet!" And he talked about the controversy in Norway between a certain clergyman of the old school who has fiercely rebuked the bishops of Norway for not believing in Hell. I then asked Dr. Bull—for he seemed so luminously good and all that a Christian should be—what his religion was. "Well I suppose you would call me an agnostic and a humanist," he said.

And he told me how Bishop Berggrav, head of the church in Norway, had written a book and asked if he could inscribe it to himself, Francis Bull. "I said why yes. Why I was very, very pleased that he should want to, and very, very grateful. And I thought also it was so fine that a Bishop would pay me, just an unorthodox and secular man, this respect—I mean not that I am anything to deserve it but I thought that this spirit was so very fine."

We had coffee in the restaurant at the airport. And then

we walked out to the sun-drenched airfield to his plane—that monstrous, gleaming steel bird. He carried a thick book to read on the plane: "about the New Criticism and T. S. Eliot and others, although I am not of that school," he said, "but so interested in what they have to say."

And then with the most absurdly generous thanks for my kindness (it was not kindness at all but I was the lucky one to have had five minutes of his company) the tall, large, fine looking, gentle, poetical man, his long black hair a little awry, his soft face flushed pink in the sun, his light blue eyes flowing with smiling tenderness and joy—

"Thank you, thank you! Tak, tak! Kom til Norge! How kind you have been. Thank you again and again. How kind all Americans are . . . How fine it is to be here and what a wonderful and happy experience to be with you all! Tak. Tak! Farvel! Adieux!"

❖

# DR. PIET KOLTHOFF

I had lunch with Dr. I. M. Kolthoff of the University, a distinguished scientist, a chemist known all over the world. He is Dutch-American; not married; rides horseback on dancing, uneasy horses. He has a round face, childish in its circle like the drawings of French children: brown eyes through plastic glasses; a faint limp from a riding accident; an almost inaudible voice speaking through a line of lips, smiling and tenderly awry.

He was angry at the day's headlines about the Russian "spy" held in Oregon. "So have *we* spies in Russia! Our Intelligence service is there—of course it is!" He thinks the working up of anti-Russian feeling is criminal: "And it isn't innocent, the way it is timed. *Somebody* wants it." It is so sinister—"We may be on the brink of destroying the world. Say that we *do* fight. Can we beat Russia? And would that settle anything? Not at all.

"There'll just be another world war and another, getting always worse, newer and bigger enemies forever and ever, until man is destroyed. I'm afraid I'm a pessimist"—with a kind of sigh.

"Oh there's too much greediness, egotism in us, nations grabbing more and more" (because they are the monstrous expression of each tiny citizen—of you and me, and our stupid automatic selfishness). "We now have Pacific bases in a semicircle all around Russia, ready to pounce. Don't you think Russia has reason to be scared? You know in France the Gallup Poll found 26 percent of the people distrust Russia most, but 25 percent distrusted the United States most. That's a kind of joke on us, isn't it? We can control everything but man, and if we can't learn to control man we're lost. It is hopeless until countries and people give, not grab. But go back to the Bible and what it says!"

Should the secret of the atom bomb be shared? "You

must put "secret" in quotes. Because there isn't any. The real 'secret' was when Otto Hahn and Lise Meitner discovered the fission of the uranium atom. A discovery is made and others get to work on it, that's all. The Duponts have the 'secret' of nylon, but there will soon be cropping up everywhere hundreds of things exactly like nylon."

But he has some hope. What does he think of the United Nations? "It is already 10 times as strong as the League of Nations. The one obstacle to world government is 'sovereignty'" (i.e. every country ferociously claiming it can do as it chooses and never saying, "In certain things, we will bow to world law and give up a piece of our sovereignty.")

I think he hugs a miserable hope that the atom bomb is so full of doom that it may actually terrify each country into giving up a tincture of sovereignty—for the world's sake. "If the nations will only subscribe to the international control of the bomb, then we would have the vestigial beginning of world government. We must work for it."

He spoke of things to save us and the best idea, he thinks, is "a kind of unprecedented exchange of younger people— sending them to study and work in each other's countries, so that we can all learn to like each other a little bit. The state department has a bill for this," he says.

I have a notion that great scientists and rhapsodists are struck with celestial bolts of "inspiration" like poets and prophets—getting things straight from the angels. From what he says I think it is so. He says his students don't like it much, but in his examinations he gives them all the facts and then asks them just to draw conclusions from the facts to find if they have a nickel's worth of imagination. A stupendous memory for facts isn't worth much. As the working man said: "Everything's true but them facts."

He says the less he works the better the *work*. The war made him more frantically busy than a waltzing mouse over practical things, "facts," and so his work is far less good than when he had four times as much idleness. "I'd sit in the sun and stare at the blank sky in Holland for three hours, and my nieces and nephews would say, 'Look at Uncle Piet dreaming.' Really

I'd be working the hardest then." His religion? The tender slanting smile and he said, "I guess I probably have more religion than anyone, but not in the conventional sense."

◆

# DR. WILLIAM O'BRIEN

D r. William A. O'Brien said that I could see him at the University hospital. On the telephone his manner is a combination of blunt, forthright statement and such quick, monosyllabic friendliness that it takes your breath away. "Sure! Come over." At the hospital I asked where his office was and, finding it locked, I waited. Then a huge big man, the brim of his hat turned down, with a broad face, glasses, enormous shoulders, came to the office door and stooped to fumble in it with his key. ("Dr. Foster went to Gloucester," I thought; "No, he's Boswell's Dr. Johnson.")

We went in and his wide expressionless face gazed at me (a half hour later it wonderfully smiled) and I thought how the eyes, wide apart and very clear and soft, and the golden eyebrows were Irish—that soft puzzled look in them, full of feeling. "A tranquil, poetic nervous system," I thought, "and no wonder, after a thousand years of the green bogs and wet tides of Galway."

He told me that his grandparents came from Ireland "because of the potato famine," landed at New Orleans and went up the Mississippi to Cincinnati. Then to escape a cholera plague they fled west in a covered wagon to southwest Illinois. "My grandfather, like so many of the Irish, took what was one step removed from the farm—he bred horses." (Percherons and work horses). "And then, the next generation would go into the professions."

He went to Notre Dame and then to St. Louis University to study medicine. "One of the oldest medical schools west of the Mississippi." Then to Detroit. "My sister was a social worker there." And that describes the kind of family it was—those wonderful social workers, feminist girls of a generation ago! Then he went into the First World War and after that he wanted to do graduate work. "Dr. Lyon was here at the University and also a graduate of St. Louis. So I came here and have stayed ever since."

What we do in our lives is decided by some vision, some admiration we had when we were young. "I once saw a clinic conducted by Dr. George Murphy of Chicago, the great surgeon, you know, and I never forgot it. After that I always wanted to explain, to teach people. Now in medicine there are two things. First, research, and second the *interpretation* of the research so that the public can understand it. That's what I do, that's my work—lecture, talk on the radio. (The important thing is don't talk down to people; respect them, have affection for them.)

"We have the Center for Continuation Study where grown-up people—doctors and so on—can come and do more studying. We don't call it 'refresher courses.' Don't like the word, 'refresher,' because it suggests that you learn something again that you have forgotten. But really we never forget what we have learned, but are always learning, advancing. All life and knowledge is a continuum. . ."

As for his choosing a life in a university rather than practicing medicine— "Some people say that we can't take it in competitive practice and that is why we are here. No. University work is right for some, that's all. You can only explain it if you experience it—the detachment and search for disinterested truth." And he said the University is not really as browsingly calm as outsiders think—"These thousands and thousands of people struggling to learn something, to learn more, more." His short sentences made me see the fever of effort and passion and energy in it. "It is such a fight . . . Much unhappiness too . . . Many of them terribly forlorn . . ."

Then presently he was defining the difference between "good-hearted" people and "kind-hearted" people. To give an example: Sometimes in the newspapers an account of some poor little unfortunate person is given and people write letters and give help. There are pictures in the paper, photos of gifts donated, and all hearts wrung and everybody bleating with a kind of sentimental satisfaction and not much cost to themselves, all getting more out of it in the way of free advertising, emotions, etc. than they give the poor little unfortunate.

"Well, they are good-hearted people," said Dr. O'Brien. "But kind-hearted people want to help *everybody*, to think, give money and work for the health, the good of *everybody* and without credit."

His first sentence to me had been: "In your family you kept the good old Viking names. I think that's right. That's good. Many Irish and immigrant families give their children new kinds of names, not names like Bridget—" but probably Hazel or Merrylyn. So I asked the names of his children: "William, Patrick, Kathleen, Michael, Peggy and Molly." Molly is the baby, six months old.

◆

# KATE TUCKER

I t was Katherine Tucker (Director of Nursing Education at Pennsylvania University) who gave me a bright astounding picture of American nurses. And what they do. And she said, "A girl who has both a college education and a nurse's training can make from 6 to 8 thousand dollars a year."

"How? for Heaven's sake!"

"She can become an executive in that huge public health army." And she began to describe that scrubbed, starched, intelligent, fresh-faced army of young women of which Dr. Thomas Paran, the Surgeon General (a wonderful man, a great man) is the commander-in-chief.

It is this way: The United States has about 3000 counties. About half of these have a public health office (some time all of them will), and in it there are a few public health nurses. They go out and take care of sick people in the countryside, and also, they teach them—that is the important thing. You see to prevent sickness you must start with the person who has the disease. If he can learn about his own case, and take care of it and isolate it, and if you can teach his family how to prevent the same disease, that is the way to lift the permanent health and soundness of the whole country.

Take one major cause of death: heart trouble. It is often caused by rheumatic fever in childhood. This runs in families and also it recurs periodically. And while the child who has it may grow up, its effects may impair him seriously in middle life.

Well, say the county nurse finds some farm child with rheumatic fever. While the doctor can diagnose it and prescribe, she is the one who comes day after day. And cures him. And teaches his family everything about it so that it will not injure his heart, and how to watch for its recurrence. And she'll be showing them all kinds of things about diet, hygiene, about psychiatry even and how to treat children. You can see what a tremendous force these wonderful nurses are for enlightenment!

Now nurses' aides—What are they? Their national director is Mrs. Walter Lippman. (223,000 have been trained this year.) And in Minneapolis, Mrs. Anne Mariette is in charge. (Her husband is Dr. Mariette of the Glen Lake Sanitarium.)

She says that 526 Minneapolis nurses have gone to war and so we must have nurses' aides. The course takes seven weeks. You wear a pretty blue and white uniform. You can enroll at the Red Cross or the Citizen's Aid Building. Now my friend, Dorothy Lewis, became a nurse's aide. She has five grown children and was experiencing that invisible anxiousness and pained conscience: "I am not contributing enough . . ."

Here is my diary:

*Thursday, February* 26, 1942. Below zero. Dorothy came to tea. It was her first day at St. Barnabas. Three hours only. "Soon I'll be working twice a week for seven hours a day. Whew. After today, I don't know if I can come through. Well I guess I can." She means that it is such dodgasted hard work.

"What is it like, Dorothy? Like housework?" I meant, is it just carrying trays and so on.

Then she tells about her job. Her first patient was an old, old man with a very bad heart. ". . . so he had to sit up in bed, the bed bent at a sharp angle. And I was told to bathe him. Well (he is stone deaf) I go in there. Now how to make a bed and bathe him—I have learned that. I take down his sheet. He has had an abdominal operation and there it is—a great thick forest of tubes and drains. And to make his bed bent at an angle like that, and to change the sheets with all those tubes! Well I was just staggered," (she burst out laughing), "but I plunged in and did what I could. I did it all right—my heart pumping. And he would droop his head and look kind of faint and deathly pale. 'I seem to be kinda tired' (She imitates him.) "Why I thought he might die at any moment." And at the conclusion of this Dorothy fixed me with a flashing indignant eye and said, "So it is *not* like housework!" adding however, "Thank God."

That angel of a Dorothy! She likes it so much. "It opens up

my whole life. And I have an advantage over the kids, the younger nurses. I know what to talk to the patients about... and you will be making a bed and perhaps they will just touch your hand, gratefully, pat you, ever so weakly... How this makes you feel you cannot imagine," she says. "It's such a sensation that you do some good, some wonderful *good*. Gosh!"

❖

# In Memoriam
## Kieth Emery
### January 2nd, 1980

Darling, incomparable Kieth Emery died. It seems astonishing, a shock. Almost unbearable. There is a vacuum. It will be hard, so sad, to live without him.

I had come to know him very well because, out of their unstanchable kindness, Ella and Kieth took me swimming twice a week to the Blaisdell YMCA. Now that meant being with Kieth three hours a week—genially arguing, talking about children, grandchildren, War, Salt II, Truth and Beauty, Feminism, outrageous nukes, violins, Jimmy Carter, heroes, skunks, world history.

But the point is, Kieth himself. I must try to tell that. That extraordinary man, so alight with imagination, ideas, with miraculous good nature, with jocularity; Kieth, with his wide tireless mind, his entranced interest in everything. Just coming down my front steps on Wednesday and Friday, Ella getting out of the front seat (those two married saints!) so that I could sit with him—I wish I could describe to you my eagerness. Oh here he is! Kieth! What a Holy Circus to talk to Kieth!

He was a fine strenuous swimmer. There are several lanes in the pool, you know, mine a slower one, what you might call "the Sixth Grade," but Kieth was farther over near the Olympic fellows. He would thrash along, steaming through the water like a side-wheeler, splashes rising to the ceiling: the Australian crawl, the back-stroke, and that violent stroke that I call "the Sea Monster." It is a breast stroke where you sink under water each time and with a convulsive paroxysm of backbone and muscles, you come up glaring and snorting, mouth open like Neptune's or a shark's. We had time to swim nine laps, a quarter of a mile.

Now I must tell you something important about him. He was very handsome. He had great Beauty. This was a part of him—his physique, nose, eyes, shoulders, legs. He looked very young. Comely. Compact. Limber. It was exactly like his spirit. Flexible. His lovely ease. The wide smile.

Leonardo da Vinci said, "The soul makes the body, and the artist's inner creative mechanism is so insistent that when he paints a portrait he makes the sitter look like himself." And somehow Kieth expressed this among all our swimming friends. There are Jesuits, bartenders, invalids, fatties, stern girl athletes, Olympic champions, wonderful witty blacks. We are all absolutely devoted to each other.

Now I am very romantic and this adorable and remarkable Kieth, so arch-intelligent, so sane, honorable—I have often thought: "Who was he in another life?" He was certainly Somebody. Spell it with a capital S. Who was he aforetime? Maybe he was Herodotus. Maybe Roger Ascham. Could it have been Condorcet of the French Revolution? Was it Thomas Jefferson? Maybe he was George Washington's friend, John Mason, who invented such a wonderful thing to make the Thirteen Colonies coalesce and stick together, i.e. a vote for every person.

Anyway, there he was, a man with an everyday familiar life, retired, living on Upton Avenue South, loved by his dog, a DFL delegate, a Norman Thomas Fan, a man who actually knew (a rare bird indeed!) the difference (they are hundreds of miles apart) between Socialism and Communism, "that Socialism, hang it all! is NOT bureaucratic collectivism!" A man who gravely, seriously, radiantly loved and admired his grandchildren. Kieth, so dear, so grand, so important in his soul and life, so symbolic of Minnesota in the United States of America in 1979, this perilous and appalling time. Never mind. Think of Kieth and don't be frightened. His ilk are among us. This must mean something about this terrible world boiling with crises and incipient horrors.

Now here please overlook a little mysticism. The tragedy is that death came too soon. We should have had twenty more years of him, of his jocund, stalwart presence. You know much brighter souls than I, Blake, Swedenborg and Jesus, great souls more pervious to the Invisible than I am, say that when we die we are not dead. I cannot help but believe that. It is a certitude.

I cannot get away from the notion.

Death is unbearably tragic and grievous because it is a kind of farewell. But it is not forever. Those who are Yonder, in a queer way—I have discovered this myself—are more puissant than ever. They are more befriending, more strengthening, more helpful.

Then there is this thought. Rudolph Steiner, the Hungarian mystic, said that the Catholic prayers for the dead are so right, so true, because the person who has died at first is a little lost. Our love helps him, makes it easier for him to find his way. I believe it.

So we must send Kieth our love day and night. And he will return it. He will give us his towering magnanimity, his light-heartedness, his love.

He will help us all.

I know it is so.

❖

# My Brother Torvald
## Part I

M y darling brother Torvald died in a New York hospital in the care of his doctor, Dr. Bickerman, who (he told me many times) was as good, as wise, as Dr. Kenneth Taylor of long ago, our incomparable brother-in-law and a world-famous doctor. He had emphysema and was very much handicapped for two years and more, taking oxygen several times a day—all that. Then there was several weeks ago an infection in one lung. Dr. Bickerman was able to mend it, but Torvald died. I imagine he had made that final inner decision to do so. It makes me feel better to think how he was always surrounded by an incomparable family, especially Karen and Tora, his daughters, such handsome, able, competent, loving beings, always mightily at hand. And Connie. No one on earth can equal Connie.

A death is always so strange and terrible. A farewell! an amputation! But it also is a kind of paradox; on one hand one has an utterly terrible and dreadful feelings; on the other hand maybe it is not sad at all and one begins to think how Yonder there are all those people (and far more of them than here) who are far more grand, more beautiful, merrier than any of us left here on earth, how fine it must be over there!

I now try to write a column about Torvald, such a magnificent, jokey, kind-hearted fellow, so original, brilliant, so alive with astonishing ideas, I mean new and good ones.

He was born in September 1901, the youngest, of our seven children. He came trailing along nearly four years after Rolf. As I remember it I think we were all a little chagrined that there was going to be another one. Six children already! I think that even my mother kind of wished things were otherwise. But immediately after he was born he became a kind of pet adored by all. A magnificent child, perfect, laughing, eyes like brown velvet pansies. Remarkably strong and well-proportioned, a lovely infant Hercules—chest, shoulders, legs, plump cherubic feet. My mother (two generations ahead of her time) put him in the sun. Barefooted on the lawn, in the lake, and in the woods beyond the pasture.

He was, unlike the rest of us, sort of tenderly, gloriously neglected, I mean never admonished, because he was so nice, so utterly amiable and because he was the youngest. All rules seem to have been suspended. For example, when he grew up and went to high school and then (briefly, alas) to the University, my father had at last bought an automobile. He had resisted such nonsense for decades. We had our horse and pony and then Bessie and the Brougham purchases from Mrs. Frank Foreman our neighbor. That was entirely good enough for anybody my father thought, a Norwegian Stoic and as philosophically haughty and independent as Jefferson and Thoreau.

But then at last he bought "the Marmon" costing $5,000. A very fine car indeed. We kept it into its final decrepitude but it was always in my Father's thoughts magnificent, and say that the President of the United States came to town, he would grandly offer it for the occasion, in case they wanted it.

At this time my mother was going daily to the State Capitol in St. Paul, to the Legislature, trying to persuade Ole Sageng and horribly hide-bound legislators to have woman suffrage, to pass child labor laws, minimum-wage-for-women laws. She went there always from our house on the south side of Lake Calhoun on the streetcar, often transferring downtown to do a few household errands. Torvald had the car. She did not mind in the least. She came home in the late afternoon on the Selby-Lake, transferring at Lake Street and Hennepin to the Oak and Harriet. She liked those Twin City Rapid Transit streetcars—ah! so beautiful they were, like yellow fairy palaces with a motorman in front and a conductor in the rear (Scandinavians always with kindly accents) to collect your nickle. (If you were adroit at transferring you could do the whole Twin City circuit from Lake Harriet to Lake Phalen for five cents.) And Torvald, as I said, always had the Marmon. That adorable charming rascal, Torvald, always talking and joking through his wide-stretched smile, of *course* he had the car, a splendid driver, a mechanic (often lathered with black grease).

Then Torvald flunked in the middle of freshman year at the University, thus breaking a record among the Ueland children, all with their college degrees, some like Sigurd with all A's at Harvard Law School. Torvald cheerfully went to work as a flour salesman for Pillsbury's.

❖

# MY BROTHER TORVALD
## PART II

A s I told you last time my youngest brother, Torvald, died and this is Part II of the column I wrote about him.

Now this is interesting about Torvald. He was apparently extraordinarily bright, especially in things like mathematics. I think this talent came from our grandfather, Ole Gabriel Ueland, the Norwegian statesman who was also a poor farmer in the mountains of Heskestad. The folk around there used to say—with astonishment—that when Ole Gabriel was a young man he "could even read in a book he had never seen before." And he taught himself mathematics, as much as possible, and even some astronomy, making maps of the stars in the sky.

When Torvald was five years old he could beat my father at chess, at least now and then. He went to West High School and accomplished the four year's course in only three. When he went to the University suddenly he became very very big, over six feet, very tall and somewhat fat, a great broad chest, long legs like the pillars of Hercules. These violent physical changes of adolescence (and this is something we must always consider in the young, when they alarm us by becoming temporarily lazy or dull) seemed to obliterate all mental fervor for a while. He had the car, cruised about, much loved by all friends, but he couldn't *think*. He could not do his lessons, skipped classes, did not pass tests. There was a game at the Alpha Delta house where one tossed pennies at a crack and when you got the nearest to it, you got the pennies. He did a great deal of that. He was flunked out of the University.

But as I remember it, there was no caterwauling or lamenting. He went cheerfully to work for the Pillsbury Company, going to Omaha and other places, selling flour or trying to. My mother had pangs about his possible loneliness and said in every letter to us, "Be sure to write to Torvald. . ."

And presently he married Constance Puffer, a delight, a star of a girl. Apparently he made a kind of living. They went to New Jersey where he worked as a salesman for Pillsbury's. Enchanting children were born, Karen and Ranny and when they hit on that handsome name for him, Ranulf, my brother Sigurd said, "A very fine name! Half Ole Virginie and half Viking."

There was the Depression. Connie and Toke came up from their rather decrepit old house with its yard full of weeds, from Plainfield, New Jersey, to visit Anne and Kenneth Taylor in New York. Torvald had lost his job. It seems that he told a certain Mr. Prince, his boss, in a friendly way, that he (Mr. Prince) was not smart enough, that he suffered from a paucity of ideas. Mr. Prince didn't like it. Anyway, Torvald was out of a job and there they were—the Depression, a third child (Tora) about to be born. I remember that time: We were all at Anne's house on Sutton Square in the green library, the French windows looking out on the East River and the great liners going by. You could almost trail your hand along their sides. There was our tender anxiety about his lost job, the ominous general situation in the world, about poor Connie going to have a baby. But presently Torvald said drawling (he talked very, very slowly through his very wide smile): "Well it's all right. One thing we do awfully well is to have children."

Fired from Pillsbury's, Torvald became a kind of free-lance flour salesman. And he had such an interesting idea I thought. It was what he called, "salesmanship reversed." That is to say, instead of pressing and bullying and exhausting customers to buy flour, he did just the opposite. He would visit all the small Italian and Jewish bakers in south New Jersey and New York. Talked to them, liked them, got fond of them. They admired his judgment, his prognostications. They began to like to see him coming. He baked bread very well himself. He was so interesting, a lot of fun. After a number of months they would buy flour from no one else.

He rented a tiny one-room office on squalid Front Street in lower New York on the Hudson River near the Battery. The rent was about fifteen dollars a month but his telephone bill was four or five hundred dollars a month, and on this telephone he would buy a carload of flour in Buffalo, say, and then guide it, by telephone, around a blizzard in Elmira ("Go through Birmingham...") and see that it arrived at 8 a.m. on time at a doughnut factory in Harrisburg, Pennsylvania. As I remember it I think he sold great shiploads of flour to Brazil, to Italy. (I tend to be wildly romantic about such things and may exaggerate.)

Anyway he was immensely successful. He bought a 200-acre farm in Monmouth County, New Jersey and there was a fine old pre-Revolutionary house on it; deep woods and pastures; a house for the farmer. Presently he had forty cows and a milking parlor and a great pond in the pasture. His office was in his house overlooking lawns, gardens, tennis court. The Shrewsbury River was not far away and he would skim us out to the New Jersey coast where we could see Sandy Hook and the faraway ocean liners.

All through these years, this is the way I see him in my mind's eye: endless geniality and mighty energy. On jerk-water trains sitting on his suitcase in crowded aisles all night; smoking, rumpled clothes. That energy and goodnature! The kind of man who will be mowing his lawn at eleven o'clock on a Sunday night in the rain. There were always two or three adoring dogs, very large, galumphing around him on the way to the barn. Wagging tails thumping the rungs of his chair. Asleep on his bed.

Once as a reporter for the *Minneapolis Times*, I went to a business lunch at the Minneapolis Club, beside me, an eminent chemist, Miss Betty Sullivan, very important at Russell Miller's.

"Ueland?" she said. "Is that your name? I correspond with a man named Ueland in the East. He has so many good ideas." It was Torvald of course.

But the most vivid ever-recurring memory of that darling little boy, Torvald, is this: He is nine years old. We are all in the dining room having lunch. Torvald comes home from school. He comes into the dining room from the kitchen. He is laughing, laughing. He is staggering with laughter. He laughs so hard he bumps into the sideboard. We ask him what he is laughing about. At last he gets it out. "Miss Brooks says we can write a composition and make it just as funny as we want to!"

As a writer who has spent a lifetime hoping to be funny now and then and seeing how hard it is to be Mark Twain, this shows you the hope, jocularity and exuberance that was Torvald.

◆

# MR. BRUCE CARLSON OF THE SCHUBERT CLUB

T hree years ago Bruce Carlson wrote me a kind and cordial letter asking if he could take me to see the Museum of The Schubert Club—a piano that Brahms had played and other remarkable things. I wrote that I was not as athletic as in former times and disliked troubling people to lug me around.

Then he came over to my house bringing Patricia Hampl—both of them young, slender, comely, lively. After that he came regularly—say once a week and never failed. It was a strange and astonishing thing, a kind of eerie faithfulness, really love. He always brought presents—Yeats, Mozart's letters. I gave him Swedenborg, Blake.

He is a listener and I would talk far too much. He had read my biography written in 1938 and a smaller book, *If You Want to Write*, one of those awful "How To" books. But it is better than that. Its true title should be "Helped by the Nine Muses." He and The Schubert Club published them both.

And now I come to the power and mystery of this extraordinary Bruce Carlson. I was immediately projected upward into a kind of famousness: letters from San Francisco, visitors from everywhere, a young woman, (frighteningly handsome, stylish) came from Chicago, a kind of advertising tycoon who flew from Brazil to Santa Fe to New York and back, and she quietly wept, wiping and wiping her eyes because I "was so great" (I had told her in a letter she could never write anything worth a damn as long as she wrote advertising.)

Well now Bruce Carlson, my incomparable friend. (Patricia Hampl calls him "our Swedish nobleman" and that is just the way he looks.) He has that talent for promotion—for the bright and beautiful enlargement of any person or thing. Now usually I dislike it, indeed despise it, because it is the flattening out of persons and events into a kind of monstrous vulgarity.

(As I say of the Cowles Newspapers: "They have such a talent for being uninteresting.")

But the thing about Bruce is his taste, his instinct for what is first rate in music, beauty, historical events. He knows why Mozart is great, and Schubert. He has flawless taste, as certain and unfailing as it is in all great artists.

His parents were Swedish. His father, M.C.R. Carlson, worked for the famous Lucian Sprague, the railroad president who saved the Minneapolis and St. Louis Railroad. He had been a ten-year-old call-boy for the Burlington, getting up at five to rouse the engineer for his run.

In 1935 the M. and St. L. owed a million dollars. Lucian Sprague, as a receiver, came to watch the autopsy, but he decided on a shining miracle.

The railroad goes from Minneapolis to St. Louis but its branches go East to Peoria and West to South Dakota. Goods coming from the East could go on board at Peoria and then slip through the smiling green plain of Illinois with ease and save 37 hours and great expense. They took as a motto "The Peoria Gateway." It was painted on the freight cars.

Lucian Sprague said to Mr. Carlson and his discouraged young staff, "No more telephone calls for business. Go out and get it. So will I. But you've got to have enthusiasm. You can't pull an engine with cold water."

Bruce's mother was Margaret Helen Nelson, also Swedish. They married in 1930 and bought a house near the Mississippi River. There were three children: Bruce and two sisters. They were all (Swedish) good-looking, (yellow hair and light green eyes). They had a happy home life. There was good music always. They were a type of Swedish Lutherans, serious inwardly and happy and generous outwardly. "We were all good skaters." His mother played the piano in church. His father enthusiastically supported his family.

And here Bruce tells how his mother "was a fine tennis player. She won a state championship." And in his mild admiration you begin to see she also had great style and delightful effrontery. "She bought herself a red convertible—a bright red one."

Bruce was born in 1940. He had a talent for friendship, a searching, smiling interest in everything. He went to public school, took impassioned music lessons. And, like all the children of poor first-generation Scandinavian immigrants, they were all bound for universities, for Phi Beta Kappa and probably Doctor's degrees.

They sent him to a college in Chicago from 1958 to 1962, North Park College, and here he met more beauty and Swedishness, Deanna—born on an immense farm in Iowa. They were married six years later.

In the small Chicago college he read Milton's *Paradise Lost*, Dante's *Divine Comedy*, all the great Russians, Henry James, Shakespeare, Shelley, Keats, Byron, Carlyle, Sir Walter Scott, Yeats.

When he was 22 he came home and went to the university for two years for a Master's Degree. In 1964, he went to law school for three years and a law degree, and then at 28 he started to work for The Schubert Club, his first job.

The Schubert Club—it was a group of unpretentiously intelligent persons—women—who loved the music of Schubert, who also was divinely unpretentious and had died young.

Now he has been there 16 years. Their concerts expanded and grew. His great museum. The wonderful recordings, (Serkin), the scholarships. Great performers and virtuosi. The very large audiences at O'Shaughnessy Hall, published books. Promoted composers like Libby Larsen and worked out collaborations (oratorios) with Patricia Hampl, the beautiful concert at Plymouth Church.

The small gently amateurish Schubert Club began to pull abreast in eminence, with the Minneapolis Symphony. When he first worked with them it had an annual budget of $20,000. Now it is $1,000,000 a year.

Bruce and Deanna were married in 1964. They bought a house near the Franklin Avenue bridge on the Minneapolis side—a warm hospitable house with grave dark woodwork, most of it an expression of his tireless physical energy and unswerving labor for taste and his idea of perfection. There are two children, Vanessa aged 15, slim, golden, with a rare bashful smile, and then there is Max, two years old—Maximillian Frederick. I remember when he was named. It is like the enormous expanse of Bruce Carlson's imagination to associate a child with pale silken hair, shyly walking, staggering, with a sixteenth century German Emperor of the Holy Roman Empire.

Here I must tell an interesting thing about Deanna, (quite tall, walks lightly like an insolent goddess). She is an eminent tap-dancer. My insistent idea is that tap-dancing is the most beautiful of all dancing and Fred Astaire, one of the greatest artists who ever lived. It expresses so much better than solemn ballet, happiness, reckless freedom, enchanting rascality, the victorious human spirit. The summer before last, one of the hottest of all time (96 degrees) Deanna in the tap-dancing corps of the Aquatennial, danced one and a half hours, (at least four miles) and there were two cloud bursts. I saw Bruce when he drove his car to rescue her at the end. That has made me her fan for all time. My dream now is that when at last I can run a marathon I will tap-dance it and the beauty of that is that at the end one would never be tired but full of earth-spurning joy.

To tell a few things about Bruce: He seems to have a constant unchanging unclouded mood of smiling happiness and golden success. I have never known anybody just like that.

A young relative of mine had an important job in Philadelphia. She wanted to work in Minneapolis. I asked if he could find her a job. "Sure." Within an hour he had talked to Mrs. James Ford Bell, chairman of the board, on the telephone about a new head of MacPhail School. Mrs. Bell said: "If she's your man, she's my man!"

I think his great talent for success is explained in this way: His final objective is always so distinguished, so beautiful, so unflawed. There was an oratorio written for Plymouth Church by Patricia Hampl and Libby Larsen. Another instance: A lot of "modern" poets were going to read their own work for a prolonged evening. Bruce added a musician with an ancient seventeenth century harpsichord. Thereby the evening became alive, very, very interesting, marked by special beauty. He goes to innumerable plays, concerts, meetings, and the odd thing is he is most often alone. There he will be on the top row far over to the left.

And he is so radiantly and delightedly suggestible. I say: "Drink a pint of hand-squeezed fresh orange juice a day." And he does it. I say, "Read Swedenborg." He not only does it at once but plans a museum for the great Swedenborg at Landmark Center.

He has two arch-especial male friends (he sees that his friends know his other friends): Art Mampel, a poet and a clergyman in Seattle, and Tom Tredway, the president of Augustana College in Illinois. They meet and talk with great seriousness several times a year. And they come to see me.

And so from all this I hope you will see what he is like. He makes me think especially of what George Bernard Shaw said in *Back to Methuselah*: "Discouragement is the only illness."

❖

# ◢ CHILDREN ◣

## CHILDREN: HOW TO BE GOOD TO THEM

I have always felt that very small children, even a child of two, is wonderfully intelligent and always understands things clearly if you express them well enough. Their understanding is as good as ours, perhaps better, but we are not aware of it because they have not the vocabulary or the experience.

And that is why grownups so often do not explain to small children, the reason for things, the logic. Take stealing. All small children steal at first in a gay light-hearted way. Indeed, it seems to them a very sensible thing to do.

But what are the underlying reasons for *not* stealing? It is not that you will get caught and get into trouble, be put into jail. (Anyone who refrains from stealing for that reason only, for only his own miserable skin, is no good at all!) And you refrain from stealing not just because it is bad, terrible, naughty. Well, it is. But *why* is it? What is the underlying reason?

Because it is cowardly—you want to get something with no risks and no generous effort—and selfish (what you steal is for your own self-indulgence); and it is unaesthetic, i.e. it requires sneaking and padding about and pussyfooting in the most slimy unattractive way. But most important of all, and the only true reason for *not* stealing—it is so mean, so unkind. It causes much pain and deprivation to some innocent person.

Well, children see these underlying reasons so quickly—far more sensitively and quickly than we do—if grownups will just explain these things a little bit. In the same way, good manners should be explained.

I have seen scores of children automatically doing something they consider embarrassing, asinine, affected, such as shaking hands and saying; "How do you do?" and they don't know why. Their nice parents say they must, but it seems all hypocrisy to wise, sincere little children. But if you explain the underlying logic of it, then it all clears up. It was like this with my own child:

On Christmas Day we were going to Mr. Carl Taylor's fine house in the country at Westport, Connecticut. I had that maternal uneasiness that comes because a small child is not polite to strangers. That is, strangers beam and offer hands and ask questions and the child stares back with no response, a cold fishy look. There is the impulse, as the mother, to say: "Now what do you say, dear? Now say 'thank you,' dear, to Mrs. Q." But I never could. The words rose in my mouth and I could not let them out. Because it was humiliating for the child and perfunctory and forced if she *did* smile, embarrassing for the company. And embarrassing for Mama who wants all to feel happy and at ease.

As we drove up to Carl Taylor's I talked to Gaby about it. She was 4.

"You know there will be lots of people up there—Anne and Kenneth and others—and they will be glad to see you. But look, darling. This is something I want to talk to you about. You know grownups always feel fond of children and interested in them and make exclamations and smile and ask questions. But children are apt to feel bashful. And this is what they do: They just look back like this—I then acted it out.

"But I'll tell you—if you possibly can, smile back and speak to them pleasantly. Or anyway, just smile. Because you see when you *don't*, it makes them feel that you don't like them. And that hurts their feelings."

She listened to all this thoughtfully and suggested some thoughts on the subject which I cannot recall, but I could see that it had cleared up for her the whole reason for all politeness. When she got up to the Taylor's, all pressed around. She smiled at everyone in the kindest, brightest way. She answered all questions sympathetically. She has had tender-hearted and good manners ever since.

# DISCIPLINE AND CHILDREN

 lthough I have always tried so hard to discipline myself, I never discipline children. Thank Heaven for that. My motto for child raising is: "Always be careful never to cross a child." And I never did. And from the very first I have always bowed low to children and respected their wishes and differences from myself.

I always tried to do this: to tell what I *thought*, but never assume or feel that I was necessarily *right*. My child, for instance—she might feel differently and think differently. If so, fine. Then she must defy me, stoutly and with an honorable courage. Of course it made it easier that she was an only child and there were not other children to commit injustices among each other, and to compete for my attention. And because I had no other children, there was none of that parental policing to do.

At Christmas and on her birthday I bought her an avalanche of presents:

"Gaby"— I find I have written in an old letter—"got her turquoise-studded watch and she was delighted with it. Christmas was a tremendous success: a tiny umbrella, a raincoat, a coat, books, a scooter, stuffed bears, kangaroo (and a baby in its pocket), foxes, some with glasses on.

"When she saw her presents she made a great fuss over me, saying now nice I was to give her such things. This is surprising. Having never been disappointed, it is strange she should feel such affectionate gratitude. Why didn't she say, as spoiled children are supposed to, 'Well, why didn't you get me the pony?'"

Once for a short time I had a tall, refined, splendidly educated French woman to take care of Gaby, a governess. (I had to work in New York every day.) But I could not get rid of her quick enough. And I tremble with indignation to think of it now, for she believed in "discipline," the usual firm, flute-voiced, relentless, will-breaking that is practiced all over the world by stupid, well-educated people. With splendid firmness she forced Gaby to eat fish with the consequence that she threw up and can never eat fish to this day. When four-year-old Gaby took a gum drop from a puppy and ate it, and denied it, though the Mademoiselle distinctly saw it in her mouth—well when I came home at night the Mademoiselle told me, gravely, how Gaby had "lied" to her, and what sort of a serious treatment should we use to deal with that sort of thing?

But I cannot write about it without feeling within me the running fire of a Berserk, right now. Yes, I would throw all such people in the ocean. No, let them live. But let them never come near my child or any child in the whole world, every one of whom must be free and a friend and an equal.

And I have always thought that there is nothing in the world as bad as scolding. When you come to think of it, it is the thing that we, as adults, most dread. I am not much afraid of physical pain. But to be scolded, to exchange harsh words, makes my flesh creep with fright and dreadful excitement. It seems so much more cruel than blows. Scolding means there is a temporary spiritual state of dislike, of hateful repudiation. And dislike is so much worse than good-natured physical fighting.

So I thought that children should never be spoken to sharply. And never expected to mind quickly. If anyone orders *us* like that, we are apt to murder them (if we are any good). I tried always—and only when it was necessary—to use good-natured force. If a child were too slow in going to bed I would carry him upstairs, and if he kicked and screamed I remained as amiable and jokey as could be and I would say: "I bet you can't cry for five minutes more. If you can, I'll give you a cookie." And that fake, curiously histrionic crying would fade away into the falsest effort and angry giggles.

And if my violent temper came, as it does to everyone, and I felt strong enough to pick up the piano and dash it on the floor, I would always explain it. "Don't be scared, darling. This is just my temper. I don't mean it. You are not to blame in any way."

Yes, I know that parents who discipline (so-called) their

children, make them dull, break their spirits, extinguish their ideas, initiative and creative energy, and are just getting them ready to be afraid of all the employers and bullies and mean husbands and wives of the future.

❖

# ON SCOLDING CHILDREN

I wrote a column about not scolding children. And Mrs. A. W. Harris writes:

"I have a boy two-and-a-half months and a girl of sixteen months . . . and I find that I do more scolding than is good for the children and myself. I almost feel that you wrote the column especially for my benefit, and believe me when I say I put those two 'wild Indians' to bed tonight without a bit of scolding, and neither did I object when they practically took a bath in their dinner.

"I know I am not the only mother with this scolding affliction (and it really is) so perhaps it would be a good idea for you to remind us of it once in a while.

"I will admit that the first time I read your column through, the thought occurred to me: 'Wonder how she would like to take care of Billy for one whole day.'

"Thank you and let's hear more of 'Baby' growing up."

Mrs. Harris, I know it is hard to be shut up with two wild, boring, lovely little children smashing everything, yelling. But say this to yourself six times a day:

"By rights they should be wild and free, with green acres, endless space to frolic in." Because our primitive ancestors going back a million years, had that.

And say to yourself: How can they help that fiery energy and curiosity inside them? And what if they did not have it and were entirely demure, "good"? How frightful that would be! Just a sign of vacuity and congenital low vitality.

No, the more rambunctious children are, the more wonderful the spirit and energy that is in them. And say to yourself: They have to use it, don't they? So they can learn more and more. What you learn from scolding parents is superficial and worthless. What you learn from your own search and inner life is part of you forever.

But here is a parable to throw some light on scolding and external discipline. You see meagre, unimaginative people (these are the ones who write to the newspapers on child delinquency and make me rage) can never think of anything but "discipline," i.e. knocking children around and hammering at them and forcing them in the dreariest, cruellest way.

But now for my parable: I know a wonderful little boy, a "wild Indian." He would run lightly across the sitting room and straight up the bookcase shelves and sit on the top, smiling down. His mother admired it. He became one of the most physically deft, brave, venturesome, daring athletes—a ski-jumper. He is now a fighting pilot. But most important of all, he is full of rollicking power and good nature and generosity. It is because he grew up in the wonderful sunlight of freedom and good nature.

I know another boy whose disciplinarian parents whammed into him day and night— "Don't do that! . . . Don't do anything at all—except what I tell you. Look out! You'll get hurt! Don't you dare make a noise!" (which is just another way of saying "Noise bothers *me*. Worry makes *me* uncomfortable.") "How dare you spend that nickel Papa gave you without asking us!"

This second boy is now cautious, prudent, carries his money in an anxious two-inch-square purse, and has a clammy pallor and poor arches. How could he possibly learn about his wonderful physical co-ordination (inherent in all) and develop it, and that skill and courage, without experimenting, practicing? And most of all, without a lovely delighted mother saying, "How *good*! Hurrah for you, darling!"

Yes, the scolding mothers should know this: that 90 percent of their scolding is blocking and ruining the child's practicing, his experimenting. It is just as if they kept saying to a child practicing the piano, earnestly and with excitement: "Stop that!"

So Mrs. Harris, closed in your little house with two lions, I know it is hard work and takes endurance. But try this: Try just to reverse the whole nervous process. Instead of thinking with a neurasthenic frown, "Look out! Don't do that!" think instead:

"Oh what lovely children. What rascals, what lungs! Look, kids, I can jump higher than you can. Whoa. Don't break that hundred-dollar vase, lamb. I'll just put it in the attic."

You see we get to thinking that orderliness, say, is more important than childrens' flourishing spirit. But what do you want most—20 years of a neat sitting-room? Or children who remember what fun you were, how jolly, what a darling, how generous, how sympathetic to child-excitement and joy!

◆

# Until All Teachers Are
# Angels and Geniuses

**B**oredom is very bad for children. (For grownups too, although with us it is either self-inflicted or we should be able to escape from it.) To mention just one thing, it can cause an injury to the eyesight. And of course the more children are crowded into one schoolroom, the worse the boredom is. Boredom lowers the general bodily and mental vitality, including the organs of vision. And it works in a vicious circle because the more eyestrain a child has the more he makes an increased effort to see and this increased effort, coupled with the increased effort to fix attention in spite of being bored, results in a lowering of vision and in time, permanently injures the eyes.

Incidentally, Francis Galton once made an experiment: He counted the number of bodily movements observable in an audience of 50 persons who were listening to a rather boring lecture. The average rate was about 45 movements a minute, or about one fidget for each member of the audience. Once in a while, when the lecturer deviated into liveliness, the fidget-rate declined more than fifty percent.

Now about 70 percent of our children are sturdy and well balanced enough to be able to go through school without injuring their eyesight, provided they have adequate light. The rest emerge with some defect of vision. Some of the reasons for bad sight can probably never be eliminated from the schools because they are inevitable in the process of herding children together and imposing discipline upon them. Not until all teachers are angels and geniuses can we prevent many children in every generation from being frightened or bored.

◆

# THERE IS NO RESTING PLACE DOWN HERE

**P**rofessor McWhorter spoke about the dangers of inhibiting love and tenderness. About little boys not being allowed to cry from a generous emotion (it is all right of course to reprimand the loud "boo-hoos" of self-pity), or to show their tender concern. Perhaps that is one reason that men as they grow older are so much less interesting and so much less fun than women, tending to become emotionally arthritic, rheumatic in all their emotional joints whether it is in response to beauty, to sadness, or the ability show a lively interest in everything; whether it is ardor, rapture, repugnance, blood-thirsty rage, rascality, clownishness, sympathy, or laughter.

Men tend to become more dull and sardonic and critical than women. Criticism is the narrowing weazening thing; praise is its opposite, the joyfully expanding thing. The feelings, if they are allowed free play in childhood continue to be fluid and delightful.

◆

From Eva Jerome: "The big black Labrador that is dear to everyone in my daughter's home, was responding cordially to little Eugenie's petting this morning."

"He can't go to school as all the rest of you do," I said.

"He goes to God's school," Eugenie answered.

◆

From N. N. "Letting your children discipline you, Miss Ueland, as you say, seems ridiculous to me. Parents should set them an example."

But what if the parents are not as intelligent as the

children, as often happens? What if the children are eagles with chickens as parents? I have seen it: The dumbfounded parents are nervous nellies, prudes, nagging, hamstringing, curtailing their children all the time. What if Lawrence of Arabia had had parents who did not know he was a genius? He stayed out all night; he wouldn't eat with the family; he carried revolvers; he explored subterranean sewers; he went without food for five days. He read 50,000 books between midnight and dawn. He got into horrible danger, raced over high buildings. His parents were fortunately bright enough to know that what he did was not naughty but right for him.

N. N. writes: "The children should see that the years have taught the parents something. By their larger experience they have learned not to fail so often."

But maybe all they have learned is prudence, caution. "Look out! Don't try anything, you'll get hurt!" is all they are ever saying to their children. And this is death to an exuberant and wonderful life, and to all energy. Parents should say: "Children, see what brave magnificent mistakes you dare to make. Hurrah for you!"

N. N., I am unfairly quoting only scraps of your letter and although I argue, I think some things you say are true and important. I just want to show you that when we moralize we set up fixed rules. And we like fixed rules because that ends thinking and we can rest. But there is no resting place down here.

❖

# PARENTS MUST BE MORE FUN

I find in my mother's big grey ledger a newspaper clipping that she had painstakingly pasted in there. When? August 1917. It was an article by one Dr. Forbush who, it said, was one of the best authorities on boys in America. He knew about girls, too, and he helped to start Judge Ben Lindsey's far-famed Juvenile Court.

This is what the article says:

"A Yale professor was trying to find out why it was that his class did not seem to be more interested in things.

"The trouble is, Professor, that when we get home nobody seems to care about any of the things that you talk about here."

The same Yale Professor said that when he rides on a train with the fathers of his students, the conversation includes nothing but business, real estate, and stories.

Is the home chloroforming the minds of children against education?

"What do you talk about at your house for dinner?" one school child asked another.

"All we talk about," said the other child disgustedly, "is the burned string beans, and Aunt Maria's rheumatism, and whether we must wear our rubbers when we go out."

And in the school that day, they began with the "Spring-time Song" of Mendelssohn; they studied about the way the Persians make their rugs and how cotton grows in Alabama; they drew anemones and violets in crayon; they used the stereopticon to travel in Brazil, and they closed the day by reciting together Longfellow's "Children's Hour."

From such a world-outlook the children went home to the daily grumbling-bee at the dinner table.

But why lose this opportunity? Dinner time is the only occasion when the whole of the average American family is together. Isn't the occasion too precious to waste in complaint, scolding, gossip or petty squabbling? The family table ought to be the knightly Round Table in daily life. The table should be set and the talk keyed as if for guests. The common meal was intended to be and ought to become a sacrament.

It should be cheerful. Father should not hide his head behind a paper. John should not kick Frances under the table. Nobody should talk about anything that everybody is not interested in.

What I am saying is that the meal might be more broadening and full of light. This does not mean that the tired father must give a course of lectures, or that mother must "read up" while she is ordering the groceries. The point simply is that each should bring his best to the table.

Mother has been shopping and has seen many beautiful things in the shop windows. Father has a foreign letter or has had a business caller that suggests an interesting story. The children have been told something in school that they can share. Grandma is reminded of a delightful reminiscence of her own school days.

The Yale professor said that the only persons whom a college can really educate are those who have what he calls "a family background." And every school teacher can identify the pupils who have such a background by their superior alertness, their avidness to learn, their store of information, their clear way of expressing themselves with a vocabulary freely, untrammeled, vivid!

"Background comes chiefly from the dinner table. Are you giving this at your home? Or is your child one of those who cannot be educated until somebody has lifted his family off from him?"

I have another thought to add to this: Don't ask your poor children those automatic questions—"Did you wash your hands, dear?"—those dull, automatic, querulous, duty questions (almost the only conversation that most parents have to offer). Note the look of dreadful exhaustion and ennui and boredom that comes into their otherwise quite happy faces. And don't say, "How was school today, dear?" which really means: "Please entertain me (mama) who is mentally totally lazy at the moment with not one witty or interesting thing to offer, and please give me an interesting and stimulating account of high marks."

Years and years ago when my child was four years old, I suddenly learned not to do this. I learned—a bolt from Heaven—never to ask an automatic question, so boring, so mentally lazy, so exhausting. No, I would *myself* tell *her* something interesting and arresting: "I saw Pat Greaves next door running and bawling because he was being chased by a strange yellow cat." My child's eyes would sparkle with interest, and there we were, in the liveliest conversation, and behold! she was soon telling me the most interesting extraordinary things, her own ideas. At our meals together I felt that it was I, not she, who must be the wit, the raconteur, the delightful one, the fascinated listener to her remarks, the laughter at her jokes. Now, the light in a child's eyes is a splendid gauge and tells you in a split-second if you are failing and becoming a bore and a schoolmarm. She has liked me ever since.

Another aspect of the same thing is this: I say to those youngish parents (the vast majority in these days) who are exhausted by their children and, with pale, neurasthenic frowns on their foreheads, are always pleading, "Plee-ase go to bed, dear... Plee-ase now Jack, Sally, Jane, go in the other room dear, and look at television."

"No," I say, "you are doing it wrong. You are failing as parents. You should be so vigorous, healthy, in the pink of condition (cut out all the smoking and drinking and coffee breaks), so inexhaustible, rambunctious, jolly, full of deviltry and frolic, of stories, of dramatizations, of actions, of backward somersaults, or athletics and tomfoolery, of hilarity, that your children at last, after hours of violent exercise, worn down by laughter and intellectual excitement, with a pale, neurasthenic frown on *their* foreheads, cry: "Plee...eease, Mama, go to bed!"

❖

# MY ADVICE TO A BOY OF EIGHTEEN

A boy of eighteen writes: "Now I am going to be honest in writing this. I have a terrific drive in me: That is, between getting ahead, meeting the right people, society, and that of being entirely myself. I think to myself: I want a convertible, fine house and money, and then I deviate to this: What is the sense of it all? When I die I am quite sure God is not going to ask me if I have a fine house, etc. He is interested in me, not my house. Do you understand what I am driving at? I just wanted you to know all this. Please do not put this in your column although it would delight my ego to the Nth degree. See? I am not so honest—because of thinking some of these things I have said are good enough to go into a column. Forgive me, S."

Dear S: Thank you for your letter. Don't worry about wanting fine houses, a convertible, to be somebody of social importance. Of course you do! Everybody does. That is fine. Try and get and earn all these things, if you feel like it. The only thing to worry about would be getting them in such a way that somebody else has a tough time. Or if by doing so, you add to the crassness and ugliness of the world. Or if you add to the temptations of people, especially the young and the poor.

It struck me how sometimes our businessmen and bankers and insurance men and advertising men and even our doctors do this without a qualm. The essential idea is to make money, though they may hide the fact from themselves. So they tempt people into buying things they do not need and that are, indeed, very bad for them, like liquor and cigarettes. Or they tempt people into debt by new and fancier installment schemes for houses, cars, medical insurance. I am told that the ten-cent stores have now found a way to get people to owe them $300. And sometimes these same bankers and business men—very prosperously safe and solid themselves—bemoan the "lack of character" and "thrift" in these very people whom they so grievously tempt.

In this connection and thinking of my own not-too-bad habits, I think of what St. Paul said. He was asked by his little handful of Christian followers if they should refrain from drinking wine and eating meat. He said, well, such a thing did no harm to strong souls, that were spiritually illuminated and sound and steady, but to do so "might cause one's brother to stumble." Here again I think particularly of the young. I think of Sweden which has just banned all advertising of tobacco because their young people are being so unfairly tempted to become smokers.

That is an awful lot of negative advice. But here are some things you can do: Learn all you can, but accurately and not just for show, or so that you can be a loud oratorical know-it-all. And do lots of work. Be useful. And every day be vigilantly honest to yourself and others. And don't merely dream. I mean let there always be some action directed toward every dream. Because that shows the achievement of the dream is harder than you thought and then you can have respect for other people. Everything will come out all right. You will see.

◆

# GABY, SANDRA AND GRADUATION

**M**y raven-haired daughter, Gabrielle, graduates from the University. She is going to New York, going forth like the lad in the fairy tale to seek her fortune "with horse, hound and a hundred dollars." To get a job, to be independent.

"What if I come to New York and live with you and Sandra in your apartment?" I say. Her face falls. "No. Because then you'd do all the work . . . pick up everything and we'd never learn anything."

And that is true.

Well, I am glad she is going. Though I try to wring her heart, to undermine her. "What about me and poor Ivan (the cat)?" I say. I draw a sad picture of Ivan and me walking into the sunset, his little paw in mine.

Thursday evening to the graduation exercises at the University. I never saw them before. The ceremony is surprising and beautiful. I think of our English forebears and how much of this ceremony came from long ago, from England. I think of John Colet "who took his M.A. degree at Oxford in 1490 . . . who did so much to influence Erasmus," of Roger Bacon who took orders at Oxford in 1233, "the first English philosopher and first man of science," and who found that "everywhere there was a show of knowledge concealing fundamental ignorance," and of the papal legate who asked him to write his treatise on the sciences in 1266 (he was 52). And Roger Bacon took fresh courage. "He set at naught the jealousy of his superiors and brother friars, and despite the want of funds, instruments and copyists, completed in about eighteen months three large treatises, which were dispatched to the Pope."

But in 1278 (when he was 64) his books were condemned again and he himself was thrown into prison for fourteen years.

He was 78 then and it was two years before he died.

At Commencement Thursday evening, I thought of him and the lineage of heroic scholars reaching from this moment in Minnesota to twelfth century England. And it is so clear that we and the English, and the best that is in us both, is identical, and we are they and they are ourselves and it makes one take heart to be reminded of it.

The Auditorium was filled with five thousand mothers and fathers. On the stage a row of familiar civilians like Dr. Harold Diehl of the Medical School and Dr. Raymond McConnell, all grandly metamorphosed into Abelards and Thomas Aquinases by grave black gowns with beautiful green velvet facings, and scarlet hoods, and bands of magenta silk to the floor. Behind them ROTC lieutenants in sparkling buttons sitting very straight.

The organ played Bach and Sibelius. The graduates came marching across the freezing campus, each school led by a mediaeval herald carrying a gonfalon.

Then a black-robed doctor would arise and intone: "Will the candidates for the Degree of Bachelor of Arts, magna cum laude, please rise. Mr. President, these candidates for the Bachelor of Arts, magna cum laude, have..." done thus and so.

President Coffey bade them come forward for their degrees. The gonfaloniers mount the stage and these children—twenty years old or so—walk across the stage, the girls with ambrosial curls on their young shoulders, Bachelors of Science... of Medicine... of Law. Doctors of Medicine... of Dental Hygiene. Aeronautical engineers . . . agricultural chemists. And finally Doctors of Philosophy on whom Dr. August Krey in maroon velvet, a kind of Minnesota beef-eater, and someone else festooned each one in a color-striped hood.

People clapped for the soldiers, for the nurses, for the doctors and lawyers and for all the lambs and angels so dear and so young. Seven hundred of them poured out, trained, knowing something, knowing exactly what to do about all kinds of things so that our new world can be run rightly. And when parental spectacles steam up at graduation it is for more than the fact that Jim passed his finals with a low C average.

My niece, Sandra, got a magna cum laude. It means that Sandra had good marks and then was game to stand before four professors and answer their questions like St. Joan before the Inquisitors. And she passed and so was canonized—magna cum laude silk braids on her shoulder like a bugler. "Or a movie usher," says Gaby, her cousin. "If I had known how cute it looked I would have worked for it."

Gaby was the last in line and said afterwards: "We walked by in order of scholastic achievement." But this isn't true. She can tell me just what Hegelian dialectic is in ten words and before breakfast.

❖

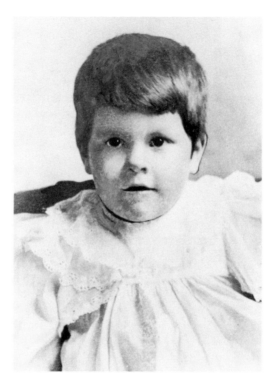

Brenda Ueland 1894, age 3.

Brenda in the 1920s

Early 1930s

1936

1937

1938

The Ueland Household ca. 1940
(*Left to right*—*top row*: Louise Ueland, Timothy Fiske,
Harriet and Margaret Ueland, *far right*—Arnulf Ueland.
*Bottom row*: Eric Ueland, Brenda, Gabrielle, and Mark Ueland)

1950

1950

1983

Portrait of Brenda Ueland by Eleanor Falk Quirt

# ◢ FEMINISM ◣

## THE REGRETTABLE HERD INSTINCT

Sometimes people complain—my children and others—that I dress so unstylishly, so eccentrically, indeed so badly. I say this: "If I did not wear torn pants, orthopedic shoes, frantic disheveled hair, that is to say, if I did not tone down my beauty, people would go mad. Married men would run amuck."

And sometimes I say this: "As a matter of fact I am so original, so inventive that I dress about 25 years ahead of the fashion. I can prove it. I was the first woman in the Western World to have my hair all cut off. Irene Castle was the first to have a rather long, albeit, demure, bob to her shoulders. I went to Henri in Greenwich Village, the French barber at the Hotel Breevoort in New York and I told him to cut my hair all off. He was frightened, appalled. To cut off that nice, very black, ladylike hair, with a pug! I described to him what I wanted. 'I want it to be like Lord Byron's—as if a high wind were blowing from the rear.'"

He did so. It was splendid. Wherever I went seas of white faces turned to gaze. That is just what I liked. Gradually it began to be copied. When I came that summer home to Minneapolis we had a great cocktail party. All the girls had me cut off their hair. I did so, the shorn hair rising to our knees on the floor. We were all laughing. The cry was (thinking with scorn of Irene Castle): "Triangular effects must go!" In fact as time went on, to my sorrow, I seem to have started a fashion that flooded the population with hundreds of thousands of girls with crew-cuts and neck-shaves, all looking like men in nightgowns.

And I really think I was the first to wear sailor pants, tight around the fanny with bell-bottoms. Very becoming and it still is. And I was the first to wear a bandana handkerchief tucked in the belt and tied around my neck, my back bare to the sun. That was the summer of 1927. I used to mow my lawn in Stamford, Connecticut, in this arrangement. Divine rosy sunburn spreading on shoulders, arms and back. My neighbors were angered at the immodesty of it and even my friends protested anxiously.

As for trousers, long pants, there soon proved to be good reasons for them. You could escape from garters and long stockings and corsets, and you could even wear comfortable flat shoes which were becoming, making one look long-legged, easy-striding and debonair. It was an escape from that frightful crippling thing, the high-heel, which ruins feet forever and makes a beautiful carriage and easy grace impossible, with the result that the comeliest young face gets a look of haggard suffering. It used to be, and still is, such a pleasant thing to see nuns voluminously clothed in flowing black garments and with flat, wide comfortable shoes and able to walk in long easy strides, their rosy faces happy, smooth and benign.

Once David Shearer and his law partner, Lee Byard were planning to go to Duluth for a few days on business and I said: "Why don't you take Henrietta (his wife) and me along—take along a couple of Skirts," and I added, "That is to say if you can still call me "a Skirt."

David said with such gallantry, such chivalry: "You will always be a Skirt to me, dear."

When we swim in the Blaisdell-Thirty-Fourth Street YMCA pool, I wear swimming garments that suit my invisible taste and arouse the affectionate criticism of my swimming companions. It is a navy-blue shirt buttoned to the neck, with short sleeves and below that I wear faded beige-colored cotton shorts. I like it. I think it is kind of becoming. In fact I dislike lady-bathing-suits and I despise bikinis with an intensity. For one thing, I don't think navels are all that beautiful, and as for the look of bikinis from the rear, their wearers do not seem to realize that they look like unchanged didies.

One day the Blaisdell Pool was being mended so that we had to swim in the Yorktown Pool. The pretty-girl Lifeguard had to say to me, with suffering, that I must wear a regular lady-bathing-suit because those were her orders. When the authorities heard that I had broken an international world record for over eighty (I hasten to say that it was not very fast) she said my outfit was quite all right. To make her feel less apologetic for possibly hurting my feelings, I said, "You see I was born with a birth defect." "What was that?" she said. I said: "No herd instinct."

Now the Herd Instinct has been very interesting to me ever since years ago I read a study that Charles Darwin had made of it. He said that human beings (my friend Helen Baxter calls us "human beans") are herd animals like so many others, and they timidly and anxiously crowd together and copy each other. Darwin's especial study was of the South African oxen, a very necessary draft animal used for pulling and hauling in teams. When the oxen are very young their owners have to watch them continuously in order to find a few rare ones who will stray a few feet from the herd, who will behave with a slight independence and not crowd anxiously with all the others. This is in order to find certain ones that will LEAD a team of six or eight oxen. Otherwise, Darwin said, South African oxen will be like a lot of gentlemen going into a fashionable dinner on some social occasion: they all hang back and do not want to go in first, to lead.

This is so interesting to me. I think of those people who will not take a front seat at a concert. Why not lead? Why not go up boldly? Why not be the first?

As for me, I think it is better not to have the herd instinct than to be always under its anxious enslavement. Years ago I would be running around the lake. A car comes. I would slow down embarrassed, fearing to shock him. But then I reasoned it out.

"Why, running is the right thing to do! I am free, healthy with a good complexion. It is that automobile addict who should be ashamed: driving in a sealed car in warmed-over carbon monoxide and smoking a seegar. I am the Goddess! He is a bug in a monkey nut!"

# A History of Women

**R**obert Graves, the poet and historian, says, "The most important history of all for me is the changing relationship between men and women down the centuries."

For thousands of years there has been a tragic situation—the domination of men and the degradation of women. We are so used to it we do not notice it. The situation has begun to change but very little, and going back, I will show you why in a minute.

This was not always so. Now there is an underlying feeling that true equality is impossible because men and women are so different. We can never be like each other. But I disagree. We once were and we must again become noble equals.

Two things stand in the way of this: the age-old egotism of men, their anxious jealousy of women as equals, their touching infantilism, their dire need—all interwoven in their *amour-propre* to dominate women. The other thing that holds back the equality of women is our acceptance of our own feebleness, our physical weakness, our work to make a kind of virtue of it as a self-sacrificing sweetness, gentleness and nobility. But this is wrong, too, as I will show.

Our weakness, smallness and athletic ineptitude has come about because for four thousand years we have degenerated. Due to what? Male domination.

Fortunately women inherit from their fathers as well as their mothers. If all women were weak, cowardly and flightily stupid it would not be so for more than one generation. But due to this imbalance, something regrettable has happened to us.

In fine wild animals—lions and lionesses, mares and stallions—there is no inequality. A mare can run as fast as a stallion. A lioness is about the same size as a lion and just as brave and capable.

Now go back three thousand years to Asia Minor, the first civilization that was somewhat stable. In those happy and far-off days women were deeply respected and loved by men and had a kind of wise command over things. This was evidenced by the greatest queen of all time perhaps, Semiramis of Assyria, a great wise and beneficent ruler. And she had another quality of women then—bravery, for she was also a great soldier. In fact that was what especially charmed her husband. She reigned 42 years. And she realized, with the modern Einstein, that the only way to have a better world was to have better people and the design of her religious system was to achieve this. We know this from the Mystery Religions of Egypt, Greece and Rome all of which varied only in superficialities. When Semiramis died, after insuring that Babylon was the most magnificent city in the world, she was deified.

Now the goddesses of the Mysteries were all believed to have been originally extremely wise human beings and owed their deification to this fact. Ceres was said to have brought agriculture to mankind—which was one of those talented inventions of women. Cybele the Phrygian was described by the enlightened Emperor Julianus as "the Intellectual Principle," the very fount of wisdom. Her symbol was the Dove, later the symbol of the Holy Spirit.

This love and earnest respect for women was evidenced in the matriarchal Greeks. Remember their Goddesses—Pallas-Athene, the Goddess of Wisdom who sprang fully armed out of the forehead of Jove. That is to say, like all bright women with our sixth sense, intuition, which is the highest intelligence on earth, she did not need a lifetime of boring, ponderous academic analyses to know immediately what is the True, the Good and the Beautiful. The Goddess Diana the Huntress was adequately athletic. The Nine Muses were female. In other words the Greeks knew that great poetry, music, history, drama sprang from the wisdom and the golden imagination of women.

There were not startling physical differences between men and women then. The statue of the Winged Victory of Samothrace had not knock-knees, poor musculature nor enormously exaggerated breasts. There is a beautiful statue of

Orestes and Electra who were brother and sister, their arms over each other's shoulders. They are the same height, built identically alike with the same limber prowess and athletic beauty.

The same is true of Egyptian sculpture. The Pharaohs and their queens are almost exactly alike. Even their breasts are about the same. Secondary sex characteristics that we now consider masculine and feminine, came about through centuries of artificial selection due to masculine domination. This is wrong and very sad.

Many matriarchal societies have existed in which there was the opposite, female domination over men, though masculine historians have suppressed this and cannot bear to think it. Nevertheless, they existed and still do in some places. In Ancient Egypt, Diodorus Siculus tells us the women ruled their husbands. There is no ambiguity about it; the wives were absolutely supreme. Herodotus said: "With them the women go to market, the men stay home and weave. The women discharged all kinds of public affairs. The men dealt with domestic affairs. Men were not allowed to undertake war service or any of the functions of government. Nor were they allowed to fill any public office which might have given them more spirit to set themselves against women. The children were handed over immediately after birth to the men, who reared them on milk." In Sparta women were the dominant sex. They alone could own property. This was the case among the Iroquois, the Kamchadales in Siberia and countless others. "When women ruled in Kamchatka, the men not only did the cooking but all the housework, docilely doing everything assigned to them." According to the historian, C. Meiners, "Men are so domesticated that they greatly dislike being away from home for more than one day. Should a longer absence than this become necessary, they try to persuade their wives to accompany them, for they cannot get on without the women folk.

"There was only one way in which members of the exploring party in Kamchatka could bribe the Kamchatkan women to undertake tasks regarded by them with contempt (men's work). This was by gratification of their sexual appetite. The point is worth noting because it is so characteristic of mono-sexual domination to find the dominating sex repaying the subordinate sex for sexual services. When men rule, it is the way of men to reward women for their caresses, and the practice, of course, tends to degenerate into prostitution. Where women rule we find the reverse of this tendency: women reward men for the gifts of love."

This is why in a Men's State like ours, men despise feminine tasks. Note that with us, women are proud when they can do men's work. No woman would be offended to be a Justice of the Supreme Court, just as an Ancient Egyptian would be proud of himself if he—even little he—could do a woman's work, that is, be a tall, swashbuckling soldier.

In Abyssinia, in Lapland, men did what seems to us women's work. Tacitus, describing the early Teutons, tells how women did all the work, the hunting, tilling the soil, while men idled and looked after the house, equivalent now to playing bridge and taking naps. The heirlooms in the family, a harnessed horse, a strong spear, a sword and shield passed on to the women. They were the fighters.

And so they were in Libya, in the Congo. In India under the Queens of Nepal only women soldiers were known. In Dahomey, the king had a bodyguard of warrior women and these were braver than any of his men warriors and would reproach each other for cowardice or weakness with such phrases as, "You are a woman!" And physiologically, things were reversed: the women, more active and strenuous, became taller, stronger, tougher than the sedentary home-body men. Now I do not approve of this. I consider it as unhealthy, as disgusting as our own state of affairs, our exaggerated inequality.

Robert Graves says the greatest civilizations were matriarchal. But the ancient Hebrews were patriarchal, very anti-woman, with their stern tetchy male God, Jehovah. And so were the Romans for the most part, expressing their dominant masculinity in Law and War. But the Mycenean Greeks and Etruscans were matriarchal, far better civilizations, more graceful, gifted and kind.

The Semitic race, Hebrews, Islam, all degraded women.

They were obsessed with the idea of an all-male God and the superiority of the male sex. Moses and Abraham—in fact there is a persistent ungentlemanliness, a lack of feeling of justice and kindliness toward women, in the Old Testament. They were so terribly concerned with breeding, concubines and herds. Instead of kind, mighty and beautiful Goddesses, they had one harsh, punishing He-man God. I have a friend who says: "if only the Lord's Prayer had been, 'Our Mother who are in Heaven . . .' all would have been different."

The obsession infiltrated into Christianity through Paul. And note how the three great monotheisms, Judaism, Mohammedanism and Christianity have produced power-loving, aggressive people, revering masculine qualities with their constant wars, the subjugation of women (women, remember, were handicapped unfairly in this contest by having a child a year). They have tragically lacked the moral attributes of the Wisdom Goddess, love, mercy, purity, wisdom and compassion. They have, in fact, been worshipping a semi-Deity, half a God. And so the world has arrived at its present state. We cannot deny that it is the worst half.

The divinely balanced nature, man *and* woman, together and equal, was manifested in Jesus. He was on our side. His power was restricted to ideas of compassion, healing and mercy and never applied to coercion and punishment.

Now women emerged somewhat in the Renaissance with the rediscovery of Greek culture. It flowered with excitement—a passion for learning and the nations of the great pagans. It became fashionable for kings and nobility to give their children, BOTH girls and boys, into the care of the greatest men of the day, like Erasmus. Vittorino da Feltre, teaching the children of the Dukes of Urbino, created three generations of wonderful men and women. You see the GIRLS were included. And great women began to appear, Vittoria da Colonna whom Michelangelo loved, Caterina Sforza the soldier, St. Catherine of Siena, the great teacher and stateswoman. I am sure that Joan of Arc was a Renaissance manifestation. Shakespeare's women show this—wonderful women "learned, kind and fair" as he said of Sylvia. There was Portia, Beatrice, Cordelia, even

Lady MacBeth had a little ability and courage—bright stars appearing suddenly out of fourteen dark centuries when women were sub-nobodies. Indeed, as they are now.

Then came the Reformation and Martin Luther—closed down the magnificent ideas of antiquity and kicked women back into the kitchen. And there we have stayed since the days of Susan B. Anthony.

Now about our physical inferiority. We have seen how the dominating sex gets bigger and stronger, but this is very dysgenic, the opposite of eugenic, and very hard on us all, the whole race. To feel superior, men chose wives with low-grade physical prowess, unable to walk or run decently, with feeble feet, ruined knees and, as at present, enormously exaggerated breasts (a masculine predilection promoted now by that absurd monster, Hugh Hefner). Their offspring, of course, dwindle and become inferior. "A little woman as high as my heart," was the tender phrase. And men chose such women, as Bertrand Russell said, "because it makes them feel so big and strong without incurring any real danger."

Fear of bugs and thunder was adorable and it is still considered so, when it should arouse in men fierce scorn. Courage is the greatest virtue, because unless you have it, you cannot practice any of the other virtues. The fraidy-cat mother inflicts a terrible psychic handicap on her sons. Among wild animals the newly-born offspring has no fear at all until he sees it in his mother. Men with instinctive fears because of cowardly mothers, have to hide it all their lives, a cause of terrible mental suffering and break-down.

Now why do women not yet amount to much? Hardly a hundred years ago, what was our lot? A child a year. (Incidentally, not much time to write Shakespeare's plays, to compose symphonies.) No education. (When the University of Wisconsin allowed girls to recite in class with boys, there was a terrible uproar.) Not allowed to vote. To own property. To own our own children. Why didn't we keep away from marriage then? Because there was only one alternative—prostitution. In the Civil War they needed women as school teachers, so they gave the girls a little education. Fifty years later, they needed typists and girls who could work in offices.

We had very poor health. Heavily corsetted. Skirts fourteen feet around the bottom and dragging in the mud. No exercise at all, not allowed to "romp," as the saying was. This induced chronic ailing, headaches, the vapors, ten days a month of acute menstrual sickness. (This was one of the big arguments against woman suffrage.)

Sargent at Harvard wondered why girls were such poor stuff athletically. Girls and boys under 13 were structurally identical, agile and lively. But after that girls were clapped in iron corsets and lost three inches in the length of their thighs. No circulation. Thereafter they were weak and clumsy.

Considering these things we have not done so badly.

Now I come to a generalization. We, the women, do not have to worry about being kind. Our maternal physiology accounts for this. We are kind already and cannot help it. It is men who must worry about that. They must worry about their hardness, their dry know-it-allism, their destructiveness. (If any men in the audience have been lucky enough to inherit equally from their mothers, I do not mean you.) That is why I want an honorable equality.

For millenia, mothers have pampered their male children with the result that husbands are dreadfully aggrieved if they have not wives solely focused on their small achievements. Note that women admire men for their first-rate equalities. Men admire women not for their bravery, their intelligence, their contributions to society, but for their splendid courage in baking cookies for themselves.

Do not think our liberation has arrived. Just consider our unimportance. Being women, we abhor war—babies of 18 and 19 killed by the tens of thousands, for no reason at all. And we abhor just as much the killing by hundreds of thousands of slim little Asian boy and girls, living on a little rice, who heroically hurl themselves into death because they want their own country. (Note that, this aspect of the wars seems not to bother men too much.) Half of this country is women. The war goes right on. What women think is as powerless as a sigh, a breath, a vapor. Look at TV. Only men: soldiers, politicians, commentators, Meet The Press, football players, coaches. No women. Oh yes, now and then one of those singers moaning about love. Or some narcissistic idiot applying hair spray. If women were equal, half the postmen, policemen, truck drivers, welders, air pilots, doctors, lawyers would be women, half of Congress, the judges and so on. Why not? I think half the soldiers should be women. I don't mean WACS. This will be good because women are less docile than men and will tear up their draft cards in a fury; and probably go to the front and beat the tar out of all the soldiers of *both* armies: "Get out of here! Quit it! Go home, where you belong!"

Smedley Butler, a fierce cussing major General of Marines in World War II was a Quaker and a pacifist. After the war he went all over making furious speeches. "What the hell is the matter with you, you blank-blank women, that you allow it?. . . letting these babies of 18 and 19 go to war!" I feel that way all the time. I wonder about it.

That is why we must have equal power in our society. We want to foster life, not coerce and destroy it. Every year twenty million American men go hunting, not from necessity, not for food, indeed at great expense, but for FUN. They kill more than a billion animals weaker than themselves, helpless. Women do not. And note that, what we despise most is the unchivalry of it. The hunters are so cozily safe themselves.

That is why George Bernard Shaw said that one half of every governing body in the world MUST be women. To assure this, it will be necessary at first that every man elected has a female counterpart who goes into office with him. If Humphrey goes to the Senate, a woman senator must go with him willy-nilly. Indeed we have not much time left to save this unhappy planet.

Men are now loosening the bonds of women a little bit but they are almost hysterical with fear less she exceed them in capacity and achievement. They must encourage her to work, but not to excel. They hold on to their superiority with all their might. They are afraid she might be portrayed as morally and spiritually superior for that might lead to the long-suppressed realization that she is really quite first rate, maybe even a higher creature. She must therefore be dragged down and exposed as a near-animal, her worth being assessed by "vital statistics," her aim to titillate and degrade men.

Rev. W. Hayes, a Unitarian minister in England writes: "Biologists tell us that woman has been the pioneer of progress from the beginning. In the upward path from the lower species, she has led the way—in the decrease of hairiness, in the upright gait, in the shape of the head and face and jaw. Woman is the civilizer. It is through woman that a sense of human nobility and possible beauty and greatness is awakened in man." And the Irish poet AE wrote: "Woman may again have her temples and mysteries and renew again her radiant life at its fountain. Who shall save us anew shall come divinely as a woman." And our other good friend, Robert Graves says this, and it is so remarkable that he should be able to see it: "A real woman" he says—he points out that the word "real" is the same word as "royal"— "A real woman neither despises nor worships men, but is proud not to have been born a man, knows the full extent of her powers and feels free to reject all arbitrary man-made obligations. She is her own oracle of right and wrong, firmly believing in her own five senses and the intuitive sixth."

"Since she never settles for the second best in love, what troubles her is the rareness of real men. Real women are royal women; the word once had some meaning. Democracy has no welcome for queens. To reach some understanding of real women, one must think back to the primitive age when men invariably treated women as the holier sex because they perpetuated the race. Women were guardians of spring, fruit trees, and the sacred hearth fire. Tribal queens judged each case on merit, not by legal code, as real women do; and showed little regard for trade and mechanical invention."

Men should be happy because women will rescue us from Science, that horrible idolatry, from dry, hard analyses, the gross literalists and computers of everything. From the dry horrors of technology, bombs, automobiles, mass production and from those silly literal-minded, unloving mechanical fellows, those boring engineering scientific fellows, and measurers collecting rocks on the moon.

Women have almost no friends among men—we are always loved for the wrong thing—only a few very great ones, Pythagoras, Plato, Sophocles, Shakespeare, John Stuart Mill, Ibsen, Bernard Shaw. It seems to me one of the best ways to be a great man would be to be a true friend of women. You would be in good company. How? Neither pamper not exploit them. Love in women their greatness which is the same as it is in men. Insist on bravery, honor, grandeur, generosity in women.

And as for men, they should be kinder. Quit their silly mass-murdering, their conceit based on nothing, and their absolutely permeating, unstanchable infantilism, feeling wronged if all women's force and strength is not devoted to themselves, usually their weaknesses, their babyism.

I say this because I think there is a state of great unhappiness between us. If we can be true equals, we will be better friends, better lovers, better wives and husbands.

◆

(*Address and sermon given at the First Unitarian Society in Minneapolis on March 7, 1971, and later at the University of Minnesota and the University of Wisconsin and Augsburg College in Minneapolis.*)

# TWENTY MILLION HUNTERS
## AN ASPECT OF FEMINISM

A favorite slogan is: Sexism means there's always half the population, I, a man, am better than.

It is time to assert again that women's liberation is a dire necessity. Because women are kinder, more humane than men. Erik Bye tended to disagree with me. But I pointed out the proof of it. Twenty million hunters (male) are carrying on war of extermination against fleeing, timid, harmless inexpressibly beautiful wild animals, from squirrels to moose. Women don't do that. It makes us sick to our stomach. We think it is obscene. And we must arise with a sturdiness, an effrontery, an insolence until we welcome half of every governing body in the world, from the smallest committee to the governments of great nations. That is to say, if the world is going to survive.

This is why. Women for physiological reasons (they have children) have a kindness, a tenderness about all life. They want to foster it, save it, protect it, help it along into happiness. Men see a flying duck. "Kill it! Bang-bang. I want it for dinner."

This is the time of year 20 million men—not ten thousands, repeat, twenty million—go out and kill everything they can see. Think of it! An army bigger than any that ever existed, fully armed with long-range rifles, warmly clad in expensive and fashionable garments, opulently fed with breakfast, lunch and dinner, and comforted by a great deal of Scotch and Bourbon, declares war on all wild creatures who are unarmed, utterly harmless, always fleeing, frightened, and woefully unequipped with technical inventions or strategic, scheming brain of godlike man.

Now men argue: "Listen Honey, little girl, hunters are not really bad"—1. They love Nature and love to be out in it. 2. They love to be out in Nature with their sons, that tender companionship. 3. If they did not kill everything they see—raccoons, deer, elk, stags, wild geese, bejewelled little ducks, grebes, pheasants, partridges, crows, falcons, eagles, maybe a blue-bird or two, otters, foxes and fox cubs, evil-doing coyotes, why the poor animals!—They would starve to death because of the food supply and wouldn't that be horrid? Cruel! Oh just dreadfully cruel!

Men are sportsmen. It is "Sport" (fun). They are not hungry. This was once a reasonable explanation. But look. They could love Nature and be out in it. With their sons. Enjoy all the other nobly bucolic and arcadian joys and happy virtues *without* killing anything. It is therefore the killing that they like, that draws them.

Dr. Karl Menninger (he is a friend, sends me his books) in *The Vital Balance* talks of "aggression" as something bad. I thought to myself as I read along, "Why, I couldn't even make the bed if I weren't aggressive." But as I read on I discovered that he means by aggression "the wish to hurt." This is evil, wrong, insane, bad. He speaks of the hundreds of thousands of nice men, so good-natured, affable, so certain of themselves as beneficent citizens, who go hunting.

He says: "Reflect on the psychology of the hearty, friendly, exuberant fellow who can write with such pride the following account, referring to the gouging and tissue avulsions causing pain of the sort that, in a human being, would evoke screams or choking moans. But, says this gleeful fellow:

". . . My heart started to pound. This was the buck I was setting for. I raised my old rifle, and when the deer was broadside, I let go my first shot. It proved good. He dropped to his knees, but was up in an instant and on his way. As I hurriedly pumped in another cartridge, the buck jumped into the stream and was bounding through icy shallows to my side. I let my second shot go, and heard the solid thump of the 255 gram bullet as it hit home. But he kept right on coming. I heard my third shot smack against his ribs, but no use . . . I let him have another slug when he was broadside. It slowed him somewhat but it didn't stop him. I let my fifth and last shot go. He reared back on his hind legs and turned around trotting in my direction. About 10 paces away, the legs slipped from under him and he rolled against a rotten log and lay still. He had enough holes in him, as all five of my slugs hit home, but I don't believe the last 4 would have been necessary. My first shot had done the work. It hit low on front quarters, passed through and shattering the heart. That accounted for the crazed action."

Now this simon-pure, unadulterated wish to hunt, to kill, and enjoy it is bad, morbid, a rotten decayed part of the human soul. It is so interesting—Christ said so two thousand years ago. Now modern psychologists, after endless research, verify it as a fact and say it again. And women (my sex) knew it all the time. But being utter non-entities those two thousand years, without authority or respect, no one listened to them.

And Dr. Menninger, to bring alive in what we laughingly call "our minds," the disgustingness of the pleasure of hunting, tells the following:

"Some will hold, as did the early American colonists, that animals (like Indians) have no souls and are here for the pleasure and benefit of men. For over 200 years it was considered perfectly all right to have a little fun in the dull days of winter by hunting down Indians and their wives and children and shooting them on the run or on their knees. For documentation of this favorite sport of the whites in northern Canada, take a look at the article in *Maclean's* for October 10, 1959. The unarmed quarry was routed out of tents in the dead of winter before they got dressed, and driven naked out on the frozen lakes, where they were easier to see. Men, women and little children were shot down like jack rabbits or coyotes. This popular amusement went on for two centuries, and no white man was ever prosecuted for it. But a whole nation of handsome, proud and peaceful Indians (the Beothucks) was extinguished."

I told you how Dr. Karl Menninger said that "Aggression," the wish to hurt, is a morbid, psychic aberration and my thesis is that women, so much freer from it than men, must be in every governing body in the world because they are kinder, more humane than men. They cannot help it. It is imbedded physiologically because they have children. Now generalizations are vulgar and men, fortunately, inherit from their mothers as well as their fathers, and vice versa. But nevertheless women are kinder, want to foster and encourage life. They have a clear imagination and feel distress about pain and suffering in others and in animals. My proof is that twenty million men go hunting and kill with pleasure (and this is the point, i.e. with no real necessity) a billion animals a year.

Women don't do that, only a few Lady MacBeths and Lucrezia Borgias. Some would say it is because women are too inert, lazy, limp and unadventurous. But I don't think so, and we are gradually improving. We not only don't like to kill animals. We think it is a nightmare, horrible, a fright!

The trouble is the power of men is, after thousands of years of dominance, dreadfully swollen.

And this is why I talk about the twenty million nice fellows who enjoy hunting so much, so certain that they are brave, manly guys. But "aggression," the wish to hurt, to kill, to kill for fun, is morbid, psychopathic, evil, insane. At last our learned psychologists like Dr. Menninger verify it as a fact and say it again. And women (my sex) knew it all the time but being non-existent nobodies in a male society, nobody heard us.

Now to women here is an odd thing: The hunters feel it is so brave and admirable. Where do they get that stuff? Is aggression especially pleasurable if the killer is safe? A man I knew was troubled because when he went home at night he was so cruelly irritable and mean to his invalid wife and two daughters. "Why is that?" I said, "I'll tell you. Because they can't get away. The next time you feel mean take it out on your boss, the President of the Company. Oh I'd admire that!"

Recently CBS showed a documentary of hunting, "The Guns of Autumn." It was an unbearable, horrifying, distressing picture. There was a monstrous protest from the twenty million. Their feelings were dreadfully hurt. Four or five great corporations cancelled their sponsorship contracts with CBS. The following Sunday on TV, CBS gave an account of the protests. We saw the outraged, furious hunters protesting that they were NOT like that, not at all! A few, perhaps, they said, were gross, ill-mannered slobs "but not the regular hunters." Then TV interviewed persons on the other side of the question,

Mr. Hoyt of the Humane Society of the United States, Cleveland Amory, Conservationists. (I could not help but observe that those against hunting were so much better looking—noses, eyes, chins, physiques. The hunters tended to have jowls and potato noses and porky physiques.)

The hunters accused CBS of framing the thing for a purpose, showing only the unpleasant cruel side of hunting. CBS then presented the producer of the documentary. "No," he said, "it was not biased in any way. We just took pictures of it as it is, the facts and events of hunting."

Incidentally it strikes me that this may be a wonderful device to bring about character-change. The hunters saw themselves. It shocked them. I knew a man who saw a tape of himself drunk. He never drank again. If only we had tapes of ourselves beating a child, kicking a cat, nagging a husband, blackguarding friends behind their backs, this would be fine, so helpful in our long difficult pilgrimage on earth, learning to be decent. (Know Thyself.)

And here I must say that scolding the twenty million hunters won't do any good, but if it casts up a kind of picture of the awful damned thing, the ego-cruelty-*cum*-power, if it throws light on the automatic gross conceit, the self-admiration, the unswerving hard-heartedness, that will be good.

The other day I said to my editor, "Now perhaps we could introduce a bill allocating 300,000 acres of Minnesota wilderness where hunters could go and shoot *each other*. They'd love that. Perhaps *Posten* could promote such a cause in the Legislature."

My editor's eyes became bright as stars. "Great!" she said. And then a happy thought: "Say, perhaps we could do that to War. Set it by law in certain definite places, confine it. And they could have a wonderful War there, all the War they wanted. But not elsewhere. Why, they could kill children, the whole business!"

I said, "Oh no, we wouldn't have children there to be killed. But they could kill each other, the thing he-man guys seem to need." Then I thought for a moment and shook my head. I thought of Vietnam, the children killed, running naked, shrieking, the napalm bombs (made in Hopkins) glued to their skin and burning into them. "No. I'm afraid they would have to have the children to kill or we'd never get the bill through."

Women, fool creatures, do not think that even War, like hunting, is so essential, necessary, interesting, inevitable, and ennobling as men do. And here is a poisoned javelin hurled right through the heart and entrails of the male sex and twenty million hunters. They have the oddest notion they are brave. How come? I can see that the fun of it is the power. A living creature, awfully pretty, with bright feathers, soft fur, celestial grace, fleeing, each one a kind of bright and endearing jewel in the wilderness—Bang! Killed! "I, Bud Schmittbauer done it! Quite a guy!"

But he didn't do it. The rifle did it. He didn't run 80 miles and catch it as an aborigine in Australia catches a kangaroo. He was as safe and cozy as in his favorite bar. He didn't kill a lion after wrestling with it with his bare hands. Plato said of hunting that that alone might be a gallant deed worthy of praise.

No, it is women who are chivalrous. We are Knights. We love, adore beauty and defenselessness, and try, with passionate ferocity, to protect it.

When women are one-half of every Government, Senate, Soviet, State Department, Reichstag, Parliament, Pentagon, there may be Wars for a while. But they will not be so chronic, asinine and ubiquitous. And in the colloquy of statesmen and stateswomen, there will be many a new idea about international helpfulness and happiness, and many suggestions every day hinting at wisdom and mercy.

There even may be startling, new, fresh ideas, such as drafting, say, for the front-line, no children of eighteen, but Chairmen of the Board.

◆

# FAT AND THIN WOMEN

T hirty years ago doctors were vehemently opposed to the way women were dieting in order to become fashionably thin. "What do you eat for breakfast?" a doctor asked a patient who was worried about her very peculiar feeling of lassitude.

"I take," she said, with that rekindling of interest that even a dying reducer shows when talking about food—"I take just a little black coffee, very strong. You see, I have to lose fifteen more pounds, Doctor."

"What do you eat for lunch?"

"For lunch I allow myself all the lettuce I want, with mineral oil dressing."

"For dinner?"

"Oh for dinner I let myself go—lean meat, celery, one piece of dry toast and grapefruit."

"Well," said the doctor—a rather fat man himself as it happens—swelling with rage when he told about this, "I told her, 'The reason you are tired is that from starving yourself, you have got just a little tuberculosis, that's all. Good morning, madam, I hope you enjoy your luncheon.' "

He went on to say that at the theater he and his practitioner friends would while away the *entr'actes* by looking over the audience and picking out the dieting women who are already tubercular. "A return to Rubens is my slogan!" he said passionately.

And not only doctors but husbands and men in general all over the world were much exercised about it.

"Our women must please us, not the Parisian tailors," Nazi and Fascist editors wrote in Germany and Italy, "and we—let there be no mistake about this—like pulp, not bone. We ask the government to take ferocious measures against the peddlers of thinness. We propose to watch in our own families to make sure that no such crimes are committed by women under our direct control." So they were shouting and inveighing. But did it do any good?

Thirty years ago twenty-two of the leading physicians and dietitians from all over the United States held the first adult-weight conference. The majority of them were very grave, full of warnings. They condemned the boyish form. (World War I seems to have brought it into existence.) They said that all women seemed to be trying to put themselves into a one mold, which cannot possibly be done until, as Oliver Wendell Holmes said, "we are able to select our ancestors with much greater care." No matter what the diet, a Percheron cannot be a race horse.

They pointed out that in junior high schools, hundreds of girls were going without breakfast because they were afraid that otherwise they would get fat, and a considerable number of these children were under twelve years old; and that undoubtedly, tuberculosis is a disease that attacks the undernourished young. They also told how some women reduce so fiercely they will never be able to have children. "Some take thyroid extract, get a charming slim figure, a bad heart and frequently an obituary."

About the weight of women in the past little is known. You can search volumes about the life of Mary, Queen of Scots, for example, and discover that she was beautiful, had light brown eyes. You can get an accurate description of just how her upper lip rested on her charming under lip as though on a little cushion, and so on, but there is not a word as to her fatness or thinness except the general statement that she had a beautiful figure. But what she weighed, how she was actually constructed, measurements of chest, hips, waist, calves, ankles, such as we read now almost daily about every moving-picture actress and others, there is not a word. And there is no knowing because her portraits have clothed her in as much rigging as a ship "under full sail," as a court minister said, "with her tops and top-gallants and her upper decks and nether decks, and so bedecked with her streamers and ensigns, and I know not what."

When Henry VIII wanted to marry a new wife his ambassadors sent him minute descriptions of eligible princesses. "A marvellous good, brownish face she hath, with fair red lips and ruddy cheeks." And "she is not so pure white as the late Queen, whose soul God pardon, but when she chanceth to smile there appeareth two pits in her cheeks and one in her chin the which becometh her right excellently well." But not one word about her figure. Today such specifications would come at the very beginning: five feet, five inches tall; weight 118 pounds; perfect legs; might take a little off the hips, and so on.

The Goncourts made a study of the French beauties of the eighteenth century—the beautiful, well-fed *inhumaines* of that age—and they were all plump under their stays and billowing taffetas. Once in a rare while there was a thin one like LaGuimand, the dancer— "Plain, thin, dark." Her thinness made her hideous to everybody, and the marvel was that the painter Fragonard was so tormented by her *beauté diable* that he could do nothing but paint her frivolous emaciation in all his work. The only other thin beauty was Madame de Pompadour, whom society reduced day by day, "until she became a veritable skeleton weighing only 111 pounds." Yet since she was not particularly tall, this was not so very thin according to our standards.

Early Victorian women seemed to want to be plump and pale. Pallor and a look of ill health superimposed on plumpness was the thing, because only servant girls and dairy-maids had red cheeks. But after 1958 thin women began creeping up on us.

Now, thirty years ago there were some doctors—a small vanguard—who were in favor of thin women. They gave very good reasons. Thin women, they said, were due, first, to changes in the food supply and, second, to changes in women themselves.

Before 1700 in England all the food eaten was found on the island. None was imported. After that, tea, coffee, sugar and other things began to appear. There was tea and coffee for breakfast and a sweet confection after dinner, and meals were better tasting, richer, less monotonous, more stimulating, though Jonas Hanway, who was the first to have the courage to carry an umbrella, wrote an essay attacking tea, saying, "Your very chambermaids have lost their bloom by sipping it."

From that time onward up to the present, food became more abundant and palatable. But there have been some bad effects. For one thing, a change in the food supply destroys the ungovernable gluttons. The healthy poor man who becomes a millionaire usually digs his grave with his teeth, becomes fat, ailing, apoplectic, arteriosclerotic, the victim of such degenerative diseases as cancer and diabetes, many of which, it is held, come from overfeeding on imperfect food. For example, one of the most remarkable changes in our food habits, the dietitians say, is the increase in sugar. A century and a half ago an American ate about eight pounds of sugar a year; today he eats about 140 pounds. Physiologists say that while once sugar was about two percent of our nourishment, now it is about one-fifth of our nourishment with the result that it makes us fat and spoils our appetite for food that would nourish us much better.

And so gradually the doctors who were in favor of thin women considered the majority of adults overweight anyway, and thought that the epidemic of reducing was a good thing for it meant that there was a reaction of self-control and good sense after two hundred years of over-eating on the wrong food. It is no accident that the few persons who lived to an old age in the past are generally recorded to have been abstemious. "And it is pathetic," wrote Dean Inge, "to compare the portraits of Charles James Fox and his contemporaries as Eton boys with the gross old gentlemen 'forty years on' who bore the same names."

The circulation in overweight people is faulty. Fat makes extra work for the heart, the stomach, the lungs not to mention the legs, feet and arches. Overweight brings about a vicious circle: taking exercise is a disagreeable effort so that eating becomes one of the few pleasures. There is a general torpor and lassitude and consequently a craving for rich stimulating food such as fudge sundaes and chocolate cake in order to get more energy and, of course, more weight.

On the other hand a lean person finds exercise such a

light and easy matter that he gets out of a chair willingly and will run up and down stairs without deliberating over it for a half hour in advance. In consequence he has good circulation, a good digestion and has not the perpetual false appetite of the overfed person. And although it is often true that fat people are good-natured and acquiescent, they have not the force of will or fire of lean ones. And this leads us to the chief reason why men dreaded dieting wives—their dispositions tend not to be good.

The best way to arouse a husband is to say in an undertone to his 112-pound wife:

"I think—take off about seven more pounds and you'll be just about right." No matter if he is asleep this will bring him to his feet with a cry of protest. And I suppose you cannot blame him. I remember three strange, melancholy periods in my life that have always puzzled me, when I, a sanguine, good-natured and almost imbecilically optimistic person became for a few weeks not only melancholy but the victim of a vague neurasthenic fright and sadness. Just the fact that it got dark after twilight, or that it was the month of March, or that company was coming to dinner, seemed a terrible thing, filled me with a foreboding and a dreadful loneliness.

Well just a short time ago when I had turned the fifteenth day of a ferocious new diet, I suddenly found myself in this very same state of mind and looking back at those other periods I realized that then too I had been trying to get thin by living on coffee, nearly raw meat and lettuce. And the worst thing is that the judgement seems to fall off. A friendly, jolly, competent wife who is full of horse sense will begin to think that her husband does not like her because he reads the newspaper, or that friends give her compliments just to hide their true feelings about her, or that the man who dances with her is waving a five-dollar bill at the stags behind her back.

But as we know now it is not the reducing that is bad but the wrong methods of doing it. In other words, it is not how much you eat but what you eat that is important, and to illustrate this, Sir Arbuthnot Lane, the famous English surgeon, tells how Wellington's soldiers and their wives, who were allowed a ration of a pound of raw ground wheat a day and lived on that and nothing else, had better teeth and better physiques, though they were exposed to constant hardships, than modern English soldiers who have a wide variety of food but who probably eat and drink too much of what tastes good but does not nourish them.

Some people think that thin women came into style in one season a few years ago, like a novelty bracelet or the maxicoat, but really they have been creeping up on us for nearly a hundred and fifty years. In the last half of the nineteenth century there were Sir Edward Burne-Jones women and Dante Gabriel Rossetti women. Du Maurier's heroine, Trilby, was very tall and fairly slim. Manet exhibited his famous painting, *Olympia*, and threw all France in a rage. They were used to the soft pneumatic women of Bouguereau and to women in the paintings of the classical period who in the Greek draperies had large white legs and dimpled ankles and slim feet that toed-out excessively, and fat wrists, with a dimple where the wrist-bone is today. To us, Manet's *Olympia* is a limber compact girl. "Just right," we would all say. Yet sixty years ago all French artists and critics and the general public set up a resentful cry that she was a ghastly consumptive; they shuddered to look at her horrible emaciation.

And as far back as fifty years ago when women were still wearing corsets, underwear and long black stockings even when they went swimming in the sea, were quietly beginning to reduce. Mrs. Stuyvesant Fish, the leader of the Four Hundred in New York Society in 1910, used to walk five miles every morning in Central Park in a rubber union-suit over heavy wool garments and had tea and one bleak slice of thin dry toast for breakfast. And although her dinner parties had the requisite number of eight or nine courses, under her dictatorship for the very first time, dinners were not gorging feasts but each course was whisked away so quickly by innumerable footmen that there was hardly time to eat more than a few mouthfuls. Dinners that had always taken more than two hours she reduced to one hour. And incidentally she also introduced champagne at the third course, the entree, not in delicate stemmed glasses, but in tumblers.

But it was during the First War that thin women came in with an overwhelming rush. One reason was, as the French explained it, that it was patriotic to eat little because there began to be a terrible dearth of food. Then, because of the necessity of economy, dresses were made with the least possible cloth—no petticoats, no ruffles, no corsets. (This was the sudden innovation of that genius, Chanel.) Now the skimpier a dress is and the more diaphanous, the harder and more compact you must be to wear it. In fact for the present slimness of women we have to thank the chorus girls. Ever since the first original musical comedy, The Black Crook, in which the chorus girls wore black tights instead of long skirts for the first time since ancient Greece, people have taken a sensible, dispassionate, critical and aesthetic interest—not a facetious and waggish interest—in women's figures. In fact, women's figures have consequently become very very much better than men's who even now wear such thick coverings that you cannot tell if they are living skeletons or fat men or pitifully knock-kneed. Since men have not been exposed to criticism or admiration, they have had no incentive to improve. But things are changing.

George Bernard Shaw wrote in his day of the absurd fact that a portrait is not a portrait of a man or woman, but of a dress or business suit and a pair of shoes. "Bereaved parents, orphans and widows weep fondly over photographs of uniforms, frock coats, gowns and hats, for the sake of the little scrap of humanity that is allowed to peep through these trappings. Women with noble figures and plain or elderly faces are outdressed and outfaced by rivals who, if revealed as they really are, would be hardly human."

But as far as women are concerned, this situation is diminishing. No longer can one whose face, a small disk about one-twentieth of her surface, is kept thoroughly pummeled, pomaded and wrinkleless—"youthful" is the word—compete with a woman who may have some lines in her face but who is at the same time in her grace, vigor and construction, a magnificent human being.

Carlyle staggered humanity by inviting the House of Commons to sit unclothed so that "we and they themselves shall know them for what they really are." Everyone shudders at this, but I feel certain that within a month the figures of all would be tremendously improved and, in almost every instance, reduced. That is why as long as women's clothes are diaphanous, I doubt very much that there will be many Rubens or Renoir women no matter what the doctors say.

And this is interesting: Not so long ago stoutness was a sign of wealth and opulence and social position because it seemed to announce to the world that you could afford roast saddle of mutton every night, as well as entrees of fish and fowl and terrapin before and after the roast, and sherry, claret, and champagne coming along with the proper course. Not so long ago a man was proud of his bay window and proudly outlined its curve with a big gold watch chain. "Well favored" was the adjective applied to beautiful women and if it could not be applied, they were not beautiful.

◆

# ABORTION

friend said in a letter that she was passionately against abortion. At last, I said, we seem to be disagreeing. I know a great deal about abortion and have helped many people to get such a thing. In my experience, it has never been a gory and dreadful thing, "the murder of a fetus." It is a minimal operation not even needing an anesthetic and certainly not worth, to the physician, more than $30 in time and effort, although the medical profession, very lively about profits, now charges $150 or $200. In the days before the new abortion law, when it was illegal, it cost from $300 to $500 and one had to go to Chicago or New York, and the physician was often a third-rate kind of person, anonymous, breaking the law, inexpert, dirty.

Now all this outcry about an abortion criminally exterminating and preventing a human life—I don't agree, and I cannot seem to feel distressed about it. In the fifth or sixth week the fertilized cell is almost microscopic and yet these Right-To-Lifers, who take on like madwomen, don't hesitate to eat a large brown-eyed cow. A young friend of mine was telling me a year ago about the Anti-Abortion people holding a vigil by the Washington Monument in the moonlight, candles and all night praying to beat the band for the hundreds of thousands of souls, more or less, of murdered fetuses. I said ribaldly that perhaps we should hold vigils for the billions of unfulfilled sperm cells from males—demand that it all be preserved and frozen and kept in great warehouses.

And about your acquaintance, I said, and how distressed you were when you heard that she had had an abortion—Good Heavens, she had already had four children!

I know that only once in my life did I ever discover my mother in tears. An awful pang for me. I will never forget it. It was in the back hall where the stairs go up to the third floor. I happened to see the tears and asked, in horror, about them. She was pregnant with her eighth child and said that it depressed her that it was so, that it was quite hard to be always pregnant after years and years of it. She was very slender and seemingly frail when she was married and someone had predicted that she would not live more than two years after marriage. Imagine how grateful she would have been for some chance to prevent conception. And years after when woman suffrage had been won and a few other reasonable ameliorations in the lot of women, she was very happy about it. (The child that was born was beautiful, jolly and strong and dearly loved all his life.)

In arguing with my friend I said that my mother and hers could have afforded many children, maybe eleven or twelve. They could have sent them all to fine schools, surrounded them with the most arcadian and perfect life. But what about persons who cannot do that, who have to work hard for a living, who have neither time to think nor space to swing a cat?

I wish I had had a lot more children. A young woman once made a drawing of me—very haggard and fierce I looked—and a friend said, "That is Brenda if she had gone to North Dakota and had ten children." I have often thought, "Why that is just what I should have done (breaking horses on the side)." But I just cannot conceive of letting anyone adopt a child of mine, getting some unknown stranger, some undifferentiated boob, some prissy disciplinarian, to bring up my child. These anti-abortion people, including Senator Mondale and Jimmy Carter, are all so light-hearted about that. I would like to blow a brass trumpet and yell and proclaim that any mother who is not also by nature a wild, heroic fighting tigress about keeping her own child forever and ever, is no good!

And I said: Think of the past, of the graveyards, the tombstones telling the story: One elderly New England husband outliving three wives, each one with a long list of children, dying and dead. W. R. Inge, the Gloomy Dean of St. Paul's, pointed out in his essay on *The Birthrate* that the great English scholar, John Colet was one of an average family in the 17th century: "twenty-two children, half of whom died." It did not strike him that this kind of life, common to all women, to every last dodgasted woman in existence, must have been dreadful—a continuing pregnancy and dying children all around.

Moreover, over-population is a most dire and terrible thing. People just have not the right to fill up the world with a plethora of children, casting them into a world of ghetto pressures, of nervous exhaustion, of weazening space, into a life of shrieking, over-wrought parents. Perhaps then one should preach universal celibacy? It might be a good and noble idea, but I do not expect it of people, certainly not quite yet.

And one more thing: Women are beginning to observe that men are talking through their hats. There is Father Shenanigan, or the Reverend Peterson, telling Mrs. Dennis Johnson having her fourteenth child, how wonderful it is.

Mrs. Johnson: "He would know!"

The other day the Right-To-Lifers attacked the Minneapolis Planned Parenthood Clinic. They had to call the police. Well so far the story is true and being a novelist I will continue the account in my fantasy. The police dragged them out, pulling them by the hair and arms and legs, their high-heeled shoes grooving the floor. Now in this modern sexy world ("We have the cutest new sexy icebox!") the police raped them all and got them pregnant. Here would be an interesting dilemma, a problem, a quandary worthy of poor Hamlet or Oedipus. Think of them, all pregnant! And since they do not believe in abortions either for rape or incest, they would have to stick to their ideals. The police would all be hauled into court but the Judge would acquit all of them (perhaps with huzzahs) because the Right-To-Lifers were so provocative and sexy.

Right-To-Lifers, rejoice that after untold thousands of years, women are not, one and all, the total victims, the galley-slaves of the biological process!

❖

# ON PROSTITUTION

hree years ago I met Margot St. James. She is one of those who raced up Pike's Peak on August 3rd. She is an ex-prostitute or maybe a practicing prostitute and she is also a remarkable and even a distinguished woman—altruistic, dogged, brave, public-spirited. She lectures in universities and to conferences of sociologists.

I was so glad to meet her. She has a kind, quite maternal countenance. A little haggard. Deeply tanned legs and arms (muscular). Clad in ragged sawed-off jeans and carrying an immense 30-pound back-pack. She had come down from San Francisco hitch-hiking and sleeping in the fields if necessary. Everybody likes her immensely.

There are many days of practice runs up the Terrible Mountain and sociable gatherings in our various motels. She gave me copies of her newspaper, COYOTE and it describes her effort to de-criminalize Prostitution since it is "victimless," to organize prostitutes so that they have some defense and are befriended in their struggle for a livelihood. At last, after thousands of years, there is the new notion that if women are bad and must be put in jail for Prostitution, the men who use them are just as guilty.

I find a letter I wrote to her in 1975.

Dear Margot:

I could write you pages about your work, (wonderful courage, bearding all those judges!) and I see the first-rate justice of it: 1. Prostitution is a class war against women, waged by men. 2. How you fight to organize a decent labor union. 3. How marriage is also a Prostitution (though not always). 4. Your much needed kindness and defense of the pimp, so often the only friend of the girl. 5. About the outrageous "legalization of Prostitution" in Nevada. (I saw that, I know about that.) 6. How Prostitution is a temporary marriage, honorably given and paid for. (Your argument is touchingly convincing.) 7. The practical, common-sensibleness of it, the useful training in expertness of the sex act. (I shudder with disgust.) 8. How Prostitution must be de-criminalized because it is a natural agreement and neither party is injured. (Although of course they are.)

At the same time I have many thoughts about it. They are Victorian, but I think they are also true and okay. Here are a few: Sex is a perfect sink if it is merely a bargain. There should be neither Prostitution in marriage or in Prostitution but true love, i.e. imagination, generosity, passion, insight, responsibility-for-the Other, honor, loyalty. If there is not, then know that you are doing the Other a lifelong harm, (see Tolstoy) and yourself. It is a soul-killer from Hell. Then there is that great notion that seems to have come in with early Christianity that sex love is a sacrament; a mysterious and great miracle i.e. the Incarnation of the Spirit into a new creature. There is the Christian notion that the family is holy. (I like that, a great help to poor old Mankind.) And monogamy. How grand! (Think of the lion and lioness). As for promiscuity—think of the vague slobbering life of lying, cheating, eating-your-cake-and-having-it-too (being a damned coward!), drowned day in and day out in the grossest insincerity. It diminishes and belittles the whole world of Mankind. It brings about an absolutely certain deterioration of men, women, their children! of whole cities, states, nations.

Then consider the grandeur and beauty of Dante and Beatrice, Tristram and Isolde, Paolo and Francesca, Elizabeth and Robert Browning, of the countless millions of noble and happy marriages. But Prostitution is always sad and terrible for both sexes. A hateful, sterile, commercialism is the basis for it founded on fake feelings. That is what Ibsen expounded for the first time in *The Doll's House*. Now at last we begin to have a glimmer that money accepted without the honorable exchange of sincerity and affection, (I include here marriage, business, advertising, ever-higher salaries) is always a dire infection and as evil as a hidden poison.

In a long life I have known many people and their noble

loves and their inferior loves. I have observed that men are eternally marred by their first experience if it is a kind of "mutt" experience. Women too, of course. Chastity and celibacy are sometimes pretty good. Freud was an ass, obsessed with female submissiveness and the omni-importance of sexuality. He has loosened this great tide of unrestricted ugly and trivial sexuality on us. Too bad. (All the dinky, untalented writers of the world are clamorous with it.)

But for Heaven's and God's sake, Margot, to advocate that girls should be allowed to regard Prostitution as a good and worthy business, cut that out! That dreadful life, indoors, sedentary, lazy, mindless, money-grabbing; all day waiting for evening, eating, drinking, smoking, gossiping; frightful talk, practicing their pancake make-up, fomenting and creating and building up the vast silliness and emptiness of the whole female world! It is a terrible thought!

Enough now. Too much. In my poetic idealism about l'Amour one must bear in mind, especially myself, that I am 88 and not too troubled by lust. I perhaps was at one time but have forgotten it. Much love. Brenda Ueland.

◆

# FALLEN WOMEN

A few thoughts about a book, *The Dark Angel: Aspects of Victorian Sexuality*, by Fraser Harrison. (Sheldon Press, England).

Anyone, especially any woman who has been induced by Masters and Johnson of the *Cosmopolitan* magazine to worry about the attainment of the perfect sex life, should read about the Victorians. And it was such a short time ago! Consider the concept of the feminine then and it is still among us. Here it is: the good woman far above the male in nobleness of nature and the bad woman, the fallen (the work perhaps of five minutes) thereafter to be bought for a shilling.

A middle-class girl's reputation was compromised if she went unchaperoned or allowed more than a kiss on the cheek. London had about 6,000 brothels (one house out of every sixty) and 80,000 prostitutes not counting the enormous number of very poor working class women who turned to part-time prostitution when necessary. In 1875 the legal age of consent was raised to 13, after much opposition. For the cheaper girls a silk handkerchief, which could be pawned, was an acceptable fee. The virtuous woman, meanwhile, the Angel in the House, was legally her husband's personal property and until 1884 could be imprisoned for refusing conjugal rights. (My woman-suffragist mother and other women were considered outrageous because they considered this an outrage.)

The author, Fraser Harrison, studied Victorian novels, memoirs and pioneering sociologists for his material. I remember myself seeing a world-shocking play in 1913, "Hindle Wakes," in which the heroine, a young working-class woman was pregnant and cheerfully delighted to have a child and—this is what upset everybody—she would not marry the father because she did not like him; she found him not admirable.

As the author, Mr. Harrison tells the story, it seems that

what we would consider ordinary sexual happiness was very rare in those days both for men and women, for rich and poor: the good woman by her upbringing and because of the ideas of the time, had no sexual urges; the working-class woman shared her bed with the youngest children and often a drunken husband; the young men either struggled miserably against vicious propensities or bought sickly ugly illiterate girls in the alleys of East End London.

Were the prosperous married gentlemen the only ones to have a little physical pleasure, fathering huge families of children? We do not really know. Mr. Harrison's analysis of the rich or poor woman's "attitude toward her body" is guesswork. Perhaps things were sometimes better than we can now imagine.

Where he is on sure ground is in his description, genuinely documented by Booth, Mayhew, and Rowntree, of the unspeakable poverty of lower working-class life and of its relation to prostitution. Cheaply as they offered themselves, the wonder is that any girl chose virtue and life in the sweatshop at $2\frac{1}{2}$ pennies per shirt when she could earn a week's utterly inadequate wages in half an hour.

And as for Victorian urban poverty, see how you like it: the underground kitchen occupied by seven people and a dead child no one can afford to bury; the water butt serving a whole tenement where a dead cat floated for weeks; the fetid outdoor privy for a hundred people or more; the roaming, homeless children living on their wits and sleeping in doorways.

Without distracting us with the ideas of Marx, the author shows how Victorian sexual conventions sprang from economics. With increased wealth and status of the middle class, it was more necessary than ever that the "good" woman be preserved in all her purity, as a proof that she was entirely owned by her husband and also because she had to provide a guaranteed certitude for the inheritance of property. And so you see the poor and therefore usually "bad" woman not only supported the lady by her labor but was "a sewer down which middle-class men could flush extraneous sexual energies."

It is a very ugly picture. Anti-Feminists please note. The

rest of the story, the tendency to split femaleness into "good" and "bad" goes back into history for millenia. We see it in the Christian tradition. But in order to be just about this situation and account for good things in it as well as bad, alas, one would have to write six columns.

◆

# ◤ Animals ◥

## My Dear, Dear Cat Friends

I want to tell you about my cats. In my long life I have had so many of them, all dearly loved. The sorrowful thing is that we human creatures live on and on and outlive them in generation after generation. Long ago in my childhood there was Ebony (black) and Jackie (grey), also female. Arguing with a small brother, I said that she was a boy because she had whiskers.

Many years later there was the utterly beautiful Ivan, a big striped tiger. But there was this difference: the very ends of his fur were tipped with white so that he seemed to be surrounded by a kind of light, an aura, a halo. When I was on my bed reading he would lie on my chest in that noble posture of the Lions at Trafalgar Square, a majestic and beautiful creature. When I lifted my eyes from my book at intervals he would look into them and then slowly, delicately, with a great white paw touch me on the end of my nose. "I love you," he was saying.

At that time we lived on Lake Calhoun surrounded by lawns and the pasture and the woods beyond. It was his brave duty to keep all dangerous tomcats away. There were dreadful and bloody fights. As he grew older his wounds would become infected, and at last there were so many of them that he could not recover. He died. Darling Ivan! I never forgot him. He is often with me.

Then there were so many other cats, all beautiful, interesting, proudly individual, charming. There were unforgettable cats belonging to friends like Nancy Benson's Pussy in New York. On weekends she took Pussy to Fire Island. Pussy loved the trip in the car and on the ferryboat, her head out of the window in the wind, eagerly watching, sniffing the sea air. On the beach Pussy would wade out into the surf after Nancy and her friends, a little anxious about their swimming so far. And she chased all dogs away, lambasting their rears with her claws until they howled. Bathers would shout: "Call off your cat!"

There was Lion, Boyo, Finn MacCool, Madeline, Roddy, Daphne, Mowgli, Mrs. Betty, Tiger, Sascha, Flower, Goody Two-Shoes, Thistle, Bonnie and Brenda, Feather Duster. We knew a very nice male cat whose owner, a little girl, had named him Uncle Elizabeth. There was a stranger cat who came wandering by and decided to stay. "What is his name?" asked little Patrick, aged four. "Katherine," I said, "and we call him Kitty for short."

Pogo was a huge yellow lion. He belonged to my daughter who had to move to New York, and so I took him to live with me. Alas! that night an upstairs window was left open and he leaped out. Gone! Myself broken-hearted. I put prolonged ads in the newspapers. Ten days later a neighbor said that a large, mysterious cat had been at her front door. The next day, behold, there was Pogo at the top of our elm tree looking into an upstairs window.

When I had Pogo I had been recently married and my husband did not like cats. I was strongly influenced by him then (I am a little ashamed to say it) so I advertised to find a home for poor Pogo. A woman telephoned: "I seen your ad . . ."

"Pogo," I thought indignantly, "could never stand a woman who said 'I seen!'" I would not consider her as a possibility.

A young man and woman came with two small boys. They wanted a cat for the children to play with. "No," I said. "I can't let you have him. Albert Schweitzer and I are entirely agreed on this subject, i.e., the outrage of giving a creature over to the careless torture of children." Then, relenting a little I said, "Now if after a few years with Pogo you decided that you would adopt a couple of children because he would be happier that way, I might consider it."

I hasten to say that there are wonderful parents who are great enough to show their children how to befriend animals, to love and appreciate them. My mother for example: Every smallest child in our large family of seven children, an infant hardly ten months old, was taught. The tiny hand was taken and showed how to stroke Kitty very lightly and gently in the right direction. "Nice Kitty . . . darling Kitty . . ."

After a while a very nice man, a postman with yellow-red hair just the color of Pogo's took him and they lived happily together.

My dear friend, Lauritz Rusten, 84 years old, a Norwegian from Lillehammer, a Theosophist, loved cats (indeed he loved everything alive) and he told me that the Hindus had a fine saying: "Those who love cats will be rewarded. They will get more cats." He said there was something mysterious and great about cats, about their souls, that it is no wonder that the Egyptians believed them to be deities. He said that cats are all great artists. "They have this extraordinary talent for beauty." See how they cannot do anything that is not utterly beautiful, graceful, enchanting. Even washing their charming behinds. They can lift themselves to the highest shelf, to the top of my sixteenth century carved cabinet nearly six feet high. They just look up at it, lift themselves noiselessly without even touching the most fragile bric-a-brac.

I told you about Pogo whom I gave away to a very nice man, but two years later our cat was killed crossing the street. I never think of it without a pang of grief. Perhaps I should never have given him away. (Weak! Unfeeling!)

My next cat (as it turns out they are all charity cases) was Whizzer with black rings around his tail who whizzed up and down the apple trees. He was named after Justice Whizzer White of the United States Supreme Court, who earned the name playing professional football as a young man.

After a while I had to go to New York and Jenny Johnsen took Whizzer in for those three weeks (she is even fonder of cats than I am if that were possible). She brought him back the day before I returned. My anti-cat husband let him out (I have repressed dark thoughts about this) and he never came back. I put ads in Lost and Found, pinned notices in all the shops, on telegraph poles, walked up and down the alley for miles in both directions, calling.

After that there was Tom. My friend Regina said there was a young white cat with calico striped spots at her door. It was winter, often 15 below zero. "He is so courageous," she said. And so I had another cat. I named him Tom.

Tom was with me for many years, a great friend and a strong guardian. One Memorial Day my neighbors, the Misses Wolf, telephoned to say that Tom had tried to get up the low retaining wall between us and could not make it. He was dead. I could find no wounds. Darling Tom! He is buried under the oak tree. He is with me. We will meet again.

I am very happy now with three cats, Muffin, Skadoogi and Figaro. Muffin: a little boy found him. He was about seven inches long with a splash of white on his nose, white mittens ("You naughty kittens, you have lost your mittens,") and white socks, and he was sick with a great swollen lump on his flank, an abscess. If I touched him he let out huge guttural growls as if he were the size of a tiger.

He slept on my bed and I gave him "healing" treatments that my Swedish clairvoyant friend, Maybelle Fahlstrom, had taught me. Presently the abscess broke and he was splendidly well. In his kittenhood he liked to climb on my chest, his back against my face and mouth, and then nurse his own furry stomach. It was awfully cozy and nice. I think he had been taken from his mother when he was too young.

And I saved his life the second time. In his curiosity he had watched me open some old cans and turpentine splashed on him. Turpentine is especially dangerous for cats. He was terribly sick—in dreadful pain. He would come to me imploring: "Brenda . . . Mama . . . help me!" I was with him night and day again with the gentle laying on of hands, and love, and consoling talk. He got well. He is my arch-especial cat and he knows it. He always sleeps on my bed and he likes to have his saucer of food set down before him wherever he is, in the sitting room, or on the porch railing.

Skadoogi is my out-of-doors boy, big, yellow, full of glossy powerful health. He likes to be out all night. Self-reliant, scornful. He has an enormous appetite and takes up a patient sentinel position before the ice-box several times a day. I like to watch him as he walks out of the sitting-room into the kitchen. His left hind leg toes-in a little. Carl Sandburg used to walk that way. It is the way a great baseball pitcher walks when he goes, ominously, to consult his catcher.

Mr. O'Dowd at the supermarket says that he has four wonderful cats, and he said, "Cats are so grateful." I had never thought of that but now I see that it is so. Skadoogi, for example, seemingly so cold, a little bit tough, indifferent, distant, seeks me out almost every third day. He comes close, his immense heavy self on my lap. Purrs. Bunts my cheek with his handsome head again and again. Kneads my arms and knees with his great paws and piercing claws. He is saying: "Thank you. I appreciate you. Remember that and make a note of it."

Then there is Figaro. He followed me home on a Spring evening. Young, beautiful, jolly, with the longest softest, thickest plume of a tail that I have ever seen. Such a darling, affectionate, fearless rascal of a cat. In the immensity of his good-nature he isn't afraid of anything in the world. He likes to go up to Muffin and Skadoogi so boldly that they forget to snarl and tear into him and he licks them earnestly and insolently, smoothing out their ears and whiskers with vigorous swipes of his pink tongue. They like it.

And I saved Figaro's life, too. I took him to the vet to be neutered and it made him terribly sick with a burning fever so that his silken grey fur came out in handfuls. To the vet's again for penicillin. He got worse. I experienced anguish, despair. I had the thinnest thread of hope because he would eat a little delicately poached codfish.

That night—I thought it was his last one—he was on my bed, as hot as fire and dreadfully thin, and he curled against my left arm and shoulder. I did not move all night, sometimes reading a few paragraphs. I kept my right hand on his heart, abdomen, throat all night. I prayed for him—that is to say I saw and felt and impelled through him with my imagination, power, light, bright happiness, life—flowing all through him in a golden beneficent river. I did that all night. It was the turning point. He began to get well and now he is the merry jocular beauty of the Western World.

Here is a thought that often strikes me. By nature I think I am an explorer, an adventurer. I have the most persistent notion that I was a sea captain in another reincarnation. I am never so happy and exuberant as when starting off alone into the Unknown, in a feeble and uncertain old car. I should have been around the world ten times. I should have driven alone to Alaska, to Patagonia, walked the west coast of Ireland, the skerries of the Hebrides, the wildest Isles of Greece, journeyed to the Black Sea where the Scythians came from, and the Amazons. I really think all this is a true and essential part of my nature.

But what? My maternal passion has done me in. I have always been so fond of a child, of some cats and kittens, or dogs, or lonely friends, and I feel such poignant responsibility about them that an immense force overpowers me and keeps me home.

But here is a compensating reason: If the cats are grateful to me, I am enormously grateful to them and here is the reason. They give me (the thought comes to me with astonishment often) a constant reassurance that I am really quite a nice person. Now that is a thing one can never be quite sure about. But at least to my cats I am unflawed in good will, affection, trouble-taking and loyalty. It is a consoling thought that often comes in the midst of doubt.

❖

# FLORENCE MURPHY AND SAM

I saw Florence Murphy and asked her about Sam, her wonder cat, nine years old. Sam hasn't been quite well lately. As she says, "He coughs on his own purr." So she sleeps downstairs on the couch because it makes him feel happier and less worried about himself, and she gives him a pill at certain hours during the night. She says a very remarkable thing happened.

Now Sam is a lordly and beautiful Persian and has never been willing to sleep up in her bedroom because on the ground floor he can look outdoors. Anyway, he likes it there. But the other night Florence Murphy said, "Now look here, Sam. I've taken care of you for a long time and I haven't really had a good night for weeks, because this couch down here isn't comfortable at all. It seems to me that you should consider me just once and be willing to sleep up in my room so I can get one good night's sleep."

She went upstairs to undress. Sam came walking grandly into her room, waving his plume of a tail, gave her one look—almost made a face—jumped on the chair and stayed there all night.

I told her that the Theosophists have the soundest and best idea about animals. (She was at once struck with the incontrovertible truth of it.) If an animal loves and admires a person very much that animal in the next incarnation makes the jump and becomes a human being. I am sure of it! Admiration, love (said Plotinus) of what is at least a little higher, a little better than oneself, is the only agency whereby one becomes greater, better and moves a millimeter or so toward Perfection. That is the point to loving God and why it is the wrong thing to fear Him: for fear is self-interest and one retrogresses.

◆

# POGO

I have just received a brochure from the Feline Society, Inc. They have a periodical, *Meouw*. I have a monstrous pale-yellow lion of a cat named Pogo. He bounds to the mantelpiece and takes a noble pose like the Sphinx and smiles down at me with his golden eyes. When cream is in the bottom of the pitcher he dips his huge soft paws—like pale yellow muffs—into it and delicately licks it off. And he dips first one fat paw and then the others, alternately.

He is a great trial and a bully and quite a handicap, softly thundering and galloping upstairs to sit on my paper when I am trying to work and rolling pencils off the desk. My husband, who thinks I am too fond of animals, asked me one day what I wanted for my birthday. "Only one thing," I said after prolonged thoughtful consideration. "What?" he asked. "A subscription to *Meouw*."

◆

# LION FARM

I read a lovely article by Sewell Peaslee Wright about Dr. Manley B. Mathers —"Doc" he is called and has a farm in Mason City, Iowa, where he breeds short-horned cattle and—what do you think?—18 lions. They have a nice sun-warmed pasture of their own, with iron bars around it. By trading with circuses and zoos, Doc has 18 lions, 8 leopards, three tigers, 30 deer, a herd of buffalo, a pair of llamas and a 14-foot boa constrictor. It all started about eight years ago when a circus went broke near his place. "Nobody up there wanted to pay for feeding a full-grown lioness so they asked me if I wanted her. She was my first lion."

Well, what has he discovered? Lions thrive in a northern sub-zero climate (they can be in their barn or out-of-doors.) They breed prolifically in captivity. (For him! They would not for a lion-tamer, I will bet.) Old Betty, a six-year-old lioness has raised nineteen cubs in four litters, and that is probably a world's record. Doc was afraid one cub would starve unless somebody went into the cage—I should say pasture—where they were nursing their mother, and make sure they got on equal terms at feeding. Doc thought it over and wrote a note which he pinned on the door for his hired man: "If I'm not here when you get back, rake my shoes out of old Betty's cage. They're rationed."

He goes into his lions bare-handed and hauls the lions around by the mane or tail, if they are in his way. And he puts his arm in their mouths and gets them all to do all the tricks the lion tamers show us, with all their guns and whips.

It's this way: According to Doc you have a lion around and you win his confidence. You become less and less afraid of the lion. Pretty soon you and the lion are on good terms and that is all there is to it. (What a parable for the United Nations, for everyone, for lambs!)

Lions, he says, are born tame. Now tigers and leopards are not. "It takes eight or ten months to win the complete confidence of a tiger." And when a lion punched a tooth into Doc's arm once, two inches deep, he said: "Make it clear that the lion never meant to hurt me. I was riding him and using my forearm as a bit to guide him. He turned too short, and I slid to one side and stepped on the old boy's toes. Instinctively he snapped—and then went right on playing."

Sewell Peaslee who saw the whole thing, says that it is absolutely true: "The lion wasn't mad, just playing."

❖

# REPORT ON THE POOR ANIMALS

◗

T The perennial row is on in Minneapolis, the anti-dog people making a horrendous fuss about leashes, muzzles, about how dogs are biting and barking and being horrid in every way.

The world is divided into anti-animal people and pro-animal people. I am pro-animal, oh ferociously so! It is curious how the matter of liking or disliking seems to refer to a point in one's very center. It is not based on logic at all but on whatever point of view you decide to take.

I know a very great soul, a violinist, who came home to her small room in a New York hotel one night and found a mouse. Now the ordinary person would automatically and grimly set about shopping for traps and poison. But my friend —St. Francesca I call her—was just overjoyed. She at once set about making everything comfortable and interesting for him. She would buy special tidbits and leave them tactfully where he would enjoy them undisturbed. (She found that he liked freshly shelled unsalted almonds.) She and the mouse became great friends and because of her exquisite tact and sensitive sympathy the mouse became a perfect charmer of a mouse, so intelligent and droll and delightful. The mouse was very, very musical, she said, and loved especially Bach's Chaconne.

Now take this anti-dog campaign in Minneapolis: someone spoke of the fact that scores of dogs congregated at the schools, to bite and nip and snarl in their sinister way.

How strange, I thought, that people should look at it that way. To me the most touching and endearing and laughable thing is the way thirty happy dogs, all galumphing and sliding and skidding and cavorting among the children, suddenly fall limp to the ground the moment the children go into the school house—bored, limp, mournful, unhappy, dull. Instead of thinking, "Those horrid dogs!" I always think, "We should have some decent classes for dogs too. Certainly! Something progressive and stimulating. Must get up a petition to the City Council."

My ideas on how to bring up children were proved right by a wonderful cat I had, Ivan. He was a handsome tomcat who looked like a jaguar, and like the lovely Egyptian sculptures of grave, noble lions. And like the Sphinx. Ivan (and this is the way we should always treat children) was never humiliated or blocked in any way. We never shooed him off the table. No, we would lift him with the greatest slowness and tact, and with pleasant explanation, and take him to some better place, without hurting his feelings. We never pushed him through a door hastily but let him take his own time even though a zero wind was blowing in.

Well Ivan, instead of becoming a greedy, pouncing, "undisciplined" wild animal of a cat, as you might think (and as the disciplinarian know-it-alls have warned us) became brave, intelligent, distinguished. He talked with so many words in his voice. "Mmmmmmm . . . tink!" (like a tiny bell) he said when I came home. He looked at us with such tenderness (only dogs are supposed to) and put out his beautiful paw to pull us gently, to delicately touch our noses to show his feeling and friendship. You see? He had had no thwarting, no blocking, no "discipline," which is the name for the mannerless, peremptory forcing inflicted on children. No, there never was humiliation for Ivan. And this let him grow in his soul.

Now some people are fools over animals and make them neurotic. They make too much silly fuss. Babytalk. They worry and display all sorts of nervous-nellyisms. Why Ivan could go out on ten-below-zero nights and to his private night clubs and stay for three days if he wanted to. He needed only to say "Mmmmmmm . . . tink," at the door. We did not belittle him by preventing him, or by worrying about him. If you do that, animals become silly (as children do) and lose dignity. We never offended Ivan by talking silly to him, boring him.

But to go back to this inner decision, very far far in at one's center, as to whether to dislike or to like: It is a matter of your own free will. (As Dean Inge of St. Paul's Church in London said,

"Of *course* the affections are a matter of one's will.") I had two charming rambunctious big cats and they acquired as a friend a huge, battered dirty old white tomcat, with cauliflower ears and a limp. On sub-zero nights this old phantom of a cat would be sitting on the porch railing, looking in wistfully and hoping his play-fellows would come out and join him. I made every effort to get the poor old white cat in the house. If only I could get him inside and keep him warm, and charm him into not being afraid of us any more, and to be at ease—say some hot beef tea to start with!

But it was so tragic—I never could. I would open the door gently, gently, and the poor dirty old cat would run over the ice and snow, so cold that it wounded his paws, toward the rubbish pile and the freezing garbage can, and to some cruel refuge. How I would have loved to have that brave old spirited white cat: Not out of charity but out of respect and admiration. To be in the company of such a brave old cat would have ennobled me.

Some neighbors told me one evening of an ominous "dreadful looking and awful old white cat skulking around." They hoped to be able to shoot it.

One of my pro-animal friends is Anne Moffett of St. Augustine, Florida, and she writes:

Darling Brenda! This is a wild, desperate SOS appeal in behalf of Shiner. He would write and point out his woes to Foxy if he could. (N.B. Foxy is my dog.) Shiner is in a horrible condition and so are his master and mistress, the Arthur Wilsons. They don't know what to do about him. He used to be the funniest dog that ever walked the earth, a born comedian. A dire calamity has befallen him. He lost the use of both hind legs, now hopelessly paralyzed. It is pitiful to see him trying to drag himself by his front legs.

This is all the more frightfully sad because Shiner was the most proudly independent dog that ever walked. Never cringed or fawned or tried to suck up to people, or climb in their arms or laps. He was a broadly grinning, genial, comical dog, but very much the lone wolf.

Now he is reduced to a shadow of himself and it makes everyone sick at heart. He was so jaunty and amusing that it used to cheer me just to hear the tinkle of his license plate going down the street by my house. He was so absurd. But no more. Since this calamity befell him his face has shrunk so that his head is falling through his collar. He can't eat. He shivers. He lies in blankets all day. He is in pain. The Vet here said it was kidneys. The Vet can do no more. This is why I write you frantically in case you would know what to suggest. I will prevail on the Wilsons not to kill him until we hear from you. We were talking about it in front of him when he looked at me in that way a dog does that is so awful, so excruciating. So I felt I must take action. It is a matter of life and death for him. Anne.

❖

# BULLFIGHTING AND RODEO RIDERS

**R**obert Graves the poet, who lives in Majorca wrote an article on Bullfighting. He entitles it: "Enter the Leaden Age of Bullfighting." It contains some startling revelations. Apparently, Manolete, the national hero of the bullfighting arena, had the horns of the bulls he was to meet cut, just before the combat, in such a way that the bull would be out of focus in his lunges. In other instances, bulls were kept corralled so that they could not exercise, or fed constipating fodder before the fight, or crippled by picadors using illegally long lances.

This is so interesting to me—the brave bullfighter having the horns shortened so that he is quite safe! It bears out my contention that all cruelty to animals in hunting and "sport" and athletic contests like bullfighting and rodeo is *always* accompanied by an especial cowardice on the part of the human being, in this most unfair contest.

And this sets me thinking of Ernest Hemingway and the great admiration that Americans have for his writing and spirit. Now from the earliest childhood I have loved heroes, brave men, fighters, Vikings: there is Sir Tristram du Lyonesse, and Roland, Olav Trygveson and Joan of Arc, Lord Nelson and Garibaldi. But at the same time since I was six years old I have felt nothing but indignation and contempt for hunters and sportsmen. For how could what they do be anything but the quintessence of cowardice, having every advantage of brains, weapons, mechanisms and with all the carefully planned personal safety on the side of the hunter and sportsman.

And this public adulation of Hemingway is based—I could always see with half an eye—on the assumption that he is describing grand, he-man bravery and daring. In his book about bull-fighting, *Death In The Afternoon*, there is the long-drawn-out murder of the frantic and exhausted bull; and there are those poor aged old horses, blind-folded, so as to be entirely manageable over and above their decrepitude, and gored again and again and their entrails dragging on the bloody ground and sometimes stuffed back and sewn in in order to continue, and the immense crowd in its handsomest clothes cheering madly for the brave humans in the arena who were carrying on this comfortably arranged slaughter. A great drama of courage and will? Nope. Not to me.

And I never could see the "courage" in rodeo riders. The horses, if you want to know, have a wire twisted around their testicles so that they are mad with pain. It makes them buck. The brave cowboy sits on the insanely suffering horse, flapping his legs and hat. It is true, he *may* get tossed off and be hurt. But also remember that he does it for the possibility of a very large prize of money, many thousands of dollars, which may soften the possible thump.

Then there are those contests where they rope calves, those daring Western Heroes! The frightened little calf scampers out of the pen. The cowboy chases on horseback and lassoes the soft little calf. There is an utterly terrible jerk—the horse stopping sharply—on the rope around the calf's neck, a jerk that only a hanged man experiences. Quite often the calf's neck is broken. The cowboy ferociously lashes the feeble trembling legs together and swaggers off to the acclaim of thousands. Perhaps the most angering thing in these exhibitions—man cruelly conquering beast—is the entire absence of fairness, of chivalry, of knightliness, of grandeur, of grace, of *noblesse oblige.*

◆

# "THE LEAST OF THESE"

The Christian church—I mean the institution, not the religion—has never been very good to animals. There have been exceptions in individuals, like St. Francis and St. Columba, and St. Hugh. But they have no influence at all on the official position. Lecky, the historian, wrote 80 years ago: "The animal world being altogether external to the scheme of redemption, was regarded as beyond the range of duty, and the belief that we have any kind of obligation to its members has never been inculcated—has never, I believe, been even admitted—by Catholic theologians."

This statement is borne out by the words of the Catholic Dictionary which says of the animals: "They are not created by God. They have no rights. The brutes are made for men . . . who has the same right over them as he has over plants and stones. He may kill them for his food; and if it is lawful to destroy them for food, and this without strict necessity, it must also be lawful to put them to death, or to inflict pain on them for any good and reasonable end, such as the promotion of man's knowledge, health, etc. or even for the purpose of recreation."

I have found, to my dismay and astonishment, this very same opinion among devout Protestants. But Mohammed had some humane legislation on behalf of the animals. In the record of his life it says: "His humanity extended itself to the lower creation. He forbade the employment of towing birds as targets for marksmen." (I think of the turkey-shoots we have, the hundreds of turkeys pinned in boxes their long necks straining out, and the hundreds of idiotic Minnesota men and boys shooting them from close at hand on a happy Sunday morning.) "When some of Mohammed's followers had set fire to an anthill, he compelled them to extinguish it. Foolish acts of cruelty which were connected with old superstitions or were merely customary, were swept away by him. He said again and again, "Truly there are rewards for our doing good to dumb animals."

And Buddha had his great commandment: "One should not destroy life." And the first of his Ten Precepts was: "I take the vow not to destroy life." This was part of his doctrine that all life is one and inter-related, and it resembles Jesus' idea that what we do to anyone—"the least of these" (I think he meant even pheasants and fish and wild elephants and laboratory rats) we do it to ourselves and to Christ, too.

And involved in this is the idea that there is an ineffable Justice in Eternity that none of us can duck, so that whatever cruelty we inflict, either consciously or unwittingly, we ourselves will suffer in the same degree whether in this life or some other one.

I believe it. It will not be a matter of vengeance or punishment exactly but in order to make us understand what the fright and suffering are that we have inflicted. This is the only way we can widen our compassion and enlarge our insect souls. My dear and wonderful teacher and friend, Lauritz Rusten, was a theosophist and believed, like Pythagoras and Plato, in the transmigration of souls. He thought there was a possibility that the Nazis with their hideous obsessed cruelty might once have been animal souls suffering dreadfully and voicelessly from men.

In the middle ages there were many beautiful stories about the stag. When hunting, St. Hubert is said to have been confronted by a milk-white stag which bore a crucifix between its horns. The vision made it clear to him that in hunting the stag, he was adding to the sufferings of Christ and he accordingly abandoned the chase once and for all. (Do you remember how year before last, up North, a snaggle-toothed, potato-nosed man with a bad complexion shot and killed a beautiful mysterious white stag? Everybody was mighty proud about it, and so was he, and his picture was in all the newspapers.)

St. Francis is said to have persuaded the wolf near Gubbio not to eat sheep. He also used to say: "If I could only be presented to the Emperor, I would pray him for the love of God and for me, to issue an edict prohibiting anyone from catching my sisters, the larks." Leonardo da Vinci used to buy and free the birds that the Italian boys tied to strings and played with. Pythagoras sometimes purchased from fishermen all the fish in the net that he might set them free. (My dear old friend, Tom Dillon, used to say he could not bear fishing—"Here you invite the fish to lunch with you and then pull him up and eat him!")

Then in the last century came Darwin and his theory of Evolution. It horrified and angered and upset Christians dreadfully. Yet Darwin's Evolution—seeming to show that we are closely related to all the animals and even descended from them—did more to start up ideas of mercy and gentleness to animals than all our earlier, anthropomorphic Christian conceitedness, i.e. that we, humans, are God's very special pets and dears and that he doesn't care a button about anything else.

The notion that all life is one, that the suffering and blocking and cold violence to a rat's soul is a suffering and blocking and cold violence to All Creation, is expressed in William Blake's beautiful couplets:

> The wild Deer wandering here and there
> Free the Human Heart from care.
> The Beggar's Dog, the Widow's Cat —
> Feed them and you shall grow fat.
> The wanton Boy who kills the Fly
> Shall feel the Spider's Enmity.
> A Skylark wounded on the Wing,
> A Cherubim doth cease to sing.

❖

# "Humane" Societies

t is interesting to compare the open and public cruelty of Rome to animals with our own secret and hidden cruelty. Perhaps it is a moral advance that we cannot bear to know what we are doing. But I don't know. Hypocrisy (like our present one about killing in war, the unctuous notion that if we can kill and bomb enough people it isn't really murder but commendable) may be worse than honest open cruelty because there is less chance of self-horror, of changing and getting better. George Bernard Shaw said that today the commandment, "Do unto others as you would be done by," must be enlarged to: "Is this that I enjoy doing for twenty minutes injuring, exploiting, killing anything alive?"

The games in the Colosseum in Rome were attended by 80,000 people. Such a gathering, assembled to enjoy suffering and death, must have been a fearful sight. There is the story of Saint Augustine's friend, Alypius, who was taken to the games against his will by a number of fellow students. At first Alypius shut his eyes and refused to look, but hearing a sudden shout, he opened his eyes to see a gladiator beaten to his knees. His heart was filled with pity for the man. Then as the death blow was delivered he "drank down a kind of savageness" and sat there, open-eyed and initiated.

This is just what happens to young high school children when they are experimenting with wretched animals in biology laboratory—the sudden "initiation" from childhood's natural kindness and sweetness into obtuse coarseness and hard-heartedness, into "being scientific," which of course lasts all one's life.

With the exception of Seneca, not one of the writers of antiquity, not even the kindly Horace and the gentle Pliny, condemned the degradation of the amphitheatre. And the organization that fed the Colosseum was enormous (like our own procuring of cats, dogs, rabbits, monkeys by the millions for the research laboratories). All over the world the Roman Empire officials trapped and bought wild animals for the arena and the number of noble beasts who died to please the mob is said to have almost exterminated certain species from the Roman world. It is said that the elephant disappeared from North Africa, the hippopotamus from Nubia, and the lion from Mesopotamia.

Long before the Colosseum was built, this slaughter of animals used to be the prelude to the combat of gladiators. One display occupied the morning and the other the afternoon. During a show attended by Cicero in 55 B.C. six hundred lions were slain and 18 elephants tried to break down the barriers in an attempt to escape. The only animal that aroused any compassion in the heart of the Roman mob was the elephant. Cicero says that this was due to a notion that it had something in common with mankind; and the Elder Pliny says that these animals, which had been procured by Pompey, "implored the compassion of the multitude by attitudes which surpass description, and with a kind of lamentation bewailed their unhappy fate."

Unfortunately, such pity did not go very deep and for centuries to come the mob continued to watch the slaughter of elephants and every other kind of animal. The world had to wait for Christianity—passionately sensitive, implacably sincere and true to its precepts in those days—to have the courage and decency to close such places.

And this Roman cruelty to animals extended to human beings, as all cruelty does, a kind of pestilence, infecting and hardening and stupefying everybody who comes in contact with it. We are apt to think that crucifixion was something uniquely dreadful and unspeakable that happened only to Jesus. Historians and archaeologists say that there were ten thousand crucifixions a year in that part of Asia Minor ruled by Rome. And there was a very popular play in Rome that became a kind of record-making "Broadway success" for two hundred years: It always ended by having a live criminal crucified upside down. It made an unfailing hit.

The American Journal of Physiology reports (cheerfully) 30 dogs beaten to death in a medical experiment laboratory. From 750 to 1000 blows were inflicted on each thigh. The dogs lived from 50 minutes to 9 hours and 50 minutes. Not all the dogs were anesthetized and anesthetics wear off quickly. Clinical findings from this experiment: "Dogs thirsty and vomited." (How grand! How important!)

Over eight million animals are cut up alive for experimental purposes every year in the United States. That is bad enough. But here comes what is worse—the hypocrisy! The Minnesota Humane Society, the Animal Rescue League, and countless others of the largest, most prosperous, most heavily endowed "humane" societies in the United States have become procurers of animals for the laboratories.

How do you like it?

❖

# THE VICTIMS

I have been reading again *Jean Christophe*. In those hours when he was weak with suffering, torn alive away from life, devoid of human egoism, he saw the victims of men, the field of battle in which man triumphed in the bloody slaughter of all other creatures: and his heart was filled with pity and horror. Even in the days when he had been happy he had always loved the beasts: he had never been able to bear cruelty towards them: he had always had a detestation of sport, which he had never dared to express for fear of ridicule; perhaps he even had never dared to admit to himself; but his feeling of revulsion had been the secret cause of dislike he had had for certain men. He could not think of the animals without shuddering in anguish. He looked into the eyes of the beasts and saw there a soul like his own, a soul which could not speak—but the eyes cried for it:

"What have I done to you?

Why do you hurt me?"

He could not bear to see the most ordinary sights that he had seen hundreds of times—a calf crying in a wicker pen, with its big protruding eyes, with their bluish whites and pink lids, and white lashes, its curly tufts on its forehead, its purple snout, its knock-kneed legs—a lamb being carried by a peasant with its four legs tied together, hanging head down, trying to hold its head up, moaning like a child, bleating and lolling its gray tongue—fowls huddled together in a basket—the distant squeals of a pig being bled to death—a fish being cleaned on the kitchen table. . . The nameless tortures which men inflict on such innocent creatures made his heart ache.

Grant animals a ray of reason, imagine what a frightful nightmare the world is to them: a dream of cold-blooded men, blind and deaf, gutting them into pieces, cooking them alive, sometimes laughing at them and their contortions as they writhe in agony. Is there anything more atrocious among the cannibals of Africa? To a man whose mind is free there is something even more intolerable in the sufferings of animals than in the sufferings of men. For with the latter, it is at least admitted that suffering is evil and that the man who causes it is a criminal. But thousands of animals are uselessly butchered every day without a shadow of remorse. If any man were to refer to it, he would be thought ridiculous. And that is the unpardonable crime. That alone is justification of all that men may suffer. It cries vengeance upon all the human race. If God exists and tolerates it, it cries vengeance upon God. If there exists a good God, then even the most humble of living things must be saved. If God is good only to the strong, if there is no justice for the weak and lowly, for the poor creatures who are offered up as a sacrifice to humanity, then there is no such thing as goodness, no such thing as justice.

A Minneapolis woman named Mrs. Edgar Brooks shot a 1400-pound moose in Montana. There is a picture of her in the Sunday newspaper, very proud of her corpse. She wears glasses and seems to be quite a homely woman, with small shoulders and large waist measure. I mean there is no apparent strength and agility. Her rifle is very fine. Mr. Brooks and Mrs. Brooks (her name is Allie) drew a moose permit and—they are proud to say—hers was one of only two drawn by Minnesotans. They said: "The moose was trotting across a small meadow. It was a beautiful sight!" So Allie shot five times. "And the moose never broke his stride. Then it just sank down at the edge of the timber and never even kicked." Mr. Brooks said that all five shots of his wife's .280 Remington rifle hit just behind the moose's front shoulder. "You could cover all of the holes with your hand. It was some mighty fine shooting."

Allie said: "I wasn't very nervous." (Brave Allie!) "I just wanted that moose—" (The usual paucity of ideas.) "I kept on shooting when it didn't go down. I'd never have lived it down if I had missed my chance."

The newspaper says that ten thousand United States

hunters, "an all-time record"—are hunting around Rainy Lake and Fort Francis. They have gone up there in 1300 cars and average four to a car. The season opened Monday and lasts for three months. Dr. Mark Greer of Illinois bagged four in one day. Dr. Doug Moberly of Waterloo, Iowa, had three before 8 a.m. all within a few yards of his tent. There is such a swelling population of campers and hunters every year that now you can see their tents all over, as you go along any lake shore. It is really very comfortable and cozy for them now, and more and more so every year. The U. S. Customs at International Falls, Minnesota is busy checking dead moose. They count more than a hundred moose corpses daily. It is a great triumph.

Five vivisectors of the University Medical School and the University Hospital report that their experiments indicate that "cortisone administration to dogs DOES enhance peptic ulcer formations." They juggled the intestines of the animals by transplants and 3 or 4 days later injected them with 200 milligrams of cortisone daily for at least two months during which period the painful ulceration developed. The dogs, then—most of them—died. The U. S. Public Health Service and Donald J. Cowling and Jay and Rose Phillips Fund for Surgical Research financed these activities. Jay and Rose and Donald should go over and watch it all, the splendid progress made.

Minnesota experiments on animals is famous far and wide. A-V, the magazine of the American Anti-Vivisection Society (1903 Chestnut Street, Philadelphia. $1.00 a year), speaks of Dr. Maurice Visscher, of our University:

Dr. Visscher seems to have conveniently forgotten some of his own past history. He has made some very strong and positive statements about vivisection and the treatment of laboratory animals. For instance, when he lashed out recently at an inference someone made to cruelty in laboratories, he said: "I have employed thousands of animals for medical research in my life. Kindness to animals is the rule in all laboratories." (*Minneapolis Star*, April 3, 1961.)

In order to refute this statement there could be no better examples than those found in the laboratories of his own University (which includes of course the Mayo's at Rochester which is connected with it.) As an example: The experiments of Bollman, Grindlay, Flock, and Mann on the livers of dogs, or on dogs in which the liver has been totally removed. Dogs without livers are miserable creatures. They usually do not eat, become rapidly emaciated, weak, and comatose. They die in about five days.

Bollman also experimented with making what is called an "Eck fistula dog." This procedure shunts the blood away from the liver. In a recent article, Bollman gives the following description of the victims of this:

"Dogs unable to eat: emaciated, nervous, restless and excitable ... Turning back and forth in the cage, trying to climb walls and chewing on everything near them. Respiration was increased and convulsions were frequent." There was a "generalized weakness" with the dogs having to "... drag themselves around by their front legs. If the animals attempted to walk, definite ataxia was observed and they would fall ... Frequently they became blind and lost the sensation of pain, while consciousness and hearing remained."

These dogs cannot eat meat, so the vivisectors gave them meat powder and concentrates so they could observe the convulsions and sometimes death, which followed. Some dogs were given whole blood by gastric tube and all were given constant tests and subjected to many experimental procedures.

Now, experiments on the Eck fistula dogs are still popular in many Universities and yet the tirelessly experimenting Dr. Bollman says:

"In the 83 years since it was first reported, the Eck fistula has been reasonably successful in hiding its secrets ... It offers a fertile field for reinvestigation of many previous studies." (Five hundred, a thousand more dogs! This is written up in the *Physiological Reviews*, Vol. 41, No. 3, July, 1961.)

Would Dr. Visscher consider these studies in line with his claim that all laboratory dogs are treated with kindness?

And where was Dr. Visscher when five hundred and sixty-six inoffensive rabbits were beaten to death in the Noble collip drum? Oddly enough a man with the name of "Noble" invented it. It is a rotating drum that slams animals that are shut inside it into the walls of its interior. These walls often have raised rough sides to make injury more certain. The intestines of the victims are literally scrambled; often lungs are ruptured; hearts, livers and spleens also. Teeth are broken and bones fractured. (Pictures are on file of the bloody viscera of such animals. *Fed. Proc.* Vol. 18, Abstr. 1909, for rabbit experiment).

Has Dr. Visscher forgotten his own early experiments? Blinding of mice—inducing congestive heart failure in dogs? Dogs were so miserable they could not lie down; gasping for breath, legs swollen with fluid; abdomens the same.

These dogs may have had clean drinking dishes and a clean cage. Maybe Dr. Visscher put a hand in and patted on the head, saying, "Good doggie." That is what the average vivisector means when he speaks of kindness to animals.

A published experiment in which Dr. Visscher participated at the University of Minnesota, involved methods of slowly choking dogs to death by interrupting air flow to the lungs and by ingestion of salt water. (Pulmonary edema or swelling of the fluid-filled lung). (*American Journal Physiol.* Vol. 161, No. 2, May, 1950. pp. 336-341).

In the English magazine, *Animals' Defender*, there is an account of the great Scottish surgeon (an anti-vivisectionist) Robert Lawson Tait. A vigorous English society called Science Without Cruelty has established the Lawson Tait Memorial Fund to stimulate medical research without using live animals. It offers Nobel-type prizes up to $15,000 each year for work so conducted and brought to a successful conclusion.

And in the *Animals' Defender* there is an interesting article: It seems an eminent physicist-astronomer and space-explorer says there are probably in the Universe beings much higher, brighter, far superior to ourselves. "They may want to use people here on earth only for food."

It's a nice thought. It should be turned over in the head thoughtfully a few times.

# THE MEDICAL SCIENTIST'S WORST ENEMY

**⌗**

**S**helley: "To live as if to love and live were one."

Milton· "So spake the Fiend, and with necessity the Tyrant's plea, excused his devilish deed."

Mr. E. J. Rose of Edmonton, Canada, has written an article in A-V, "Vivisection's Betrayal of Science." Herewith, I tell what he says:

The practice of vivisection is the medical scientist's worst enemy, for in his wholesale devotion to vivisection, the scientist has been decoyed from his proper objectives. The ten thousand or more deformed infants that resulted from the drug, Thalidomide, is a judgment on the slaughter of animals in the laboratories of the world. Mr. Fred Mysers, director of the Humane Society of the United States, said the number of animals being used—"which means being killed"—has reached 300 million a year and is expected to reach a billion by 1970.

New modern scientific investigation is ruled by three major forces or ideas: 1. Economic necessity. 2. A religious faith in science as an absolute. 3. The doctrine of survival at all costs. All three are demonic and in opposition to both humanistic and Christian world views.

To begin with, let us examine the science of economics. Having an easy and cheap means of procuring animals, science is able to solve its economic problems at the very same time as it is able to satisfy the need of the scientists for esteem. Monkey business is, to paraphrase the words of the head of a well-known pharmaceutical firm, good business. Now science, as economics, may be examined under three important categories: 1. Federal and foundation grants. (This is the researcher's golden egg.) 2. Academic and professional reputation and advancement. 3. National drug monopolies and international cartels. (Their price-fixing practices are well known even in the United States.)

Just to show you the financial windfall that can come to any researcher, I should like to cite the case of a doctor of vivisection in California who has received more than three-quarters of a million dollars over a period of four years to study "Experimental Arteriosclerosis." (He induces the disease into countless dogs and other animals, in order to observe it.)

You can imagine what this kind of windfall can do for the doctor, for his academic advancement and his professional reputation. Most of the articles in medical and scientific journals today are written because either you must publish something or not survive academically. "Publish or perish," is the doctrine.

The advancement of a man's career because of his publications may be a good enough way to measure him in the areas of scholarship but it cannot be defended when it involves the senseless slaughter and indescribable agony inflicted on animals. And you can understand why in this pressure "to publish" and the craving for "esteem," certain experiments are conducted over and over again, with only the slightest, if any, alteration. It is not difficult to understand why experiments which have been proven to be pointless are not abandoned. Oh no! Again and again, the same old thing, with an infinitesimal variant and—*with no result of the slightest value.*

> *"Pointless, and arm-in-arm with pointlessness*
> *I pace and pace the streets of the Baboon."*

The doctors and institutions get huge, colossal grants of money. Their reputations build up vast heights although the general public never knows what they have done or accomplished. (Much less do they know what happens in the laboratories.) You can see how this becomes a business in itself. Later, of course, the general practitioner must take on faith the drugs passed on to him by the pharmaceutical houses. (These have the biggest laboratories and the needed University connections.)

The individual doctor is in no position to test these drugs. And besides, he has been schooled to trust the laboratory that has produced them. We are all—you and I—subjected to the advertising of the drug manufacturers who sell their medicines as if they were soap powders. And the object of all this pressure on the consumer is the same, i.e. to make money, to make business better. The patient accepts, as the doctor does, any drug which has been prescribed for him. (Thalidomide was one). Both the patient and the doctor must believe, must have faith.

The question of faith brings us to the second of the demonic forces that rule scientific investigation, academic reputation and advancement. In the minds of most men, women and children, science can do no wrong. The irony of this! People have more faith in science than man has ever had in any religious idea. And they cling to this idea in the face of horrors unsurpassed in any other age. With the fall-out, the Bombs, the weapons of war, the wanton experiments on *all* life, see how destruction and pain and death have become accepted—indeed, admirable—goals.

Science and vivisection make no appeal to a theological idea, much less a political one. You can argue with a theologian or a politician, but doctors are sacrosanct. They *know*: you do not. Science has its mystique much more powerful than any religion active today. And it is a law unto itself. Its own faith in itself is surpassed only by the belief it demands from others. What does all this amount to? There is only one answer: survival, survival at all costs. Economic survival, professional survival, racial survival, but above all, the survival of vivisection itself. These are the aims of the vivisector.

Now vivisection is not the same thing as scientific progress. There *is* such a thing as scientific progress. But this wholesale dedication of scientists to vivisection, which is the easy and cheap way, actually prevents them from scientific progress, for true progress is difficult and requires genius and imagination in its devoted workers. But you see it does not pay for these esteem-seeking scientists to find *other* ways than those which are convenient, and which insure their survival. It does not *pay*, of course, in any way.

When the Doctrine of Survival is well established, as it is now, it is possible to get pleasantly detached and abstract about the whole business of life. Cruelty is essentially an impersonal business. One need not bring the conscience into it. I think now of how they recently revised the Bible and the commandment, "Thou shalt not kill" to read "Thou shalt not murder." Kill all you want to—soldiers, revolutionists, Russians, Laotians, Vietnamese, Cubans, American Marines, animals—but be very very careful not to commit a murder. The consciences of all of us are now totally, and impenetrably, in the clear ("Only the fittest survive," we say in our non-thinking complacency). And it does not matter what men live by just so long as they live, i.e. survive.

A vivisector has no reverence for life. He is indifferent. Why should he be otherwise? His training has made him what he is. Only the most thoroughly objective kind of mind (a hateful kind of mind!) can destroy another living creature that holds its life by the same fragile tenure as man does, and *justify* it. And this is interesting: Though we often worry about the military and political effects of atomic tests, we seem to care little about the vivisectional character of it. When whole cities and now the whole world has become one gigantic laboratory, I think it is time that thinking human beings should examine the prime cause of this arrogant disregard for life.

I suggest that this prime cause is science's conscienceless devotion to vivisection and other forms of animal and human experimentation. For vivisection's concern is mainly for its own survival, and not for the questionable good it may produce. The medical journals show this themselves. Very little *results* from vivisection but *more* vivisection. This is not unlike the atomic tests. In essence the aim of vivisection is to perpetuate itself.


*Post-Operative Dog Room,*
*Eastern Medical School,* 1961.
Many dogs were too sick to rise, some had had two operations. One heart surgical case was emaciated, had a tremor and lacked one eye from which red flesh exuded. Dr.____ first explained the dog's condition as brain surgery,

but later decided the dog had lost his eye and developed chorea before coming to. Apparently this did not deter its use for heart surgery. The dog drank water almost continuously. No attendants were in any of the dog rooms. Asked if dogs as sick as those we had seen can get up for hosing out the cages, Dr.____ said they could. He said that none of the dogs we saw had been given any sedation. This institution received over $7,000,000 last year from the United States Public Health Service.

A *Western Medical School*, 1963.
One hundred or more dogs in windowless dark room which had just been cleaned. Dr.____ admitted that virus infections often spread in this room. Dogs too sick to get up had been hosed down with the cages. An old half-blind spaniel was soaking wet, lying trembling on the bottom of the cage. It had had major surgery. Strong dogs were barking, begging for attention. The noise was intense, the air overladen with moisture.

We were also shown the elegantly appointed meeting room next door to the huge operation room for surgical experiments on dogs. The contrast between the waste space in meeting room and the over-crowding in the dog room was shocking. The United States Public Health Service grants to this medical school were over $4,000,000.

A *Middlewestern Medical School*, 1960.
Dr. ____, the head of the animal laboratory, is a recipient of over $60,000 annually from the Public Health Service grant. He repeatedly misrepresented facts and broke promises about animals and their care. He flatly refused to supply water to guinea pigs, took an infant guinea pig up and threw it back in the cage, remarking "how healthy it is." The little animal, injured, lay struggling on its side, unable to regain its feet.


Love God and all His Creatures and live in the Truth.

❖

# FIREFLIES

n *This Week* magazine an article tells how the chemical companies are paying children to collect fireflies: "To keep the nation's fireflies burning in myriads of laboratories now clamoring for them, the Schwartz BioResearch firm of Orangeburg, New York, has been quietly organizing children in the country in bug brigades. The rate this summer for firefly tails shipped in dry ice has been 50 cents per hundred. This year's quota of a million neon tails has been surpassed, thanks to a bonanza harvest of children living around Oak Ridge, Tennessee. In two weeks the children of Oak Ridge bagged 455,000 pyrotechnical bugs and air-expressed them to the firefly tail headquarters at Schwartz's lab. The Oak Ridge firefly crusade, sparked by banners, radio announcements and articles in the newspapers, resulted in a $2,000 haul for the kids and their group leaders."

So there is another way of making monsters out of nice little children besides the tranquilizer drug, Thalidomide!

Lovely fireflies! More beautiful and beneficent on summer nights than stars and music, than clouds and fountains, than flowers and meteors! Our remote ancestors, so close to Nature and who were still capable of love and admiration, and who were charged with "the Poetic Genius which is the Lord," as William Blake expressed it, believed that fireflies were celestial and from the Land of Faery, as indeed they are.

But our modern and most unpoetic scientists, fiends in business suits I think of them, or I think of them as those Niebelungen dwarves in Wagner's operas, ugly and grubbing for gold, dyspeptic and sedentary, myopic under the fluorescent lighting, and air-conditioned, and with sinus trouble, and staring through their bifocals at slides with germ smears on them—these ugly beings have come to the conclusion (and its a chance to make a million!) that what makes the fireflies glow is "biochemical ATP," which seems to provide energy for muscular contractions. Our experiments are helping to explore mysteries of muscular dystrophy and certain disease viruses. . ."

And so they will now accomplish three things: 1. Make monsters of the children. 2. Manufacture a highly commercial drug which *seems* to alleviate (for a brief time) muscular dystrophy. 3. Dispense a drug to the public which will soon bring about inexplicable new afflictions and weird symptoms that are much worse, and all these politely accounted for by the doctors as "side effects," and ranging from cataracts to cancer.

As for the tranquilizer, Thalidomide, made in Germany and deforming unborn children (there are still more than two million pills scattered around in the United States) my question is: Why anyone would be fool enough, a feeble, leaner-on-the-doctors, a credulous, lazy weakling and hypochondriac sap enough to *take* a tranquilizer in the first place!

George Bernard Shaw said: "It is ridiculous to expect that an experimenter who commits acts of diabolical cruelty for the sake of what he calls science will tell the truth about the results."

William Butler Yeats said: "The best lack all conviction while the worst are full of passionate intensity."

◆

# How to Cut the Throat Properly

I took over a Sunday school class at the Unitarian Church for five weeks. The regular teacher was ill. I was supposed to be trying to teach children to write. ("Creative writing" is the phrase, for some reason pretentious, repugnant to me). Beautiful enchanting children! From nine years to twelve. I had forgotten how adorable children are. Those in my family have grown up.

In my first lesson I asked them if they knew the verse, "Mary had a little lamb." Yes indeed! They all knew it. I told them (surprising!) that it was a quatrain in trochaic tetrameter. We were all to write our own quatrain in that same meter. Say like this:

*I had a little pony*
*His bangs hung in his eyes,*
*And when I kissed his rubber nose*
*He didn't seem surprised.*

One little girl, Sally, seemed to like me especially. Oh such a little girl! A small eleven: round, blazing hazel eyes, brown hair curling to the shoulders and piled under the chin; a wild forelock; a short nose and a wild horizontal smile; a winking dimple one inch northeast of the mouth. She wrote in a large vigorous hand and very copiously on both sides of the page. (I gave them all A's—a large sprawling A on every paper.)

After the poem-writing I asked around the class what each one liked, what seemed exciting, interesting. What did each one like to have, or to be, or to become?

One child said that she did not know anything she liked particularly. I said: "Why I bet I can name ten things you are absolutely wild about." And did so: "A tiger. To tame wild horses. A revolver. A diamond necklace. To be an explorer in a haunted forest. To be a sea captain. To inherit a thousand-acre farm and run it." And so on. Yes! Her eyes flashed. She was crazy about them all!

Then I asked Sally: "What do you like to do? What do you think is exciting?"

"To herd deer."

"To herd deer? That sounds odd. How do you do that?"

It seems her father takes her up in the north woods and she disappears into the thicket and chases wild deer toward him and then he shoots them with his bow and arrow. My face changed, a wince of distress. And her jovial happy face immediately echoed mine—a pang!

"Oh," I said, "that's kind of hard on the deer, isn't it? Does he kill them right away or just wound them?"

She said that sometimes it is just awful: "The poor deer drags for miles and miles and there is blood over everything. . ."

Poor Sally. Her feelings were sadly mixed (she is very fond of her father) and we changed the subject gently. Later she told me that her father teaches psychology at the University. Another learned man inculcating schizophrenia—that is to say dry-heartedness, into a wonderful radiant, wildly kind little girl.

My October A-V came. It is published monthly by the American Anti-Vivisection Society. (One dollar a year; 1903 Chestnut Street, Philadelphia. A wonderful magazine!)

There is the problem of scientific experiments in schools. Mrs. Leroy J. Ellis of the Pennsylvania Society for the Prevention of Cruelty to Animals said that cruelty not only occurred in classroom experiments but in the so-called "science-fairs" put on by the schools. In one school some pupils caught a cat, killed it, skinned it and mounted the skeleton "to fulfill a science assignment."

In the March issue, 1962 of *Science Education*, page 156, there is an article entitled: *Sixth Graders Dissect Chicken*. The article is written by W. Ray Rucker, the Dean of the School of Education of East Texas State College. He said:

"Two of the girls in the dissecting group joined to write a comprehensive narrative report of the dissection operation."

(These are Sixth Grade children, about twelve). Here is an excerpt:

"Mrs. Finley (the teacher) showed James how to cut the throat properly. Finally James caught on and we were getting down to business. James cut Slick-Chick's throat and we held him down on the grass until he bled to death. It didn't take long."

◆

# ⚔ SPECULATIONS: ⚔ SPIRITUAL AND PHILOSOPHICAL

## WHAT DO I BELIEVE?

The most important thing anyone can learn to do is to reconcile selflessness with a tremendous belief in oneself. This is the way I try to do it: I think people confuse the Human ego and the Divine one. But you cannot have enough of the latter. The Human ego is conceit and obtuseness to others and it is static: "Look at me and see how remarkable I am!" The Divine ego is an eternally-moving-onward stream which says: "I am incalculably mysterious and wonderful and this is what I think and believe and care about, and tomorrow it will be something different and better I hope. And now tell me what is in YOU for that will help me to understand everything better."

*And that is why those gloomy, dolefully religious people depress me who go down into the catacombs instead of coming up into "God's sweet air" as the Irish poet said.*

Now this is my religious belief and there is a kind of logic in it. It is simple and childish, but I will put it down just the same. And just when I shrink to think how unsound it is, how without the slightest proof or foundation in fact, how superstitious, I began to think that perhaps Whitehead and Eddington and Sir James Jean have not worked out anything more likely to be true. But I don't think I am superstitious. Superstition means that one has a fixity of belief, some stereotyped notion (always based on fear). But my belief is never fixed, stereotyped, but a kind of moving open-mindedness, "The only thing displeasing to God is unbelief," says William Blake, and I seem to know what he means.

*What do I believe then? That we live forever. Some people are less good than others because they are, so to speak, still in the third grade. This is an explanation that makes it easy for me to forgive them (figuring that I am about in the fourth grade), for I would like to help them pass to the next grade. I believe perfection is implicit in all, but it takes time for it to evolve. But why fret then? God can take His time. He can wait. Time is nothing to Him.*

I have found that the superficial conscious will, jerked about between breakfast and lunch, does not do much good in expanding our spirit. But solitude and imagination do. I do not believe in grim "duty" or "discipline" because this, too, is living by a stereotyped rule and so it usually forces and drives up people's true conscience. And so much of this "duty" is living up to OTHER people's consciences. That is the reason for the cruelty and meagerness of some people, people who really wanted to drink and eat and make love and needed to for their own development, but who, trying grimly and dutifully to live up to a conscience higher than their own, and making everybody else do likewise, injured their own souls very badly.

A Shelley or a St. Francis, with a lofty sensitive conscience and life-conception, can be an ascetic and shed goodness because he does not do so from duty, but from his own lighted imagination and conscience.

*I think God is a person and not a law. Because you cannot love a law. And anyway the personality of a mouse is greater than any law or abstraction or mathematical formula ever devised.*

I believe in wonderful egotism, in being "kingy," that the malaise of the world is so-called modesty, usually a form of conceit. I believe that we should all have a reckless, indomitable, arrogant, joyful blaze of self-esteem, self-trust, self-belief. You cannot have enough pride or egotism or energy or bravery, but it must be centrifugal (generous) and not centripetal (greedy).

I believe that we live after death and again and again, not in the memory of our children or as a mulch for trees and flowers, however poetic that may be, but looking passionately and egocentrically out of our eyes.

◆

# WALTER RUSSELL, THE SCULPTOR

A remarkable man lectured at the School of Divine Science. This was Walter Russell, the sculptor. He is a broad-shouldered man, 75 years old, with a white beard like Sir Thomas Beecham's and the faintest suggestion of spikes on his mustache give him a spirited, duelist look.

He told his idea of what Life and Death are, how it came to him in a spiritual crisis resembling that of Swedenborg. "In May, 1921, God took me up on a high mountain of inspiration. A brilliant flash like lightning severed my bodily sensations from my soul and I found myself freed and wholly in the Universe of Light which is God."

He was born in Boston. He went to school until ten and then had a job as a cash boy in a drygoods store at $2.50 a week. He was a church organist at 13 and then he could afford to go to art school. One summer he became a bell-boy in a hotel. The salary was 8 dollars a month and he was told bell-boys got $100 in tips. But when the first tip was offered he could not take it. Then he had a little vision. "I'll be the only bell-boy in existence who never took a tip; and the best bell-boy the world ever knew." From that moment he ran his legs off, got up at 5 in the morning to get cow's milk for a baby. And so on.

The guests were overwhelmed, invited him to dinner, to yachting trips. He had five offers of legal adoption from wealthy families and at the end of the season he had sold $850 worth of pictures. "I have faith that anything comes to one who trusts the help of the Universal Intelligence inside—so long as you always give more to others than you expect for yourself."

Then he was a war correspondent for *Collier's*, an architect designing the Hotel des Artistes, the Hotel Pierre in New York; a famous figure-skater. At fifty he won three prizes against competitors all under 30. He would ride black Arab stallions in

Central Park with President Theodore Roosevelt and bought 27 of them from Mr. Huntington for $50,000.

He says: "If you just hate to do a thing, that hatred develops body-destructive toxins and you become fatigued soon. You must love everything you must do. That will charge your body with life and keep you from fatigue." He says that he feels a sense of guilt in discovering the slightest fatigue because it tells him he has broken the "spiritual law."

"What is it that makes us say we are tired? It is an unbalance in the body. We have done something to unbalance the body that conducts the universal electric current which motivates it. And joy and happiness are the indicators of the balance."

He thinks that joy, ecstasy even, is the normal and true state for a fine mind and soul, and lack of joy means that we are injuring ourselves.

He says that Matter is just this: Waves of the motion of Light. Electricity manufactures all things (you and me, a tree, etc.) that are really just light in motion. "You pick up one of these products of wave-motion and say, 'This is an apple,' without the realization that a sudden withdrawal of the electric power that brought that state of motion into being would blow you and it into the equilibrium from which you were electrically assembled.

"And that is what radioactivity is: a quick return to the state of rest which underlies the spiritual and invisible universe. And that is what a flash of lightning is, while a flame is a slower return, or to decay is a still slower return."

As I understand it he seems to think God is this state of rest, of equilibrium to which we return, and then emerge again (living eternally), and it underlies all things and is Light. We are like a boy and girl on a teeter-totter. God is the fulcrum in the center, the state of all-powerful rest, and we come into existence by putting ourselves slightly out of balance and then striving to get back again. Yes, there are three things in the Universe: Rhythm, balance, interchange.

❖

# DR. HENRY M. SIMMONS

**M**y father came from Norway when he was 17, dug the Washington Avenue sewer and became a lawyer when he was 26. My mother was born in Ohio during the Civil War among Abolitionists rescuing runaway slaves. She went to high school in Minneapolis and although very poor, she had great beauty and style. After high school she taught sixth grade and years later, one of her pupils told me: "I was never bright until I was in your mother's class and I have been bright ever since."

My parents were political idealists, feminists, democrats. They wanted their children to be light-hearted and athletic, to live outdoors and eat oranges and apples. My mother thought the girls should not be the menials of the boys and so the boys made their own beds and the girls were on the football team in the pasture. She thought that if mothers were what they should be, surrounding their children with every freedom and happiness and cheerful intelligence, we would have the Millennium in one generation. She taught the baby how to hold and smooth the cat. She never cautioned us. We could walk endless miles in the country, swim across the lake, ride bareback. Our adventurousness was never quashed. She would have liked Blake's aphorism: "Prudence is a rich, ugly Old Maid courted by Incapacity."

My father as a small boy herded goats in the mountains in the province of Stavanger where Lutheranism was especially full of vengeful doom. He wrote:

"We really had much fun. Looking far away at the North Sea, what fancies of adventures! I recall only one drawback. That was toward the evening when my brother went out of sight to round up the herd, leaving me alone. Then I would feel the unusual colors in the sky were signals of the Day of Judgment approaching, as in Matthew 24:30. For the moment it made me repentant and pious but I was no sooner well home before I was as worldly as ever. It was as though someone in the house could stay the Day of Judgment."

This was the beginning of his impassioned critical search into Religious Orthodoxy to rescue himself and other poor Lutherans from fear of the Devil and Hell. It seemed to him an outrageous concept, ignorant and cruel—eighty-year old women who had never said "Boo!" to anyone, weeping in terror because they were going to Hell for their dreadful sins!

In this country he came upon what was called the Higher Criticism and Dr. Henry M. Simmons. My parents became Unitarians. Dr. Simmons was the most sincere and compassionate Christian but in his sermons he also talked about Darwin, Erasmus, Plato, about the accuracies of history and archeology. The church was on Mary Place just this side of Dayton's on what is now LaSalle. We drove down there every Sunday with our big horse, Lady Mane and the carriage, a lovely street under arching elms, the only noise the thudding of horses' hooves. It was a plump sturdy church of huge red stone blocks and a fat tower at one end. The sermons were wonderful, the utterance of a true poet and scholar; they might have been written by Coleridge. Our Credo then was: "The Fatherhood of God, the Leadership of Jesus, the Brotherhood of Man." Not a bad statement, it seems to me, though it has become more elaborate since then. There was Sunday School in the basement afterwards and you might get a gold star for enough attendance.

Dr. Simmons, so quiet, luminous, kind, had a military nose and a wide mustache. He was from Wisconsin, famous as a naturalist. He had walked hundreds of miles through the forest, like Wordsworth. His personal life, I am afraid, was very difficult and sad, a wife always ill, perhaps insane. His daughter was named Echo—long flowing garments, a cloud of pale hair and mysterious grey eyes. I thought she was a dryad, a wood nymph. They had a forlorn little house far, far out south, alone on a moor. Probably it was only as far away as Dupont and Lake Street.

My parents loved him dearly and my father wrote: "He is

probably better informed about science than anybody in the Northwest. . ." and added with ardent admiration, "His discourses show his unabounded admiration for every sincere religious belief."

In Dr. Simmons' book, *The Unending Genesis*, he wrote so tenderly and beautifully about the Book of Genesis—(usually a total absurdity, an asininity to scientists and more pedestrian Unitarians.) "Science," he said, "is not so much ruining the old story but enlarging it, replacing its beautiful poetic fancies by showing that its seven days did not end. All the work of the old legend is still before our eyes, not once along, but continually. We are learning to see all around us this more wonderful Genesis."

Being Unitarian children, we were not christened. There were four girls and a boy. They called him "Boy" and didn't bother to name him. Then another boy was born so they had to find a name—Sigurd. (The greatest Norse virtue is courage and that is what Sigurd means.) But the next boy was not named for a few years—there was always the effort to find the perfect name. Finally they decided to name him Arnulf. He was old enough to protest. He said he wanted to be named Albert after the policeman's son. They explained to him that Arnulf meant Eagle-Wolf. "I'll take it," he said.

To me, about eight years old, the ecclesiastical situation was very interesting. I had a passion for English history, especially Robin Hood. Next to me in the pew there was a very large, stout man with a jolly round face and a turned up nose and quite bald. "Is that Friar Tuck?" I whispered to my mother. No. It was Mr. Hjalmar Quist, she explained.

Another very interesting thing about the Unitarian Church: there were so many fascinating eccentric people, like Mr. Buell, a Single Taxer and vegetarian, and he prodded you in the ribs to see if you wore corsets. He didn't approve of them.

Now my wonderful parents—Did Unitarianism add to their grandeur and wisdom? I think it did. We grew up more lighthearted and untrammeled than Orthodox children, over-awed and inculcated with guilt (Original Sin). The hopeless naughtiness of that! Always having to drag Original Sin around!

I think we were just as benign and good as the others, perhaps more so—more original, easier laughters, allowed to even have a little engaging rascality.

And my parents were generous to all religions—all of us poor humans groping in the darkness toward Eternity. The only thing wrong about Orthodoxy, they thought, was the grimness, the fraidy-catism, the self-righteous conceit, always trying to discipline others.

I find in a letter my mother wrote to Anne: "Torvald and I were having a little religious conversation and he said, 'Is God a bird?' "

This shows there was not much religious alarm in the family. We never said our prayers and no one told us how. The neighbor children had to say at night that frightening and dismal prayer, "If I should die before I wake. . ." And it was only when I heard people speak of church and religion and show their distressing tinted cards of Jesus and his disciples traipsing barefoot in their nightgowns, that I became scared of graves, dead bodies, sin and Hell and other horrors, quite unnecessary.

An interesting thing is that entirely unadmonished I became religious myself, quite cheerfully and naturally so. And whenever great men and women reveal in their lives and works their souls—Tolstoy, Blake, Carlyle, Bach, Michelangelo, Mozart, St. Joan, St. Catherine of Siena—there expands in me a kind of light and recognition. I seem to see farther into the mysterious gloom—perhaps not so gloomy after all.

My anxiety is that Unitarians will become only Science Idolators. Perhaps God IS becoming a bird to them—not a nice live bird but a stuffed bird. An electric bird, a gasahol bird. In fact I like science less and less. Isn't it Intellectual Pride? Maybe it's Lucifer after all. See how they are always measuring and counting, and what's so wonderful about that? Usually it is merely utilitarian and destructive—weaponry and herbicides, shots for cancer that don't work, more computers, more concrete on meadows, faster and more terrible airplanes looking exactly like those fiends that great Dante saw in his genius and appalling imagination. No. Science may be the

Tree of Death. Where is the love and beauty in it?

Just the other day in that remarkable periodical that costs 25 cents a year, the *Catholic Worker*, I discovered that both Dostoevsky and the great Russian theologian Berdyeav said exactly the same thing: "Beauty will save the world."

I believe it. Please remember and make a note of it.

◆

# MONSIGNOR FULTON SHEEN

**M**onsignor Fulton Sheen spoke at the crowded University Student Forum. He is slender and well-knit and has dark hair and blue eyes with very round irises and a blazing parallel gaze. He speaks in ringing untrammeled sentences without one hem or haw in them, and he was funny at first—quite brash. He said that once he asked some little boys the way to the Town Hall in Philadelphia. "Who are you?" they asked. "I am going to make a speech there." "What about?" "On the—" rattling off an indecipherable Latin sentence from St. Thomas Aquinas. "What does that mean?" "It means: how to get to Heaven." "You don't even know the way to the Town Hall," the boys said.

His "great foe" he began, was Communism. "But today I will speak of other things. We are living in a crisis but in such destructive times sometimes certain ideas, too, are destroyed and it is a good thing.

"The first idea being sloughed off is the belief in the natural goodness of man. In the nineteenth century it was believed that biology, economics, progress were all leading mankind in an inevitable advancement until he would become a kind of angel on earth. But let us study the periods between wars.

"From the Napoleonic wars to the Franco-Prussian war there were 55 years. From the Franco-Prussian war to the First World War, 44 years. From the First World War to the second, 19 years. Fifty-five! Forty-four! Nineteen!" shouting the diminishing numbers like the voice of Doom. "And now they talk of another war. . . a small crystal discovered the other day they say that can kill everybody in Canada and the United States. . ."

And the second idea now being abandoned, he said, is the idea of relativity. "Now it seems to work all right in mathematics. But it has extended itself into all of our notions so that we no longer feel there is any particular difference between right and wrong.

"Now in this crisis there are four pillars that may uphold us: 1. To discover the meaning of life. 2. To find God. 3. A respect for personality. 4. Divine mechanics.

"What is the meaning of your life? Well if you could take your heart out in your hand and distill out of it what you want, you would find three things: We all want life—see how we would cut off a hand to save ourselves. And we want truth. We are born asking why, why? Why am I alive? For what purpose? And we want love—someone to share and give back to us the feelings we give them."

(As for finding God, he said he could prove that He exists "by that much-despised thing, reason itself," and he did it very luminously, I thought.)

As for his third pillar, the respect for personality, he said "we live in a very, very carnal age." There is our immense preoccupation with sex. Now in the Bible marriage and sexual love is expressed in a very curious way as "knowing." "Adam knew Eve"—and that meant a mystical experience wherein they were both changed forever. And the change was irrevocable and could never be undone. And he begged the students to have "this respect for personality, to see that one cannot change another's whole life lightly and think it doesn't count, that it is a terrible responsibility to injure or change someone forever in their emotions."

And he said that if only we can come to feel again the immense, imaginative nobility and seriousness of "the respect for personality" we will not have as now in 35 of the largest cities in the country one divorce out of every two marriages. "They tell me I am urging merely a dry self-denial, a negativeness. But a diamond is not a diamond merely for lack of carbon." No. There is such a thing as passionless passion.

Afterwards I moved out in the throng of people around him to watch him and see what he is like. In the sun outside were forty nuns and Monsignor Sheen stood among them in his black hat, waiting for his car.

"Well Sisters, you didn't need that lecture," and they

laughed merrily. A little old nun said that she was sorry he did not get to his fourth point, Divine Dynamics. "But, Sister, its much better, you know, not to have time to make the last point than to have had three places where you could have stopped and didn't." They laughed like jolly children.

I was watching him at a distance of ten feet and he looked at me with his piercing parallel gaze and very naturally and sweetly bowed—"How do you do?" This was surprising. Of course he would bow to everybody I thought. In the Kingdom of Heaven there are no introductions.

◆

# Scandinavian-American Banquet and Kierkegaard

We had our American-Scandinavian Foundation banquet at the Swedish-American Institute, that sixteenth century castle built by Swan Turnblad on Park Avenue—all grey stone towers and court-yards and gargoyles. It was a Danish evening. Professor Howard Hong of St. Olaf College spoke on the Danish philosopher, Kierkegaard. And there were many Danes there. (The Danes are the most humorous and broad-smiling of all the Scandinavians. I tell them there hasn't been a melancholy Dane since Hamlet.)

Professor Hong is a strong vigorous man with a childish nose and the comeliness of a sixteen-year-old boy, though his hair is gray-white. I sat next to his wife, Edna Hong: pretty and young with something old-fashioned about her: I think it was the lifted, uncurled and thick hair under the kind of hat that Renoir painted. Then I learned that she has eight children. She said—under my cross-questioning—that the secret of bringing up eight children is "to organize things and to act quickly and fast."

"It must be very hard work——."

"Well—" and she lifted a small hard, reddened, tough pretty hand for me to see. But she says that after nine o'clock that is *her* time. No matter what happens, that time belongs to herself alone, and then she reads, writes, thinks. And her dream is this: When the children are grown she will wear tweeds and brogues and have a stick and walk—I mean *walk*— from Italy to Norway. What a wonderful person she is!

Kierkegaard died in 1855, the son of a rich, silent and heart-broken Danish father, and this is what Professor Hong said in his speech, or an approximation of it because I could take only the roughest notes on an envelope:

"Soren Kierkegaard—there is no doubt he is the key to

this century in philosophy and religion. Kierkegaard is called the Danish Socrates and he is worthy of it. He did not (like us professors) talk *at* people." No, like Socrates he just kept asking mild tiny questions, searched sweetly into people, listened and listened, each question jolting the person into deeper thinking.

"Socrates and Kierkegaard were alike because they had the same basic concern with simple human existence, with living . . . Now Kierkegaard came after Francis Bacon who said, 'My aim is to extend the power and greatness of Man: the problem of Man is to control the external world.'

"But Kierkegaard opposed this aggrandizement of Man. 'Man is his own greatest problem,' he said. He saw in the vast democratic movement in Europe then, the anxious mass-Man. He said that we have forgotten what it means to exist. He spoke with certain malice about professors, about pure thought that is separate and outside of existence, of living. And he said the same of poetic thinking—building wonderful castles in the imagination but living in a doghouse. Then, he said that older people make fun of the young for writing poetry, and the older ones grow plump and successful, steady and unperturbed, but they have forgotten ethics and morality. Better to be like the young and furiously poetic, said Kierkegaard, and in spiritual pain."

So he set every kind of person to painfully thinking. Yes, the real problem is simple human existence. Socrates called it "the tendance of the soul" and that is the true purpose of life.

And Socrates' and Kierkegaard's method were so much alike. "Take that smorgasbord," said Professor Hong, pointing to the long laden tables, "It's over there but it doesn't exist until you eat it, appropriate it. And so it is with thinking, Kierkegaard said. Socrates would say to a man mildly, "But just one little question—" You see? He'd start taking just a finger, and then a hand, then the arm, and then the whole man, and in this way he disturbed people terribly, shook them mentally to their very heels until they themselves would begin to see great yawning vistas about the possible meaning of life. He awakened people to an awareness of what it is to exist, and so did Kierkegaard."

Then Mr. Andrew Johnson, the Royal Danish Consul, told us of Denmark and how right across the line they look with dread into the slavery and mental chains of Soviet Russia. He said that Denmark has nobly amended her constitution (the first country in the world to do so) to renounce her sovereignty as soon as she can join a European Federation or, better still, a world government.

Well, it was a fine evening with Americans and Scandinavians listening and talking about lofty and thoughtful things. Such interesting and distinguished people! Mr. Alfred Bergsten: "I am just a lawyer. But I like solitude, studying and writing. I have slept in the woods many a time." Dr. A. C. Ahlen: "Brenda, I took a course in philosophy under Socrates the Second—," that is to say under the dear and wonderful Professor David Swenson of the University, the first to translate Kierkegaard. There was Dr. Donald Cowling, president-emeritus of Carleton College, who raises great sums of money for our American-Scandinavian fellowships. And Mr. Dreng Bjornaraa of U.S. Steel, our president. He has been chosen to guide King Hailie Selassie when he arrives soon now to study Minnesota farming.

❖

# THE ART INSTITUTE SHOW

Thursday evening our artists showed their pictures. A party at the Art Institute. Four hundred people. The pictures are all hung now. So go and see them.

A wonderful person judged them: Mrs. Juliana Force. For 25 years she helped Gertrude Vanderbilt Whitney (an artist and a multi-millionairess) to cherish living American artists. (Everybody will help dead ones.) They bought thousands of pictures and built the famous Whitney Museum in New York.

She is short, erect, wearing a brown dress. She has Tartar eyes that slant up. On her left forehead there is a round hat, a turban of orange feathers. She has a big imperious nose like Mary Garden's and a deep voice and she is bold and direct, kind and funny. She gave a talk to the Friends of the Institute: Mrs. Tearse, Mrs. Atkinson, Miss Elizabeth Wallace, Mrs. George Christian, Mrs. Angus Morrison and many others.

She said: "So many are Wack-ing and Wav-ing, and there is induction and abduction, but now we will talk about Art. Now artists are sincere people who have a feeling and express it. Make no mistake, they are our aristocrats." (Aristocrats are those who tell the Truth that is within them and will not be bought off.) "They have a vision of life around them and want to show it to us. You know how we are always saying to them: 'I don't like the mouth,' but they won't do it as you want it. Of course they won't! If they do they are not artists. They aren't any good. They are insincere."

She told of the lady who looked at an abstraction and said, "What is it?" The artist tried to explain saying, "Well I paint what I see and then leave it out."

"Gertrude Stein said, 'So many people are irritated by so many pictures.' But it is better to be irritated than to have no feeling, no emotion. Because then you are dead. And gone.

Now it is true as Goya said, 'I paint what I feel! If you don't feel, plough.' Yes, some of them should plough perhaps. But every one of us on earth has some fixed iron-hard ideas that will take a lifetime to be freed from. But jeering at what we do not like does not free us. Only sincerely working and striving does that."

Van Gogh said, "If you hear a voice within you saying, you are no painter, then paint by all means, lad, and that voice will be silenced. But only by working."

And she said: "Now how can you help artists? Buy paintings. Don't ask anyone's advice. If you like it, get it. If you have to spend $150,000 for an Old Master—yes, get in the experts. But a living artist's painting (so tragically often they cost $10)—just buy it. 'I like it!' Don't care what your husband thinks. Put the picture where he doesn't see it. I guess you can be independent, American women!—" with jocose fire and a haughty lifted head.

"And don't patronize the artists." (This is what rich people should remember twice a day.) "You can patronize the great art of the past. But if you buy a living artist, this is not 'doing good.'" She meant that we must not lick our chops over it as a benevolence. For we can never do enough for the artist-spirit, alive or dead. These aristocratic souls must be kept flourishing. They are more important than airplanes or cannons.

"When buying a picture, you cannot imagine how you are keeping the artist alive and working! And a pat on the back is not enough. What if business got only a pat on the back and that was all there was to it? And that somebody *wants* his painting—you cannot imagine what that does for the artist! They do not even spend the money, or celebrate. They get that faraway look; they cannot hear what you say even. Their only thought is, 'I think I will go home now *quick*! and paint another one!'"

Van Gogh made $109 from his paintings. They are now worth $3,000,000. He died of starvation. Listen to what the poor, great, impassioned Van Gogh said about all this:

"Because there are two kinds of idleness," he wrote to his brother. "There is the man who is idle from laziness, from the baseness of his nature. You may, if you like, take me for such a one.

"Then there is the other kind of idle man who is idle in spite of himself, who is inwardly consumed by a great longing for action, who does nothing because he seems to be imprisoned in some cage, because he does not possess what he needs to make him productive but he feels by instinct: yet I am good for something . . . I know that I might be a quite different man. Do you know what frees one from this captivity? It is a very deep, serious affection, being friends, being brothers, love; that is what opens the cage by supreme power, by some magic force. But without this one remains in prison.

"I should be very glad if it were possible for you to see in me something else than an idle man of the worst type."

◆

# ONE OF THE VERY FEW
# MASCULINE FEMINISTS

I love Robert Graves—the English poet, novelist, historian, a war hero, pugilist, archaeologist, scholar. He is one of the very few masculine feminists in the world. He thinks that the Matriarchies in history were far greater, nobler, more inspired than the Patriarchies. The Patriarchies, for example, like Rome (we live in one) were obsessed with War and Law. The Matriarchies like that of the Mycenean Greeks and the Etruscans, also fostered and loved grace, beauty, tender-heartedness, inspiration.

The Hebrews of the Old Testament, he says, were obsessively concerned with breeding, with concubines and herds, and there was only one woman in the Bible whom the Hebrews listened to with anxious respect. That was Deborah whose prophetic clairvoyance was actually besought.

The great Greeks, although they treated their wives and families rather badly, had a consciousness of the awful intelligence of women. Pallas Athene was their Goddess of Wisdom. The lovely Nine Muses were bright enough, imaginative enough to inspire Homer, Phidias, Praxiteles, Euripedes and the rest. And there were the great Oracles, the mysterious priestess of Delphi who could tell kings and generals and politicians what to do, a thing no practical rational male could do.

And Robert Graves says that it is only the very great courageous women who have brave sons. He speaks of Ajax and Diomedes born of fearless and jovial mothers in a small Matriarchal country in western Greece. And I think of Johnny Unitas of the Baltimore Colts (the greatest quarterback) who says it was his remarkable mother who taught him and was "his good example." She was one of those heroines who brought him up and led him into a decent education by her lifelong bravery of day-cleaning. And there is Jimmy Connors' mother and grandmother who taught him tennis.

And I like what Robert Graves says about meditation. Yes, it is a very fine thing and absolutely necessary in our day, when our lives, our silence, our spiritual freedom, our sense of beauty, our haughty independence, our originality, are almost entirely snuffed out by gasoline and the combustion engine. (How great it will be when they are no more!)

But there is such a thing as meditating so much and so long that it is a mistake. I have known meditators who browbeat their souls into "harmony . . . into positive thinking, into relaxation . . ." when they could have walked 8 miles in the same time and really have been attacked by an idea.

Robert Graves wrote a rhyme about it:

*In a small heap triangular*
*Our budding Buddha meditates.*
*Gates of Nirvana stand ajar,*
*He stares unwinking at the gates.*
*Brown rice his food, water his drink.*
*Hey, quit that meditating! Think!*

◆

# DIFFERENT WAYS OF PRAYING

*n an old notebook*: Everybody prays in a different way. Jesus "fell on his face." Lord Ashley in Cromwell's army just before the charge at the Battle of Edge Hill: "O Lord, Thou knowest how busy I must be on this day. If I forget Thee do not Thou therefore forget me." The poet Cowper: "Sometimes I seem to myself to be banished to a remoteness from God's presence in comparison with which the distance from East to West is vicinity, is cohesion." Bunyan: "Oh, the staring holes that the heart hath in time of prayer! No one knows the byways the heart hath, and the back lanes to slip away from the presence of God."

Hugh Latimer's letter to Ridley, just before they were burned at the stake: "Pardon me and pray for me; pray for me I say. For I am sometimes so fearful that I could creep into a mouse-hole; sometimes God doth visit me again with his comfort. So He cometh and goeth."

Dean Goulburn: "When you cannot pray as you would, pray as you can. Sometimes when you need rest most, you are too restless to lie down and take it. Then compel yourself to lie still. So if you are averse to prayer, pray the more."

Madame Guyon said that sometimes vague groping for God *outside* us leaves only emptiness—one finds only emptiness. It was so with her until a Franciscan friar said to her, "Madame, you are seeking *without* that which you have within. Accustom yourself to seek for God in your own heart and you will find him."

From William Blake: "I am not a God afar off but a Brother and Friend. In your bosom I reside and you reside in mine, forgiving all Evil, not seeking Recompense." Blake said that when he could not write or paint, when he had no inspiration, he "was devoured by jackals and hyenas." He was asked what he did then. "I pray, Sir." He also said: "Anyone who loves can feel Love descend into him and knows it is the Lord."

The trouble frequently with even nobly intellectual and rational people is this: Their effort toward Truth, Goodness, Love can be merely analysis, dissection. But when you analyze and dissect Truth or Love it can be merely an autopsy. There it is, all laid out on the table in parts, but the Truth is fled. I say: "Go ahead. Analyze, analyze, study, negate. That is fine. But at the same time you must pray to *love* the truth that you are seeking. Only Love, descending into you from the Lord, turns the analysis into a synthesis, a recklessness and a grandeur so that the Truth becomes a part of you, transfigures you and leads you to a higher one."

❖

# ◢ WELL - BEING ◣

## ON MAKING CHOICES

T he choices turn up every few minutes, every hour. "To be or not to be?" To choose bravery or flight? To choose your natural carefree, rollicking self, or to choose your cautious, pussy-footing self?

This making of choices I have mulled over all my life. My thought is that if your choices are lofty, noble, daring, perhaps even dangerous, the line of your life will go along a higher level than, say, if your choices are lazier, more self-indulgent, cozy and imitative. Your choices determine whether your life will go along at a distinguished, noble level or a lower level, duller, more namby-pamby. Or the level may be very low indeed—in the mud. Or it may be an opportunistic, crass, vulgar level.

We must try to make wonderful choices. Now this is not easy. For one reason, we don't know who we are. As Boethius, the philosopher and Christian martyr of the 5th Century said to his torturers: "You have forgotten who you are."

I feel that I am about seventeen people. How to single out one's True Self? I seem to be sometimes my mother, some-times my father, sometimes a whiner, a great queen, or a slob, a mother, a simpering lady, or an old rip, a minister, a lion, a weasel. I have this concept: We are like onions, in layers. Many people live from the outer layer of the onion. They live in what other people think is the thing to do. They are merely imitative or conventional. Their Conscience is that still small voice that tells them someone is looking.

But we must try to find our True Conscience, our True Self, the very Center, for this is the only first-rate choice-making center. Here lies all originality, talent, honor, truthfulness, courage, and cheerfulness. Here only lies the ability to choose the good and the grand, the true and the beautiful.

But to find your Center? It is very difficult in our cacophonous times; fractured with yelling activity, feeding, drinking, galloping, of frantic uncertainties that lead to psychiatry and booze. But you must try to find it. It is the old stuff—Know Thyself. But it takes solitude and there is none. I knew a remarkable woman who had a famous boys' school and she made them, every so often, watch the sheep alone and all night. A good idea. Gandhi's rule, like that of all the saints, was to be silent for twenty-four hours on one day a week—not to utter one word. Then one was bound to look inward and the Center begins to appear. To find it you must ask yourself all the time: "What do I love? Why am I irascible? Why am I so afraid of old age and death? How odd, for both seem to be very common. Maybe I should not be afraid of them."

Now when you find this Center, or as you approach it, it is much easier to make choices. Here I must say that Unitarians may drive me out of the fold for heresy. I am a Unitarian (yet not a Humanist at all) and I am also a fantastical mystic. I must tell you that, with Plato, I think the purpose of life on earth is "the tendance of the soul," that is to say, we are in school. And like Plato, I believe in the Doctrine of Reminiscence or Reincarnation, and that in this life we are supposed to learn something, to advance, to become better. As in Ibsen's mystical drama, *Peer Gynt*, I think our soul, or Solveig, is waiting for us at the end of life and hopes that we have passed with a good mark and have learned something through striving, mistakes, suffering, and the like.

And therefore I believe that our choices should not be practical and pragmatic, founded on business achievements in the world, or success, or public acclaim, but we should try to make choices in the direction of nobility and bravery, if possible.

Now some of us do not want to be noble. Fine. If your True Self says, "Don't be noble," don't be. But if it says, "Be noble," and you want to be that, you will go insane or have a nervous breakdown if you don't make those choices. Now since our Conscience is a tiny compass inside us, our duty is to keep this little compass as sensitive and imaginative as possible, clear and alive, to keep as nervously steady as possible.

How to do that? Two generations ago solitude was a normal part of every life. Now it hardly exists. There is not even the solitude of walking, of going from here to there on our legs. A lady was parking her car and she did not get it in perfectly and she said to her friend, "Never mind. We can walk to the curb."

Some people try to live up to a Conscience higher than their own, say that of Jesus or Calvin. A terrible mistake and it accounts for the persecutions and cruelties of Christianity, and the suffering of endless generations of children. For one thing, it can't be done. Because the Conscience of many people tells them to be quite ordinary, eating, drinking, fighting and having a good time, but their artificially assumed Conscience won't allow it and it makes them not only dreadful and cruel, but idiotic.

Now in making choices, never be grim. Think of life as a river, a smooth-flowing, golden Heraclitean river. Know that you will make dreadful mistakes with almost every choice. Hurrah! Congratulate yourself for making daring, honorable, ridiculous mistakes. Children are so terribly afraid their parents will prevent them from making their most important mistakes.

There are tests to submit your choices to. Tolstoy said that a great man is one who has the highest Life Conception of his time. Well, I say to myself: "What is my Highest Life Conception?" I make myself define it, describe it. Or I say to myself, "In this trying situation, what would God do?" Hamlet should have asked himself that. The answer would have come immediately. "Don't kill Claudius. Or your mother. Be kinder to Ophelia. Don't fake madness. Intelligently plan the overthrow of Claudius and establish a good administration."

The original great test for choices was the Ten Commandments. Still very good. Although some of us think that we have transcended some of them, like the one, "Honor thy father and mother." Well this is an anachronism. You can be wonderfully good to them but you cannot honor them if they are not honorable. My friend, Ammon Hennacy, a Catholic and a religious anarchist who breaks the law in every war and goes to jail, said to the shocked policeman who asked him what he was, "I am an anarchist." "What is an anarchist?" "An anarchist is a person too good to need a policeman."

Jesus's two commandments, "Love thy God with all thy heart and mind, and thy neighbor as thyself," are helpful. Although a young philosopher said that to do unto others as you would be done by "would be rather catastrophic in a society of masochists." George Bernard Shaw had an even better commandment, an advance on that of Moses and Jesus. It is: "Is this that I enjoy doing for twenty minutes hurting any man or creature in the world?"

I have my own two commandments to propose to the world and curiously enough they are not stressed in the Bible; they are not even included in the Seven Deadly Sins. They are: No Cruelty. And no Lying. That would take care of everything. Ignorance-inducing newspapers, advertising, war, stealing, murder, vivisection, adultery. For example, the true vicious-ness of adultery is not the romantic love—there is no objection to Tristram and Isolde—but the cruelty and the lying, for lying is so bad for the liar and it is such an injustice and cruelty to the person lied to.

And if my two commandments prevailed there would emerge a world without psychiatrists, salesmen, and nervous breakdowns. A British officer was shot down in Germany and they put him to work in a Nazi insane asylum and he wrote: "I am convinced that there are only two kinds of people in the world, the Kind and the Insane." I believe it! And how clearly one can see, when we look inward, that whenever we are unkind we are insane.

Another important test for choices in ethics and morals is aesthetic. Whatever you do, test it for beauty and grace. Beauty is the Lord. Cowardice is ugly. Plug-ugly. So is tyranny and exploita-tion, the stronger bludgeoning the weaker. So is lying ugly. Chekhov said that lying is dirty and that it is even worse to lie in fiction than in conversation. Snobbishness is so disgusting-ly unlovely, such an indication of pinheadedness. Caterwaul-ing and self-pity—such a revolting sight for human eyes!

In protesting against censorship nobody points out that works of sexual freedom, of pornography, are often so extraordinarily ugly. And ugliness is an infection, pestilential thing. It invades people, just as Beauty heals and lightens them. It depresses them, lowers them, muddies them, changes them for the worse. Ugliness is Devil Worship. This should be a test for modern art and music. Much of it should be prohibited.

My final admonition in making choices is: Study especially what you *think* is your goodness. Is it self-sacrifice? Being meek, long-suffering? Watch it. It may be cowardice. And the meek do so much harm. A docile, put-upon wife ruins the nature and soul of her husband. Better to knock him out with a lead pipe. There would be no tyranny if nobody would put up with it. Or do you consider your greatest virtue a piercing critical sense? Watch it. It may be self-praise, or an inability to love, or a pervading hate. Are you doing work that is profitable but ugly and shoddy and a deceiving of the public; and do you explain it by saying, "One has to live." Ask yourself: "But do you?"

And never rest in any rule. No stereotypes are allowed. There is no resting place down here. George Herbert in a poem tells how at Man's birth God gave him Beauty, Courage and so on, and at the bottom of the cup was Rest. God started to give him that but put it back. "No, he can never have rest. Eternal restlessness will at last throw him to My Breast."

My conclusion is then: Avoid in your choices all cruelty and lying. After that, I say to my children, "Be Bad or Good whichever is best for you."

And here endeth the First Lesson.

❖

# TELL ME MORE

I want to write about the great and powerful thing that listening is. And how we forget it. And how we don't listen to our children, or those we love. And least of all—which is so important too—to those we do not love. But we should. Because listening is a magnetic and strange thing, a creative force. You can see that when you think how the friends that really listen to us are the ones we move toward, and we want to sit in their radius as though it did us good, like ultraviolet rays.

This is the reason: When we are listened to, it creates us, makes us unfold and expand. Ideas actually begin to grow within us and come to life. You know how if a person laughs at your jokes you become funnier and funnier, and if he does not, every tiny little joke in you weazens up and dies. Well, that is the principle of it. It makes people happy and free when they are listened to. And if you are a listener, it is the secret of having a good time in society (because everybody around you becomes lively and interesting), of comforting people, of doing them good.

Who are the people, for example, to whom you go for advice? Not to the hard, practical ones who can tell you exactly what to do, but to the listeners; that is, the kindest, least censorious, least bossy people that you know. It is because by pouring out your problem to them, you then know what to do about it yourself.

When we listen to people there is an alternating current, and this recharges us so that we never get tired of each other. We are constantly being re-created. Now there are brilliant people who cannot listen much. They have no ingoing wires on their apparatus. They are entertaining, but exhausting, too. I think it is because these lecturers, these brilliant performers, by not giving us a chance to talk, do not let us express our thoughts and expand; and it is this little creative fountain inside us that begins to spring and cast up new thoughts and unexpected laughter and wisdom. That is why, when someone has listened to you, you go home rested and lighthearted.

Now this little creative fountain is in all. It is the spirit, or the intelligence, or the imagination—whatever you want to call it. If you are very tired, strained, have no solitude, run too many errands, talk to too many people, drink too many cocktails, this little fountain is muddied over and covered with a lot of debris. The result is you stop living from the center, the creative fountain, and you live from the periphery, from externals. That is, you go along on mere will power without imagination.

Well, it is when people really listen to us, with quiet fascinated attention, that the little fountain begins to work again, to accelerate in the most surprising way.

I discovered all this about three years ago, and truly it made a revolutionary change in my life. Before that, when I went to a party I would think anxiously: "Now try hard. Be lively. Say bright things. Talk. Don't let down." And when tired, I would have to drink a lot of coffee to keep this up.

Now before going to a party, I just tell myself to listen with affection to anyone who talks to me, *to be in their shoes when they talk*; to try to know them without my mind pressing against theirs, or arguing, or changing the subject. No. My attitude is: "Tell me more. This person is showing me his soul. It is a little dry and meager and full of grinding talk just now, but presently he will begin to think, not just automatically to talk. He will show his true self. Then he will be wonderfully alive."

Sometimes, of course, I cannot listen as well as others. But when I have this listening power, people crowd around and their heads keep turning to me as though irresistibly pulled. It is not because people are conceited and want to show off that they are drawn to me, the listener. It is because by listening I have started up in them their creative fountain. I do them good.

Now why does it do them good? I have a kind of mystical notion about this. I think it is only by expressing all that is inside that purer and purer streams come. It is so in writing. You are taught in school to put down on paper only the bright things. Wrong. Pour out the dull things on paper too—you can tear them up afterward—for only then do the bright ones come. If you hold back the dull things, you are certain to hold back what is clear and beautiful and true and lively. So it is with people who have not been listened to in the right way—with affection and a kind of jolly excitement. Their creative fountain has been blocked. Only superficial talk comes out—what is prissy or gushing or merely nervous. No one has called out of them, by wonderful listening, what is true and alive.

I think women have this listening faculty more than men. It is not the fault of men. They lose it because of their long habit of striving in business, of self-assertion. And the more forceful men are, the less they can listen as they grow older. And that is why women in general are more fun than men, more restful and inspiriting.

Now this non-listening of able men is the cause of one of the saddest things in the world—the loneliness of fathers, of those quietly sad men who move among their grown children like remote ghosts. When my father was over seventy, he was a fiery, humorous, admirable man, a scholar, a man of great force. But he was deep in the loneliness of old age and another generation. He was so fond of me. But he could not hear me— not one word I said, really. I was just audience. I would walk around the lake with him on a beautiful afternoon and he would talk to me about Darwin and Huxley and Higher Criticism of the Bible.

"Yes, I see, I see," I kept saying and tried to keep my mind pinned to it, but was restive and bored. There was a feeling of helplessness because he could not hear what I had to say about it. When I spoke I found myself shouting, as one does to a foreigner, and in a kind of despair that he could not hear me. After the walk I would feel that I had worked off my duty and I was anxious to get him settled and reading in his Morris chair, so that I could go out and have a livelier time with other people. And he would sigh and look after me absentmindedly with perplexed loneliness.

For years afterward I have thought with real suffering about my father's loneliness. Such a wonderful man, and reaching out to me and wanting to know me! But he could not. He could not listen. But now I think that if only I had known as much about listening then as I do now, I could have bridged that chasm between us. To give an example:

Recently, a man I had not seen for twenty years wrote me: "I have a family of mature children. So did your father. They never saw him. Not in the days he was alive. Not in the days he was the deep and admirable man we now both know he was. That is man's life. When next you see me, you'll just know everything. Just your father all over again, trying to reach through, back to the world of those he loves."

Well, when I saw this man again, what had happened to him after twenty years? He was an unusually forceful man and had made a great deal of money. But he had lost his ability to listen. He talked rapidly and told wonderful stories and it was just fascinating to hear them. But when I spoke—restlessness: "Just hand me that, will you? . . . Where is my pipe?" It was just a habit. He read countless books and was eager to take in ideas, but he just could not listen to people.

Well, this is what I did. I was more patient—I did not resist his non-listening talk as I did my father's. I listened and listened to him, not once pressing against him, even in thought with my own self-assertion. I said to myself: "He has been under a driving pressure for years. His family had grown to resist his talk. But now, by listening, I will pull it all out of him. He must talk freely and on and on. When he has been really listened to enough, he will grow tranquil. He will begin to want to hear me."

And he did, after a few days. He began asking me questions. And presently I was saying gently:

"You see, it has become hard for you to listen."

He stopped dead and stared at me. And it was because I had listened with such complete, absorbed, uncritical sympathy, without one flaw of boredom or impatience, that he now believed and trusted me, although he did not know this.

"Now talk," he said. "Tell me about that. Tell me all about that."

Well, we walked back and forth across the lawn and I told

him my ideas about it.

"You love your children, but probably don't let them in. Unless you listen, people are weazened in your presence; they become about a third of themselves. Unless you listen, you can't know anybody. Oh, you will know facts and what is in the newspapers and all of history, perhaps, but you will not know one single person. You know, I have come to think listening is love, that's what it really is."

Well, I don't think I would have written this article if my notions had not had such an extraordinary effect on this man. For he says they have changed his whole life. He wrote me that his children at once came closer; he was astonished to see what they are: how original, independent, courageous. His wife seemed really to care about him again, and they were actually talking about all kinds of things and making each other laugh.

For just as the tragedy of parents and children is not listening, so it is of husbands and wives. If they disagree they begin to shout louder and louder—if not actually, at least inwardly—hanging fiercely and deafly onto their own ideas, instead of listening and becoming quieter and quieter and more comprehending. But the most serious result of not listening is that worst thing in the world, boredom; for it is really the death of love. It seals people off from each other more than any other thing. I think that is why married people quarrel. It is to cut through the non-conduction and boredom. Because when feelings are hurt, they really begin to listen. At last their talk is a real exchange. But of course, they are just injuring their marriage forever.

Now, how to listen? It is harder than you think. I don't believe in critical listening, for that only puts a person in a strait jacket of hesitancy. He begins to choose his words solemnly or primly. His little inner fountain cannot spring. Critical listeners dry you up. But creative listeners are those who want you to be recklessly yourself, even at your very worst, even vituperative, bad-tempered. You are mentally saying as you express these things: "Hurrah! Good for you!" and they are laughing and just delighted with any manifestation of yourself, bad or good. For true listeners know that if you are bad-tempered it does not mean that you are always so. They don't love you just when you are nice; they love all of you.

Besides critical listening, there is another kind that is no good: passive, censorious listening. Sometimes husbands can be this kind of listener, a kind of ungenerous eavesdropper who mentally (or aloud) keeps saying as you talk: "Bunk . . . Bunk . . . Hokum."

In order to learn to listen, here are some suggestions: Try to learn tranquility, to live in the present a part of the time every day. Sometimes say to yourself: "Now. What is happening now? This friend is talking. I am quiet. There is endless time. I hear it, every word." Then suddenly you begin to hear not only what people are saying, but what they are trying to say, and you sense the whole truth about them. And you sense existence, not piece-meal, not this object and that, but as a translucent whole.

Then watch your self-assertiveness. And give it up. Try not to drink too many cocktails to give up that nervous pressure that feels like energy and wit but may be neither. And remember it is not enough just to *will* to listen to people. One must *really* listen. Only then does the magic begin.

Sometimes people cannot listen because they think that unless they are talking, they are socially of no account. There are those women with an old-fashioned ballroom training which insists there must be unceasing vivacity and gyrations of talk. But this is really a strain on people.

No. We should all know this: that listening, not talking, is the gifted and great role, and the imaginative role. And the true listener is much more beloved, magnetic than the talker, and he is more effective, and learns more and does more good. And so try listening. Listen to your wife, your husband, your father, your mother, your children, your friends; to those who love you and those who don't, to those who bore you, to your enemies. It will work a small miracle. And perhaps a great one.

❖

# ON USING NEW WORDS

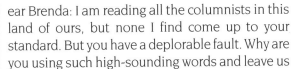

ear Brenda: I am reading all the columnists in this land of ours, but none I find come up to your standard. But you have a deplorable fault. Why are you using such high-sounding words and leave us standing here and gasping when you swing up to higher regions? What do you take us for? Learned Professors at Oslo University?

Come down, dear Brenda. Mend your steps so we poor creatures can follow you. We could easily race you around Lake Harriet and win, but when it comes to language's foggy labyrinth, we are regular Mutts and Jeffs. Yours, Agapetus.

No, Agapetus, you must look up the words, write them down with the derivation and then use them every day until they are a part of you. Now new and perfect words are a wonderful thing. They need not be long (I don't like them long) but apropos. And you see the secret of being interesting is to be continually shocking the reader as he goes along with tiny shocks of surprise. When you are interested in talk, or in something written, there is a pull-along every second. You wait for each word, each phrase—because of the tiny shock of surprise in it—gratefully and eagerly as it comes.

And here is another reason you must look up new words: See how children (and tens of millions of adults) have only two adjectives "dumb" or "keen." But how sad that is. How little they can express!

I read once that a little South American bird that biologists are studying because the bird seems to utter actually three syllables, and the theory is that it is speech that develops the brain, and not the other way around.

Well I think it does work that way. The more words you know, the better, the more delicately, opulently you can *think*. Shakespeare, I was once told, used 39,000 words. Goethe was next with 24,000. And most of us have a few thousand, if indeed 500. Take the verses of this poem by the great poet, the Jesuit mystic, Gerard Manley Hopkins:

> Elected silence, sing to me
> And beat upon the whorled ear,
> Pipe me to pastures still and be
> The music that I care to hear.
>
> Be shelled eyes, with double-dark
> And find the uncreated light;
> This ruck and real that you remark
> Coils, keeps and teases simple sight.

Well, what if he wrote with the average vocabulary: "I dunno I kina like to be alone sometimes because it seems like I sorta like it. It makes me feel peaceful, kina, and I like to shut my eyes, sorta sometimes and just think and think because I dunno, I kina think that when you're alone you feel more peaceful it seems, not rushing around like a chicken with its head chopped off," this last, a fine, lively, graphic phrase, but not original of course—borrowed, hackneyed.

No. Speech is the only thing that distinguishes us from animals, but few bother to extend it by a word or two. You get to work, Agapetus.

◆

# ON FIGHTING AND BRAVERY

ourage is the greatest quality of all and I am absolutely sure it is the rarest. There is much of the automatic stuff that passes for courage, an instinctive rage and malevolence and quarrelsomeness; and there is a "patriotism" that calls itself courage in each of us. But if you examine it carefully in yourself you will see it is associated with a sneaking conviction that some nineteen-year-old soldier will do all the fighting and bloody stuff.

I have heard people speak sentimentally and with dewy eyes about the "courage" of motherhood, of having a baby. Well if one is well advanced in pregnancy I don't think there is much else you can do about it and one might as well go through the pains of childbirth as cheerfully as possible. It is like saying, "She was the first woman in North Dakota who had the courage to use a vacuum cleaner." Even if one were condemned to die before a firing squad and there was no alternative I imagine that it would not be too hard to refrain from yowling. On the other hand if there was a possibility of escape, one might run and sob and plead in a most craven fashion.

Yes, true courage is a most remarkable thing and one must bow to it. I think that in true courage there is always an element of choice, of an ethical choice, and of anguish, and also of action and deed. There is always a flame of spirit in it, a vision of some necessity higher than oneself. I think this is what the poet Blake meant when he said, "Active Evil is better than passive Good," for in passive good there is no element of thinking and daring and generosity at all. There is even no discomfort but quite the contrary. I think that is why prosperous Americans now make such a great virtue out of sweet comfortableness and superficial amiability. Indeed, there are great typically American religions that would persuade us that any divergence from comfortableness and a sweet acquiescing spirit, and a willed amiability is not at all wholesome and even in need of psychiatric attention.

And all this is why there is such a universal confusion and misunderstanding associated with the words "pacifism" and "non-violence." They can so easily be interpreted as Blake's "passive Good." As a matter of fact in modern war it is the soldiers—seemingly so active and brave—who go docilely and passively like meek sheep into a multitude-slaughtering war.

Professor Mulford Q. Sibley of the University of Minnesota, a Quaker, was making a speech against war and armaments. A questioner asked: "Well, what about Norway invaded by the Nazis in 1940. Do you mean to say that we should not have gone to war to help Norway? If your wife were attacked by a thug, wouldn't you go to her assistance and fight the thug?"

"Of course I would," he said. "But your example is not at all analogous to the situation in modern war. Let me show you a far more accurate analogy: Say that I am walking along some night with my wife and she is attacked by a thug. What do I do? I throw a bomb at the thug which blows up the whole city and kills everybody in Minneapolis and St. Paul. That is the pattern in modern war. It has nothing to do with my private battle with the thug."

In 1909 there was the first great international discussion at the Hague about the problem of war and the possibility of nations reducing their armaments. They argued and dithered about it—Russia with her Czar, Germany with her Emperor, England with her King, France, the United States, Japan, all of them. They argued about how much each country would or could reduce its army and navy. Then somebody asked the great Count Tolstoy in Russia, the pacifist whose mighty voice was heard all over the world with the greatest veneration, and he was so greatly loved that even the Czar dared not silence him. They asked him what he thought the nations should do. He said: they should all get rid of *all* their armaments. They should not have any armaments at all.

They then asked him this—to beg him to be reasonable:

"Now if in order to save the lives of a million men you had to kill one baby, wouldn't you do that?"

Tolstoy's answer was something like this: No, he would not kill the baby. "First, because no decent man *could* kill a baby. Second, you say the killing of the baby in the present moment, now, would save a million men a day, or a month, or an hour hence in the future. How do you *know* they would be killed? You know this much—that you cannot and will not kill the baby. The million men may not be killed in the future; something may intervene. I would refuse, as we all should, to do a horrible present deed to prevent a possible *future* evil."

And he said that this was the great underlying flaw in human wisdom and it led individuals and governments into this eternal legalistic balancing of present evil with possible future good, to this practical lawyerlike argument that a little evil *now* will do a lot of good *later*. Wrong. Mistaken. Unchristian.

And this is, I believe, what the prophet Isaiah and Jesus were trying to explain to us: Refuse to do this cruelty, this evil right now, at this moment, even though it seems "preventive" and impractical to do so. The very astounding and unexpected honorableness of your immediate act may bring about some utterly unpredictable magic. Who knows: A miracle might intervene, something very surprising indeed.

Say that in 1945 the United States, with the Bomb, refused to drop it on Hiroshima. Say that we warned Japan, told them to vacate a certain barren mountain and we would show them the terrible ability of the new weapon. But say that we had *refused* to bomb innocent people. Well that very nobility and forbearance would never have been forgotten. It would go reverberating down into Eternity. United States' world leadership would never have been in doubt again.

❖

# Being An Optimist

Optimism is a temperamental thing because there are just as many arguments for being cheerful as for being gloomy. Though here is a curious thing: The pessimists always seem to feel that "soundness" and rationality are on their side. But I can prove this is not so. The pessimist assumes he knows what is going to happen and that it will be bad. The optimist is open-minded and while the future may be bad, he knows it is a logical fallacy to be sure of it and is ready for wonderful miraculous surprises.

On top of that, the optimist with his cheerful, flexible, liquid, open, bouncy mind is in much better condition to deal with terrible things as they stick their heads up.

An optimist thinks in this fashion: "The last war was terrible, but what did it give us? Some fine things! The League of Nations." "It didn't last," cries the pessimist atrabiliously. "But the idea of it did," says the optimist, "and other leagues of nations will appear, each correcting the failures of the last one. And think how the last war taught England and America how to make people stronger, healthier! Women are freer in mind and body, more exposed to the sunlight. The whole level of education was stepped up a little bit and it will be stepped up more so after this war." And so on.

The optimist thinks of life as a continuous being delivered from evil (not pressing evil, massacring evil) through experience and illumination. That is why an optimist doesn't insist on "purity" on things being perfect, but moving toward perfect—with terrible setbacks. And so he never caterwauls or inveighs or scolds.

To people whose children are suffering in the war this seems like the sugary mental armor we Pollyannas put on to stay comfortable. Well, it may be. Nevertheless, you cannot possibly be an optimist if you take death as an unmitigated tragedy and doom. In a way, you have to take it as a commonplace.

I know that with two-baths and central heating, there is a tendency to think there is no such thing as death, but perhaps the saints were wise. Sir Thomas Moore wore a hair shirt all the time, under his magnificent Tudor doublet and hose, so that he would be aware of the ordinariness of death and, paradoxically, that is what made him so witty, affectionate and lighthearted.

Socrates, who had the finest intellect perhaps ever on earth, had that point of view. Condemned to die he said to his judges: "Let us reflect and we shall see that there is a great reason to hope that death is a good; for one or two things—either death is a state of utter unconsciousness or, as men say, there is a change and migration of the soul from this world to another.

"Now if you suppose that there is no consciousness but a sleep, death will be an unspeakable gain; for eternity then is only a single night.

"But if death is the journey to another place and there, as men say, all the dead abide, what good, O my friends and judges, can be greater than this? What would not a man give if he might converse with Orpheus and Musaeus and Hesiod and Homer? Nay, if this be true, let me die again and again. Wherefore, O Judges, be of good cheer about death and know of a certainty that no evil can happen to a good man, either in life or after death.

"The hour of departure has arrived and we go our ways— I to die and you to live. Which is better, God only knows."

◆

# ON DRINKING, NAGS, AND SCOLDS

I wrote about muckraking and the necessity for acid criticism last week, about Mr. Jenkin Floyd Jones of the *Tulsa Tribune* and his Jeremiad against our present society, its art and education and turgid immorality on stage and screen. I am a critic and scold myself, none worse. Yet criticism is useless, in fact a disgusting thing, unless one can see the other side of the coin, the radiant ways *out* of the problem.

It is interesting that Mr. Jones did not mention drinking, the polite and enormous consumption of alcohol by the most highly educated and gracious people of our country, with drunken catastrophes in almost every family. I think the complacency and the inability to change things for the better (in one's self or one's country) may be due to this. Drinking keeps people in their comfortable grooves. Moreover if you are dulled to a state of sedentary conversational torpor for two or three hours a day (cocktails and dinner) that means that one-sixth of your waking life is spent without the faintest stirring of intellect, of noble discontent, idealism and vision. No wheels are turning in one's happily chatting anesthetized brain for those several hours.

To change oneself or the world for the *better* requires two things: 1. a continuing vigorous restlessness of the intellect and the imagination, and 2. a continuing jovial courage.

I have been told that the endearing and talented French seem to be incapable of change, that their institutions are almost exactly the same as they were at the time of the French revolution in 1789; that, for example, they will not accept taxation, to mention just one thing. Their consumption of alcohol, imbibed charmingly, aesthetically, is the greatest in the world. Could that be the explanation? I think of Mendes-France, poor Mendes-France, the prime minister for a short time, bravely drinking milk at public functions, trying to be a good example.

I often wonder why there are not a hundred or even ten Eleanor Roosevelts in this country. Could it be because she had the immense good fortune to be a teetotaller which came about because her childhood was made wretched by an alcoholic father? In my mother's day when they were struggling for woman's suffrage, there were so many great women of Eleanor Roosevelt's calibre—stateswomen who were public-spirited, daring, scholarly, gentle, tireless and lovingkind. Today our most well-born and highly educated women have cocktails as regularly as breakfast. Go to a Smith College luncheon, or a Wellesley luncheon or a Radcliffe luncheon or any other high-brow fête of well-heeled people. Those very ones who have inherited the best genes and chromosomes in the world and the longest tradition of distinction and culture are, for two or three hours a day, reduced to a gracious idiocy. What a waste of ideas and action! What a loss for the country!

Another primary cause of our national decadence is, of course, the automobile, that is to say, all American legs are weak and fast becoming rudimentary. This leads to weak hearts, nervous jumpy minds, weak arteries, poor circulation, the universal pallor, countless new diseases, check-ups everywhere and long attendance at the psychiatrists.

But Mr. Jenkin Jones, you should also attack the soft drink industry, the liquor industry, the drug industry, the chemical industry instead of blaming it all on "Progressive education" and poor John Dewey. People do not feel well and they are drinking too much and not walking at all. When a person feels healthy, *any* kind of work is a fascination and a delight, whether it is digging a cellar, cleaning toilets, or studying for a Ph.D.

❖

# WHY MEN ARE CROSS WHEN THEY
## COME HOME AT NIGHT
### OR
## WHAT MAKES THE TIRED BUSINESS MAN TIRED

T his was a long discussion and I find some notes on it: Men are in the office all day milling around with people, with talk, with external things. It isn't unpleasant or uninteresting work but it jerks the mind about rather nervously. By the time they come home there is an instinct for emptiness and silence. But at home, what? Children, the radio, TV, dogs chasing cats, the front porch broken—it is just like more of the office, and there is no space for that timelessness and contemplation. There is not a squeak of an interval for the soul to recuperate, to get "recharged."

Some men blow up. My father used to say, "A thousand barrels of devils! Who left the orange peeling in the cellar?" (The boys had scooped hundreds of pumpkins for Halloween.) Some men recede into themselves in quiet misery. In our discussion, Mrs. Jenkins' chin trembled because, she says, Mr. Jenkins won't eat his dinner if the children quarrel. He is not cross at all, but he won't eat. It struck me suddenly: I bet that he is like me and likes to watch his own thoughts, idling and peacefully whirling in his head, just once in a while.

Then the women said: "But what time do *we* find for solitude?" But women do have that "timelessness," I claimed, no matter how hard the housework. Because if you wash the dishes or scrub the floor you are dreamily alone and it is not taxing the attention. I think how I brush my hair and chew gum for hours before my typewriter, and gaze out the window at the blizzard. It is just bliss, and I have come to see that it is a very important part of writing, just as it is to dawdle in dressing or to mend stockings in the midafternoon. But for office men there is no such thing.

Mr. Johnstone (who has eleven horses, cows and two farms at Lake Minnetonka) said that when he comes home at night he has a frightful temper because his many beautiful daughters "don't volunteer to do one thing ever. If only once one of them would just come forward and say: 'Daddy, I will feed one horse a day,'—he would be happy, he said. He said that is what makes him lose his temper. It is the eternal cry of men about home life: N*obody helps*! "And they're all being ruined . . . Cynthia took violin lessons and had talent but didn't practice." And so on. But all this he says *before* dinner. *After* dinner he is so amiable his children could all chew his ankles and he would just giggle."

"No," I said. "There is absolutely no logic to your terrible temper," and we began to psychoanalyze him.

*Question*: Would you be happier if your wife were not there when you arrive home?

Mr. Johnstone: Cripes no! I wouldn't like that at all. (A pause.) I guess I am just a so-and-so and want her there to take it out on her. (Another pause.) I will come driving out Superior Boulevard and I feel quite happy. I'll pass the Golden Valley Stables and count the horses—five horses and two colts. And then I come home and begin winding up our driveway and just as I get to the house—Pow! I am in a rage. There is a piece of Kleenex on the ground. Arabella left it there and I have to pick it up."

"But it can't be just Kleenex," we said. "It must be something deeper."

I claimed it was because he had had his mind jerked all day and then he comes home vaguely expecting mental freedom. But no, the Kleenex is on the lawn, and he gets angry because the adrenalin squirts new energy into his veins so that he can pick up the Kleenex *in spite* of fatigue. It is like a whip on a spent horse.

So we concluded the tired business man should be guaranteed a pleasant room, a pleasant impenetrable silence for say, twenty minutes, when he comes home. No puericulture going on, no playing Chopsticks on the piano, no automatic questions whose answers are not listened to.

Of course another element can enter into it. An irascible man, Mr. Cruikshank, said: "Why is it that when I go home I am terrible to my family when they are the very ones I am most fond of?"

I said: "Because they are the only ones who cannot get away and who will not hit back in any way. It is like this: say you are driving a car and you come to a situation where you must either run over a nice soft fat lady, or run into a telegraph pole. You will choose the fat lady because you won't get hurt yourself. Let me propose this: Next time you feel bad-tempered be nice to your family but take it out on your boss."

"Now you're talking!" Mr. Johnstone admired my reasoning. "You are quite right. There is something utterly wrong about it, utterly irrational. Because after dinner I always feel fine—so long as I don't feel like shooting myself from remorse for getting cross before dinner," said poor Mr. Johnstone.

◆

# Confessions of a
# Badly Dressed Woman

think that peoples' clothes and appearance express them very deeply in a symbolical way. For instance, those who are too neatly, finickingly dressed, with a kind of tight anxious exactness, are often that way about money, or tiny rights and wrongs. Or they have a meagerness, a lack of rushing vitality and warmth and opulence.

There are people who dress vaguely, drably—belts a little too loose, skirts a little too long, shoulder seams too drooping. Well, they may tell themselves it is a sign of intellectuality or a commendable lack of vanity. But really it is an inner lack of aesthetic talent. There are people who are very daring and gay in their clothes, and wonderful to look at, like plumed horses at a circus. Well, I like them. Because so they are in their souls. They aren't afraid to attract attention, and to sing out with their voices, and to be ridiculous, and to lead a parade. I love the majorette spirit—to dance and prance and be full of exuberance and hallelujah. Those are invaluable people.

Sometimes people are the quintessence of modishness—each hair in place in the plucked eyebrows, and the scalloped permanent—but they are neat as corpses, as toupes. Automatically there is no style at all. Because style always comes not from what you do to your shell, but your inner spirit. Have you dash, freedom?

Now I think it is fine not to be consistent but rather to have a variety of personalities in you, the more the better. It is fine to be your lineal ancestor, William the Conqueror, and your Aunt Nellie, and a couple of pirates, and your Uncle Hank. And give them all free rein in their turn, as you feel them pressing in your bosom. And if you have this kaleidoscoping variety of temperament in you, the more interesting you are. Why naturally! It means you are both funny and tragic, gentle and murderous, graceful and angularly sincere. Well, then, your clothes, as the outer symbol of all that is happening inside, will express this variety.

That is why I don't admire (as I used to feel I should) the unvaryingly, correctly neat people, or try to emulate them. They have not that Shakespearian, that Beethovian gamut in them from violence to sweetness. So I have told myself it is all right to dress up and to dress down. Sure, be a duchess when you feel like it: diamond tiara, silver spike heels. And be a burglar with a shaggy mane and dungarees and sweat shirt.

My diary shows that one's outer change in clothes, appearance, follows one's inner changes of personality. "Now my hair is all off; one inch all over the skull." (I write this kind of thing a thousand times.) "I am sorry about it. Well, never mind. It will soon grow. My haircut has something to do with combativeness. Why is that? Contrariwise, rough he-men should improve themselves by wearing their hair fluffier. A chignon would tone them down just enough."

Sometimes my daughter wanted me to dress exactly like everybody. When I first visited the Lake Harriet school I dressed for her approval—pearls, hat, etc. My first step into the fourth grade room, she rushed up to me, quickly pushed my bangs under my hat and then went back to her seat, wig-wagging and smiling at me proudly from the distance. I looked okay—like a regular mother. But, in general, I don't think she minded my appearance. Her ten-year-old friends once said: "Brenda looks like a robber." And this pleased her (and me, too).

I used to have an old joke with the kids, when they were in high school, which is the pinnacle of the most ravishing, persnickety perfection in lipstick, tight belts, sculptured curls. At the university there is a curious change to sloppiness and too-big sweaters.

"The reason I dress as I do," I'd say, "is that I have to tone myself down. Otherwise people would go wild; they would be so crazy about me. Whenever I appeared downtown they would run amuck—men leaving their wives, etc. And have to protect them from themselves. And so, children, that is why I wear bog-trotter shoes and all. I should really wear thick glasses, I suppose, to make it even safer."

And sometimes I would boast to them: "Well, I may not seem fashionable. But it is just because I am 10 or 20 years *ahead* of the styles. In corroboration of that I would point out that I was the first woman in the country to have a short haircut, to wear sailor pants (introducing slacks thereby), to wear double-breasted tight-fitting chesterfield coats, to wear shorts to get the legs tanned, and to tie a handkerchief around my neck leaving the back bare. Why, this is really true.

I remember when I mowed my lawn in Stamford, Connecticut—I wore shorts, a silk bandana tied around the neck and stuck in the belt in front—and sophisticated people like Lucille Buchanan of *Harper's Bazaar* gave me the devil for it because it was shocking. And did it herself in three years. And not many years ago, two of us went downtown in Minneapolis with socks on (we wanted golden legs) and got out of the car on Ninth Street, and it was so staggering to the public we lost our nerve and had to get back in, and go home.

But now about that first haircut. Irene Castle had a long Joan of Arc bob. But I cut mine all off short. Once as a child, I had seen a little girl who had had typhoid fever and she looked charming in these short standing curls. And I never forgot it.

But long hair was really sacred then. At night you braided your two long, heavy tails over each shoulder. There were hair-receivers and rats. When you come to think of it, this seems shocking now.

Well, one day when I was living in Greenwich Village, I went to the Brevoort and sat in the barber chair. Henri was the barber's name, a rather coquettish man with a long, soft, virgin beard.

"I want it all cut short. Like a boy. But not exactly like that, but as though the wind were blowing from behind. Like Lord Byron."

He didn't know Lord Byron. "Like a bad boy," he said finally. He started to cut. I directed him with a hand mirror. He was frightened. I felt as though I were being beheaded.

I was utterly delighted with the result. And so was everybody (so I thought). Everybody looked at me and that was nice. My pug was gone, my maternal pug. Gone was my weakness, motherliness, my please-look-out-for-dear-little-me meekness. Honest and free now.

Well, it led to some fearful sights because presently every woman in the country had mannish hair. They all began to look like men in nightgowns, though at first, most of them had the courage only for a long triangular Irene Castle bob, with no shingling up the back.

One summer when I came home to Minneapolis, somebody gave a cocktail party for a lot of girls. I had an expensive pair of real haircutting scissors. So I went home and got them and in the ribald, cocktail hilarity, they began letting me cut their hair—shingling it, standing it on end and hacking it off in the most skillful fashion. And it worked up into a kind of hysterical bacchanalian recklessness, so that I cut every head of hair on the premises. "Triangular effects must go!" was the reiterated cry. I was standing in shorn locks up to my knees.

❖

# CONFESSIONS OF A SECRET TEETOTALLER

I wonder how many people there are in the world like me who have never had the courage to speak up? Perhaps thousands, millions. But now I will tell it and it may give others courage. Although we seem like people to be socially shunned we are not actually so bad inside. Yes, that is what I want to show: that we are at heart friendly and affectionate and even have some jolly recklessness like other people.

But now here comes the confession. I just hate to drink. One cocktail—I don't like it at all. It has the most awful effect. First, my fine water-clear physical state—it muddies it all up and then chews at my nervous system for twenty-four hours, so that the next afternoon (and it is just at this point that most people quickly down another cocktail) my nice bouncy good-nature becomes suddenly jittery and tetchy and dreadfully apprehensive and anxious. In a pettish, schoolmarmish way, I feel meanly critical and want to rap people on the skull with my thimble. But worst of all is what it does to my soul right at the cocktail party itself. It does not free me at all (though people may think it does from all the noise I am making). Actually all the nice things about me have been automatically blocked and inhibited and I am in mental chains.

Now since this is so, what do I do about drinking? I have been pretending to drink and did not really do it. Sometimes I had to. I would be absolutely forced to gag it down under the eagle eye of my hostess and with all the subsequent misery that I have spoken of. And sometimes at a party I have been tired and the will is weak then, and if the cocktail is very sweet like a Manhattan say, or a Daiquiri, and tastes as much as possible like an ice cream soda, I have downed it, and perhaps two of them. But Oh, I dread that sort of thing!

For there is not only the physical effect that I have spoken of but it injures my character right on the spot. I deteriorate so! I become such a loudly-clacking, self-assertive party, getting off things I have said a hundred times before, grinding out yesterday's records. I am a flatterer and cozener and a sap and a fool and a knave. I cannot listen to others but must talk myself. And my talk is not the result of quietly thinking something and saying it in a friendly way but it is mere mental evacuation. Say that I hear somebody say the word "war" or "detente" or "Federal Reserve Bank," my mouth flaps open and a rattling stream of vague, loud, hearsay comes out. It is not even misinformation but it is far vaguer and louder than that. "Why yass, take Europe. Take your balance of payments. You are simply bound, I mean, to have conditions like that in your totalitarian state . . . Because if you haven't neutrality in Norwegian waters . . . I mean they have just simply GOT to . . . Because it is a case now, I mean, a question of your raw materials . . ."

This happens to me just after one cocktail. So I try not to drink. Well then how do I get out of it? There are many ruses. Sometimes if it is a very large and very loud party I just leave my cocktail for the hostess to scavenge, or one of the guests. Or I pretend to go upstairs to telephone and then dump it in the washbasin. But sometimes you are up against it.

For you can understand how you cannot say right out bluntly, "No thank you. I don't drink." This would be so mean, so ungrateful to the host and so chilling and depressing to everybody all around. And quite naturally so. Because either people think you have liver trouble, or that you are a "reformer." And that is a very queer thing about reformers. Reformers are usually very shy, apologetic people who bashfully like to be good themselves. The trouble is that it is the sinners who catch the reformers being good who get so mad and intolerant— because their consciences make them know the reformer is right and it throws them into a perfect fury of indignation. And sometimes if the reformers persist in secretly being good all by themselves (for no true reformer or saint ever scolds others for not being good) the indignant, righteous sinners have to kill them or burn them at the stake as they did Socrates or the

Christian martyrs. But that is a digression.

Anyway, I don't mind at all other peoples' drinking. I would feel terribly sorry if others did not drink. Say people took to serving lukewarm Ovaltine or iced Postum at cocktail parties—No, I just love cocktail parties. The thought of stepping into a room full of amiable uproar with pretty women with new hats on—that is one of the most pleasant things in life.

And I give cocktail parties myself and if I had time or money I would quadruple them. And when I do, I always want everybody to drink to beat the band and keep pouring it into their glasses even against helpless protests. Thank Heaven, I always feel indulgent toward other people. Just as I was always saying to my children, "Never, never eat candy, Pet. Only raw carrots. Here is a fine two pound box of candy." I mean that as soon as I recommend any reform I feel so guilty for preaching that I implore people to go on with their vices and double them.

Besides, I know that others may be different from me. I am perhaps extra-sensitive to stimulants. Coffee, for example, affects me like a painkiller. I once went to a New Year's Eve party, danced all night and hit balloons across tables at strangers, and at eight o'clock in the morning when the others said, "We must go to bed," I knew that I would not be able to sleep because I had had a demitasse for dinner.

I told you last time how one reason that I dread drinking is that I am too sensitive to stimulants. A half a cup of coffee keeps me awake until Sunday. From this you will say that I don't know anything about drinking, about the psychology of it, about the good it does to dry, tired, empty people who need so badly the freedom, the warmth, the broad-smiling that seeps into them from drinking. Yes, that is true. I have never passed out, I have never leaned against a lamp-post. For one reason, after three cocktails my epiglottis closes and I cannot down any more.

And so you will say that before I talk about drinking I should first try to understand it, to put myself in drinking peoples' shoes. Well, I think I can. I suppose drinkers feel as I do sometimes about fudge sundaes. About once in three months I have a frightful craving for fudge sundaes. After being stern with myself for a long time, suddenly my resistance to fudge sundaes breaks down. My will breaks. You could no more stop me than you could a cannonball. I go downtown to the most opulent, sinful ice cream emporium in town and have a double fudge sundae. Then ashamed to ask for more I go home, change my clothes, put my hat on backwards as a disguise and come back and have another one.

But of course, this is a form of drunkenness. This is dipsomania. I know some very churchy, fine, respectable women who do the same thing, intellectual women who read scholarly papers for their study clubs. I have caught them doing the same thing. And I tell them in no uncertain terms that it is just plain drunkenness. "You feel very respectable reeling up Nicollet Avenue with a pound of candy under your belt. In reality, my dear Mrs. Peebles, you are drunk."

So you see I know how a person who likes drinking feels. But my point is this: if fudge sundaes are hard on my constitution, as they most certainly are, and blur my fine, clear translucent spirit, cocktails do the same thing.

And now I come to a description of what drinking does, how it inhibits and enchains my rowdy, free (sober) personality. How instead of being a release, a freeing of my spirit, it is a straight-jacket.

If you are a teetotaller (both of cocktails and fudge sundaes) presently you get a fine, childlike, water-sluiced state of clarity and sensitiveness. In this state the spirit or the intelligence or the imagination (whatever you want to call it) is like a little fountain continually casting up new thoughts and ideas. If you are very tired, strained, overworked, you have no solitude, run too many errands, talk to too many people, eat too many pancakes, drink too much coffee, cocktails, this little fountain is muddied over and covered with a lot of debris. Pressure, too much action—all those things throw sand on the fountain.

The result is you stop living from the center, the creative fountain, and you live from the periphery. That is, you go along on mere will power without imagination. You become a mere corrector of peripheral things, such as your manners or your hair arrangement. There is no new wisdom in it. And you swing back and forth between being cocktail-party jolly and (the next day) being sober-cross.

Say you are a tired business man. You work nine hours a day, turning off factual accomplishments, dictating, talking, pulling ten-foot telephones-on-scissors to your chest and barking into them. After eight or ten hours you notice a slight feeling of emptiness that even the tenth stogie cannot dispel. So you go to a cocktail party with not a single, dry, little thought left to rattle around in your brain. Cocktails. You feel warm. You feel bright. You feel affectionate. You feel witty. You FEEL all these things but it is all subjective. It is not from the fountain, your true self, but just peripheral. I mean you are NOT all these things. And you would know it if you had a Dictaphone record your talk. "Why, yass, take Europe . . . You are simply bound, I mean, to have conditions like that. (5 minutes) . . . Totalitarian states (10 minutes) . . . Inflation is here to stay (12 minutes) . . ."

You see? You do not say what you are quietly thinking now, as we always do when sober and clear, but something you said or heard yesterday or twenty times before, something automatic and merely remembered. The true, clear fountain always casts up something that has thought-content in it. And this is the true secret of being interesting. The secret of being boring is to say something that is automatic, not meant.

That is to say, if only I can be a teetotalling sneak and side-step drinking at a party I am so much nicer. I can listen to my friends and hear and understand them without shouting at them or pressing against them with my own ego. Sometimes men, suspecting me, say uneasily, "Here! Now you have a drink!" They are afraid I will be cold and critical if I don't. I say—and they don't believe it—"But sober I am much more reckless, gaily wild, affectionate, unguarded, flirtatious, I am a thousand times more appreciative. I can see all your wonderful qualities so much better and tell you what they are." And this is true.

Last time I told you how all the jovial shouters at a cocktail party are uneasy if I am quiet, friendly and intelligent.

They suspect I am not drinking. They can't stand it. No. They won't have it! They insist. Down goes the glass of poison and there I am grinding off old records. I adjust the needle and put on my you-ought-to-play-the-piano record, or I don't believe-in-bossing-children record. I have a lot of old joke records, jokes I have got off surely a thousand times. I do not mean that these records, if sober, cannot be expressed often and be interesting and helpful. Our ideas and life-convictions—of course we must say them hundreds of times and up to the end. But when we say them sober, with the clear, little fountain working and with the thought-content there, they always affect people and are worth listening to perhaps. But when they are ground off automatically, why that is merely ego-pressing. That is to say it is only fun for the speaker. The poor so-called listener's eyes have glazed and he is waiting, as tense as wire, to spring in and spout his own old record.

Now there is a physiological explanation of all this. Here it is roughly: Alcohol is not a stimulant but an anaesthetic. You are not being stimulated (though you think so) when your voice rises and clatters out of you but you are being slowly dulled and put to sleep. First, it anesthetizes the highest brain centers (the cortex) where the finest perceptions are i.e. the faculty of 1. self-criticism, and 2. decision-making. (These are the highest mental functions that man is capable of.) The cortex, now put to sleep, the second brain level is the one that is working: the emotions. This is when you giggle, whack men on the arm with your fan and say, "Naughty boy!," when you talk in a loud, unhearing voice about "conditions all over the world." (If your cortex were working it would tell you how many times you have said this and to the same person.)

Now it is at this point that each person THINKS he is stimulated because he has the sensation that he is suddenly witty and bold, and this is why he always claims, "I am not really myself unless I drink. That release! *In vino veritas.*" In wine, the truth. But it is really all an illusion. *In vino mendax:* In wine, a liar. You THINK you have released some recklessness and ardor but what you have released is just something very loud and usually not true. ("I have always been madly in love with you, Edna. I never cared for my wife.") You THINK you have released deep, emotional suffering about war or Senator Goldwater but probably you have released only the pleasurable emotion of indignation, one of the most sensually indulgent of the emotions.

Then the anaesthetic keeps working. The second brain level, (the emotions) is obliterated. The emotions sleep. The third brain level still works and this is where the motor functions are. So you can still walk. At last the anaesthetic is complete. You slide from the lamppost into the gutter.

And you wake up to what? Gloom, pain, jangled nerves, misanthropy, anxiety, dreadful cowardice about the future, and despair. The door pushes open and a young kitten comes in. "Damn you!" you roar in rage, "Don't you come in here stamping around!" A half hour later it is your poor wife. After that your frightened children, in terrified unhappiness at school all day and trying inwardly to explain to themselves inexplicable things.

And now as I write this I suddenly begin to feel sad and guilty. How do I know what drinking means to people? Think of all the nice people I know who get such jolliness and warmth out of drinking! How terrible if people didn't drink any more. How I despise blue noses, those prudes, those holier-than-thou, those dyspeptics with congenital low vitality, those people who masticate with their front teeth! I take everything back. If I am a teetotaller, please forgive it. The only justifiable admonition for anyone is: Be bad or good, whichever is best for you.

And now perhaps it is time to quote Pascal, that great Frenchman and mathematical genius and philosopher and saint: "Man is a reed, the most feeble thing in nature, but he is a thinking reed. The entire universe need not arm itself to crush him. A vapor, a crop of water, suffices to kill him . . . All our dignity consists of thought. By it we elevate ourselves and not by Space and Time which we cannot fill. Let us endeavor then to think well; that is the principle of morality. By Space the universe encompasses and swallows us up like an atom; by thought I comprehend the world."

Alcohol—it is the perfect world-wide medicine to prevent thinking well. Or perhaps I should say, nobly and lovingly.

# On Two Kinds of Moderation

In this talk of "moderation" we must remember that there are two kinds. There is the "moderate" but extremely able man who has a deadline for his achievement. He means what he says. The deadline for his achievement may be a year hence or five years hence. But he is implacable. He will achieve it. The other kind of "moderation" offers only soothing talk. Or it's like this: Moderation Number One: A father says to a child: "I am saving money and working hard to send you to college three years from now. You will get your college education and can count on it." Moderation Number Two: A father says: "Well, son, I believe in moderation and will not make any rash statements at this time, though I think it indeed a splendid idea"—and he does not save the money or take a step in that direction.

People say to the Negroes: "You must give desegregation a little time." It has taken, so far, a hundred years. The Negroes think that's quite a lot of time. (So do I). A Moderation-Number-One man or series of men would have achieved their goal of desegregation, fairness, respect, education and non-exploitation at the very latest, in one generation—1895.

I think so often how if only the imperialist countries like Britain, France, etc. who have colonies would, or could, give honest, implacable deadlines as to when the Africans and others will be entirely free. The bloodshed, rage and misery that we see now is due to just that—the natives not believing their oppressors and having no reason to believe them.

Some day the United Nations will be able to do this: To guarantee a deadline. They will be able to say the following and mean it: "Africans, what you need and ask for is just. In five years you will have it. We will both work toward it definitely, actively, vigorously, with observable progress made each six months—you to educate yourself to run your own country, we to loosen our economic hold without too much suffering and ruin for ourselves."

❖

# NEW YEAR'S RESOLUTION

t is New Year's Day and what to resolve? They say one of the very first things you must not do is to make resolutions because that does not work at all but leads to the ditch of psychological defeat. The resolution-maker is merely saying to himself: "Oh, how nice are the things that I am *not* going to do, how delightful, and what a dry, terrible strain this is *not* to do them! But I will stick it out for a year!"

But the imagination beats out the will power every time, William James says. So the thing to do is this: Say that you resolve not to smoke. Think, "Oh the bliss, the freshness, the athletic bounciness, the clear slippery eyes, the iridescent sparkling intelligence when I don't smoke! Think of it! To get out of that horrible old straight-jacket, sucking in that stuff until your mouth tastes like a motorman's mitt and you feel that you have a combined case of slow poisoning, gangrene, steeple-head and impacted teeth."

Then if you think and see these true things, you will probably give up smoking.

On the contrary, like the Alcoholic Anonymous, you should make a humble, meek little vow just to try to get through one day at a time. In the morning you say mentally to some unseen Helper, "I would like to get through today without a drink—that would be fine." And if you do, why say at night with happiness. "Good. I did it. Sir, thank you!" And on the morrow try to get through one more day. Then the task does not seem so immense, bleak, and dismally impossible.

But now what shall I resolve for New Year's? I would like to have a minute-to-minute awareness of what is true, good and lovely in everybody and also in myself and to throw out of myself the tiresome, cantankerous self. And to do this not only in solitude when the temptations to be muddy, self-absorbed and confused are easily avoided, but even in the most churning, crowded, active life, in all the outward-turning activities, so that there is a transformation of them and they become illuminated, you might say. And to do that it is necessary to have an unsleeping awareness and one must have, in thought, feeling and conduct, the constant exercise of something like an artist's tact and taste. "*Si volumus non redire, currendum est.*" "If we wish not to go backwards, we must run," said a man named Pelagius 500 years ago.

◆

# A Spree on Gasoline

A little philosophy about running. More and more people do it. It is an addiction. They cannot stop it and do not want to. The ability to run a Marathon seems to be built in. It is slowly acquired after days and months of trotting and jogging around. If you keep running, there you are—able to go 26 miles. A scholarly friend (young middle-age) now finds herself running six miles a day in one hour. And the queerest thing of all is her sorrow, indignation, when it is 20 below zero and there is a blizzard and she cannot do it. She misses it grievously. It has become a pleasure, a delight, an absolute necessity.

And here is the most mysterious, the most paradoxical thing of all: Instead of subtracting or of taking away from the sum of one's energy, it seems to double it, to quadruple it. (Housewives say defensively: "I get plenty of exercise as it is"— i.e. snuffing up dust under the bed). They all have *more* energy ever before. Bad habits slough off—cigarettes, booze. They find they cannot bare to feel, like most people, bum, languid, plaintive, depressed, cross, down-hearted, hung over. Diseases disappear. Fat sloughs off; it just melts away, about 30 pounds of it. Hearts become strong. Dr. Ernest Van Aakan, the great German physician and athletic trainer, says that running seems to bring oxygen, not only to the lungs, but to all the cells. No more cancer. Cells without oxygen get cancer.

Why does it become such an addiction, and why cannot people stop running? I think it is perhaps our original, primeval way of motion, that it is really natural, right for us to gently run. We are then like happy deer, antelopes, wolves, wild horses. Running is the way we *should* move. And for miles. From here to Duluth.

And please remember the awful experience Americans have been through for two generations: riding in cars. From here to New York and from here to the drugstore. You make a rather inadequate parking effort with your car and you say apologetically to your passenger: "Never mind. We can walk to the curb."

No wonder immense hospitals tower to the sky. My fortunate Uncle Martin of a happier time, came from Norway, took out a claim in North Dakota near Cooperstown, dug himself a shelter under sod and walked forty miles to and from Valley City to get his groceries.

I often wish I could establish a kind of monastic order among high school students, say one like that of the Cistercians in France in the eleventh century. They made a vow never to ride. Richelieu's foreign minister in the fifteenth century, Father Joseph, was a Cisterican and an extraordinarily able man. When he went to see the Pope about affairs of state, he walked—over the Alps, through mud and snow, barefoot. When he had to see the King of Spain it was over the Pyrenees. He had a lot of time to think. And he always prayed all the way (that is what you do unconsciously when you walk) earnestly asking for illumination and love. Not a bad idea.

Now if our high school students walked and/or ran every where, think how wonderful they would be! Red cheeks, long legs, wide flashing smiles: Dauntless and helpful. And they might even have some good ideas such as distaining rock, marijuana, revolting sexual idiocies.

I often think of man's history on earth as the round dial of a clock and say that twelve o'clock is the Year One Anno Domini, the birth of Christ. Now man has existed on earth millions of years. The hand of the clock indicating our era, 2,000 years, would be about a hundredth of a hair beyond twelve o'clock. It is really just an Eyewink of time, an Augenblick. And this Eyewink, our even briefer period (sixty years) is the Age of Gasoline. It is our Spree on Gasoline. World Wars, Hiroshimas, airplanes, bombers, neutron bombs, H-bombs. Millions dead, billions frightened and wretched. Just think! Maybe in another Eyewink gasoline will be exhausted. All gone!

I know that when that time comes I myself, the blue birds, the cardinals, the wild animals, the frogs, the cowlips, the naturalists, the poets, the prophets, the peacemakers will be delighted. A few darling weeds will begin to push through the ugly, sterile concrete. No more gasoline! Thank God! Hurrah, hurrah!

◆

# ON RUNNING UP PIKE'S PEAK

**W**alt J. Stack has the 100-mile running record for persons over 60. He is 67. We are friends, write back and forth, answering letters like pistol shots in a duel. He says that I must be in the Pike's Peak run on August 3rd. He says I will get the world's record for my age. (Why of course I would, being twenty years older than any competitor of my sex). Being such a bold, tough, brave and intelligent man, he is the only complete male feminist perhaps in the world, except Robert Graves and Ashley Montagu. He keeps telling me, "It is the Year of the Woman. It is your consummate duty to your sex"—the millions of them, the timid, sedentary, sweet and dear women, taking relaxation pills, washing out their nylons, warned throughout a life time not to "over-do." They are not to blame. They have been taught that way, diminished, belittled for 2000 years.

I wrote to him on June 23.

Dear dear Walt: I am indeed your friend, admirer, and fan. I received that wonderful paper, *The Jogger*. And always your *San Francisco Dolphins Long Distance Runners'* bulletin. And Dr. George Sheehan writes and sends columns. And really how great are all the brave and merry runners, men, women and children. It is really a great thing. It may save the country, the world.

And I know how you have not much time: two Marathons (26 miles) a week; carrying 5000 lbs. of cement-asbestos to the 15th floor of a high rise; 5000 letters, editing. Good God, I just think of the telephone calls: that alone would kill Hercules. Supernatural. And you know I am never mean enough to expect an answer. Telepathy is the ticket. But here are a few thoughts. (Answer telepathically).

1. In a week or so when the editor gets back from Norway, I am sending you my columns in the Norwegian-American

newspaper, *The Minnesota Posten*. Sometimes they are good. Sometimes not. (If I had time they would always be good.)

2. About Pike's Peak. I don't like negative thinking but there are a few hurdles to take. I am walking 3 to 6 miles every day. If I had time I would walk 13 a day, (the distance up Pike's Peak). Weight (the middle) is sloughing off pleasantly. I have a microscopic defect, a twinge in the right hip. About 4 years ago I was changing storm windows. A table tipped over and I twisted it. Never bothered to fix it; i.e to see why it gave this small pain. (It adversely affected foot-work in tennis—makes one careful in stepping so there will be no twinge.) Last fall, just for the fun of it, I thought I'd find out which muscle it was so I could mend it. Went to a tolerable doctor. (I don't like them much—unimaginative fellas.) An X-ray. Interesting. He told me he thought I had broken the hip. Also I had six vertebrae below the ribs while most people have only 5. But then he said race horses have that so I took it as a compliment. I was wearing a little day-time decoration in lapel, some red ribbon and a silver coin, a Saint Olav decoration given me by King Haakon VII of Norway. He asked me what it was. "I am Sir Brenda Ueland, a Knight of St. Olav." (An exaggeration). The doctor said: "No wonder you were knighted—walking on a broken hip 5 miles a day for 4 years."

Well the hip is really no handicap and I am now walking it into perfection. The 13 miles up Pike's Peak is no problem. The thin air and altitude probably are. I believe you have to train for it somewhat in advance.

Problem 3: I am supposed to make a living or a partial living. Lack of money is the Brotherhood of Man. I work pretty hard. I have a feeble car with asthma and cardiac trouble. I have a serious complex about accepting money, borrowing or being lifted around. Have four intelligent and wistful cats who feel awful if I leave them, etc. etc. Now all these matters I leave up to my Teachers, my invisible and most helpful Angels. I will leave arrangements to Them. They will get me there if it can be done honorably.

I tell you this so that if I don't make it you will still like me and not be infuriated. And it amuses me to think of Ibsen's

*Brand*, a great drama and poem. Brand, the hero, is supposed to be the philosopher, Kierkegaard. Well in the play Brand, the fiery idealist, climbs a terrible high mountain, his wife and child dying on the way but Brand is such an idealist he doesn't give a damn. When he gets to the very top, a terrible wind blows him off the Peak and a Voice says out of the Abyss: "He is the God of Love!"

Now that may happen to me. I rather like the idea. It is adequately dramatic. Well enough. True love day and night.

Brenda.

Walt Stack's letter just came. I'll print it next week.

◆

# MY FAILURE AT PIKE'S PEAK

etter to Sandra:

L The Pike's Peak run: great excitement, fun, fatigue. Then we drove home Monday. Now about my athletic triumph, conquering Pike's Peak. It didn't quite come off. That was sort of awful—not to get to the top. And a slightly disgusting aspect of it that I actually thought I could do it. The boneheadedness, the feebleness of imagination! But Wow! That Peak! Acclimatized to Lake Harriet and Linden Hills Boulevard I did not quite comprehend Pike's Peak.

But never mind. I was approved of, indeed praised by the runners (348 completed) and I was useful to them in public relations (a thing I hate—a typical Nixon). That week in Colorado I did "train" for it dutifully—walked up, up, up the unbelievable Hill for seven and nine and then eleven miles a day. I got a round cloth badge to sew on my jacket to the effect that I had been to Barr's Camp halfway up—six miles. (Barr was the man who built the Trail.) Now if I had had, say, three weeks to quietly practice I think I could have done it.

There were three difficulties: 1. I am not used to walking UP at all (Lake Harriet) and the muscles at the top of the legs—lifting up my weight of 130 pounds a foot or two—were not strong. The first day I would walk 32 steps and have to rest, the next day 100 steps, and so on.

2. The psychological pain and fright of looking DOWN from a great height. Awk! The path was narrow, about 3 feet, gravelly (slippery) and on my right, there it was—the Abyss, the ghastly deep chasm and valley, and you could see practically to Minnesota. And say you slipped, there was nothing to hold on to but a flower.

3. The altitude. Even the little town of Manitou Springs is 7,000 feet above Minneapolis. Pike's Peak rises above that to over 14,000 feet. You feel quite odd: dim, dreamy, imprecise,

uncertain. I am sure that in three weeks I could get used to all this. In Minneapolis I walk at the rate of a mile in twenty minutes steadily for 9 miles, without a rest, and do not get tired. The lower legs are splendid.

I went up one day with Kay Atkinson and Annabelle Marsh (aged 54 and 58) who are San Francisco Dolphin Runners. They were extraordinary—nimble, bouncy, talkative, tireless. They took (kindly) too much care of me. I mean I am a solitary and do things better alone. They were thinking, "Her age, her heart!" I'd slip a few inches on some gravel and they would leap to seize my arm. "She'll break a hip!" I kept waving them on. "Don't wait." It was even a handicap, an extra effort to talk, to be gratefully polite. Although we walked ten hours that day I had not the faintest qualm about the hazards of old age, I mean of getting sick, heart, etc. Larry said, to assuage my disappointment at not finally standing on the Pike like Balboa: "There is not a doctor in the U.S.A. who would ALLOW you to go up on the top *even in a car*, because of your age." (Larry is a doctor, married to Alex, my granddaughter.)

Eric and I did that. We drove to the top in a kind of limousine-bus. Terrifying! The road is over 20 miles—up, up around the dreadful sharp curves, the hairpins. The young driver explained happily that there were no bulwarking the edges "because then people would not drive carefully enough." It was something it would take Shakespeare, Goethe, Milton, Dante and Lord Byron and all the thunder of Wagner's operas plus William Tell to describe. Black clouds miles below, riven by lightning. Thunder, rainbows, fat gilded clouds like cherubs. Shafts of sun like harp wires. And when we got to the top, three miles above the timber line, there was a blizzard, thick, wild, blinding, snow. I thought of that painting by David of Napoleon on a snorting horse going over the Alps.

Well Kathy Fahl (a dear—she and her husband manage the race) told me that when I was up there I should study and practice a little on the descending Trail "just to get the feel of it." She is 74, has been up many times. Rudy, her husband, was the champion in 1956. Showed us his solid gold cup. He is now 77, limber and bounding with a pink face and a dauntless blue eye.

I didn't even LOOK over the edge! I couldn't! Never! There is a trembling in the back of the legs. They turned to water. To look over that tiny iron rail, that Jump-Off into Eternity!—Eric and I went into the Cafeteria and had a nice hot dog.

Sunday morning at 7 o'clock Rudy Fahl fired his pistol and all Runners started leaping up the mountain. We knew the winners would come down after three hours so we were waiting at Manitou and Ruxten Streets. Pretty soon he came leaping down the road in nine-foot strides, between two police cars, all lights flashing. We cheered, waved handkerchiefs. It was Richard Trujillo, a geologist. His time was 3 hours, 31 minutes and 5 seconds. He had clipped 5 minutes and 5 seconds from last year. Hurrah! Hurrah!

Soon after came Joss Naylor of Wales. "I couldn't get my breath. I was gasping. I just couldn't get enough oxygen in my blood." He was very, very thin, as lean as wire. Even his nose. His hair and wide-whiskers were a kind of fawn-colored fuzz. He looked exactly like one of those other good runners, an Afghan hound.

Note to all the fatties of America: None of them are fat. And their legs are utterly beautiful: long, straight as plumb lines, set close together at the top; calves and thighs exactly the same size. Knees are small, perfect, beautiful, fluid, debonair and lubricated as something in a 37-jewelled watch.

And I learned something. I think it is running that is so miraculously strengthening. So Sandra, stick to it. Think of Annabelle and Kay lightly gambolling and frolicking uphill for 13 miles like Spring lambs.

◆

# ON WALKING

The lake is turbulent and grey and cold. The sun at the horizon lights up the dun world with shafts of living gold light. And just crossing the bridge between Lake Harriet and Lake Calhoun I overtake Mr. Lyman Wakefield. He says he is walking from his house in Lynnhurst to the Minikhada Club. He says he agrees with me: It is much better to walk alone. Then is when you get recharged and it does wonders for you.

Well that is what many walkers have said. "A walking tour should be gone upon alone," said R. L. Stevenson, "because you must have your own pace and neither trot alongside a champion walker nor mince in time with a girl . . . There should be no cackle of voices at your elbow to jar the meditative silence of the morning."

And now if you begin to study the question, it seems as though every man who amounted to anything was a walker. "Shakespeare," said Sir Leslie Stephens (English biographer and literary critic) "knew the connection between walking and 'a merry heart.'" His friend Ben Jonson walked from London to Scotland. Another gentleman of the period (I forget his name) danced from London to Norwich. Tom Coryate hung up in his parish church the shoes in which he walked from Venice and then started to walk (with occasional lifts) to India. Isaak Walton, the Compleat Angler, and his friends would start a day of fishing by a walk of 20 miles.

As for John Wesley, "One secret of his powers is not always noticed. In his early expeditions he went on foot to save horse hire, and made the discovery that 20 or 30 miles a day was a wholesome allowance for a healthy man." The fresh air and exercise put "spirit into his sermons" which could not be rivaled by the ordinary parson of the period.

"The literary movement of the eighteenth century was

obviously due to the renewed practice of walking, if not mainly," Sir Leslie Stephens said. Wordsworth's biography shows how every stage of his mental development was connected with some walk. Carlyle is unsurpassed in his descriptions of scenery. He walked one day 54 miles. So did Sir Walter Scott, though lame. Coleridge walked 40 miles a day in Scotland and is known to have walked alone over Scafel (England's highest mountain). And see how wonderfully he described night walking—that lovely alive feeling of being scared:

> *Like one that on a lonesome road*
> *Doth walk in fear and dread,*
> *And having once turned round walks on*
> *And no more turns his head;*
> *Because he knows a frightful fiend*
> *Doth close behind him tread.*

But the most valiant walking was that of the seventeenth century Capuchins who took a vow never to ride. Father Joseph, Richelieu's statesman and ambassador, walked far north into Germany, down to Rome, into Spain, on the most weighty ambassadorial journeys. It is as though Molotov walked from Moscow to Italy to talk to Pope Pius and then home and three months later set out plodding to see Churchill.

❖

# Bill Roessler and
# How to Walk, Dance

I was asked to write about "*How To Walk*." Now there has come to town a youngish man who seems to know all about the whole history of motion from Homeric times down through the Czar's ballet, Isadora Duncan, Martha Graham and modern dancers. This is William Roessler, who went to the University, won a scholarship to study with Ruth St. Denis and now is teaching in New York and knows the theory of motion such as that of the great Dalcroze, the sort of thing that all young actresses should know (not to mention housewives, business men and children). I asked him about the famous Bess Mensendieck in Holland whose exercises were adopted at Yale. He has been her pupil too. He is a friend of Shangkar, the Hindu dancer, who is more graceful and perfect than a leopard, a panther, who is truly a great artist and a thinker as well. And Shangkar wanted Bill Roessler to teach in his school in the Himalayas. And the Danes offered him a job. But the war came.

I went to his class in Elliot Park Neighborhood house, with twelve Minneapolis women in it (among his pupils are Maria Montana, the singer; Mrs. Liebenberg, Louise Lupian Jenkins, the pianist; Helen Bach, Mrs. Leber, Mrs. Ditter, Mrs. V. Stanchfield, Mrs. Rosenblum, Mary Ellen Sturdevant, Mrs. Julia Putnam Andersen). All groaned when I appeared, because they assumed that I'd write about them. It seemed to be taking such an unchivalrous advantage.

I took off my shoes and joined the class.

Mr. Roessler makes you know yourself (with Hindu-like introspection) what is happening inside your body. Say that you take one step: He makes you feel the weight of your body thrown ever so slightly forward until you are forced into another step.

He makes you feel how your foot should feel, every tiny

stress and strain in it. Indeed, he tells you what a foot *is*; how you should consider your two feet together as a pedestal; how the smaller the base in your stance "the greater the loftiness, the grace, the freedom of spirit, the thinking power."

Now we are usually told that to reduce our waistline we should put our toes under a bureau and then pull ourselves up and down (which probably just thickens the whole trunk beyond redemption). But Mr. Roessler explains how in the abdomen there are three (or is it four) big muscles from breast bone to pelvis. It is these three muscles pulling, and these alone, that you must feel when you pull yourself up and down. You learn to separate them out from the general confused mass of muscles. If these three muscles get strong (with all others kept limp at will) behold! you can begin to design your own body yourself. And there you have it! A small waist, small clenched buttocks, straight legs, a round divine upper arm (no backward-bending arms, no knock-knees), a round neck like the Diocletian Venus. And more important than mere measurements, you will move with unutterable grace. (Note how all dieting is just to make one *look* all right and not to *be* all right, i.e. full of pneumatic agility like a goddess.)

Most people think a good posture means a ramrod position. No. Good posture, he says, is a light, easy, graceful thing. "And when you wait for a streetcar don't let your *muscles* hold you up"— He slumped into the usual horrid pretzel we all know in our tiredness— "Let your *bones* hold you up; your legs like *pillars*. Rest in your own boney pelvis . . . " In other words, be an engineer about the thing.

As for "modern" dancing, he disagrees with Martha Graham, "although she is a genius . . . It always expresses something bitter, turgid and glum." And modern dancers have a snobbishness about interesting and charming the public, he says. (Like "modern" artists, sculptors, composers).

Martha Graham can fill a New York theater about one night a year, but Shangkar or Isadora Duncan (or indeed, Fred Astaire or Bill Robinson) can fill a theater every night and people are just insatiable for the bliss of watching them. "Well then," he says, "something must be wrong with modern dancing." And he thinks it makes bodies uglier. (True and great dancing from classic ballet to tap dancing improves them.) "Their seats get big, the cords in their necks stick out more and more," —strain, anguish, tensions. "There is something wrong with it." Yes, a good name for it would be "the cords-in-the-neck" school of dancing.

◆

# Every Fine Garden Had Such Things

Today we think of a garden as a pretty place to look at. In the old days it was a place to live in all day long, in the lavender haze of twilight, in the evening, in the moonlight. It was a place of retirement, for sweet sacred seclusion; a place where one never seemed to tire of walking, as people today never seem to tire of walking on golf links; a place for poetical and intellectual reflection, for conversation, gaiety, garden parties, fetes, and for making love.

Fountains are not much in style (I wish I had a fountain), yet what is more beautiful than a fountain, the flying water showering diamonds in the sun? Or a marble-rimmed pool in a dark glade, the water reflecting the black yew hedges like a somber funereal mirror. Every fine garden had such things. They would have fountains that would play practical jokes. There would be a *jet d'eau* in a sundial. While guests were looking at it, somebody from a distance would turn a wheel so that they were sprinkled, the ladies emitting charming screams.

And today we don't give much thought to perfume in a garden, but once that was very important.

There were always little orange trees in tubs for this and, in certain parts of the garden, jasmine, heliotrope, tuberoses, mignonette. And they felt that the music of the birds was a part of a complete garden. A man would have a mulberry tree with its dark purplish fruit so that all day long multi-colored birds would be flashing in and out of it.

And who thinks of the importance of an echo in a garden now? If a man had an echo he was as proud of it as if he had a fountain sculptured by Donatello. Often artificial echoes were contrived so that the words were repeated many times. John Evelyn wrote of a seventeenth century French garden: "It was never without some fair nymph singing to it. Standing under a tree, or in a little cabinet of hedges, the voice seemed to descend from the clouds; at another place to come from underground."

In one American garden there was a wonderful natural echo, but no one appreciated it until a French visitor pointed it out. So they had a carved stone bench placed under a great beech tree. If you sat there on a still night and called, a sad beautiful voice would come out of the dark woods three times.

◆